DATE DUE

The British and their Successors

THE BRITISH
AND THEIR SUCCESSORS

A Study in the Development
of the Government Services
in the New States

by

RICHARD SYMONDS

NORTHWESTERN UNIVERSITY PRESS

Evanston 1966

First published in the United States of America in 1966
by Northwestern University Press
under arrangement with Faber and Faber, Ltd., London
All rights reserved

Contents

CONTENTS

PART 4. COMPARISONS AND REFLECTIONS

Preface

During the past twenty years I was stationed intermittently, or made extended visits, in India, Pakistan, Ceylon and several countries in tropical Africa shortly before or after they became independent. Watching the process of decolonization, it became increasingly interesting to speculate how far a pattern could be traced, and to what extent the British had applied or ignored the lessons, real or apparent, of Indian experience in West Africa and of West African experience in East Africa. In particular the history of the succession to the British in the public services seemed to have been inadequately studied.

I wish to express my appreciation to the Committee for Commonwealth Studies of the University of Oxford for appointing me as a Senior Research Officer from 1963 to 1965 in order to enable me to study this question, and to the United Nations Technical Assistance Board for giving me leave of absence for this period. While I was on leave the United Nations had, of course, no responsibility for any views which I expressed, nor were confidential United Nations materials used.

I should also like to thank those who have helped me. I owe much to Professor J. Gallagher and Mr. George Bennett, who read the whole text; and to Mr. Colin Newbury and Mr. Charles Swaisland of Oxford; to Mr. H. Laurentie of Paris; Mr. R. Coomaraswamy and Mr. A. Joseph of Ceylon; and to Sir Paul Patrick for reading and criticizing parts of it. Among others who have been good enough to find time to discuss various aspects of the study have been Mr. A. L. Adu, Sir Eric Ashby, Dr. Thomas Balogh, Lord Caradon, Sir Andrew Cohen, Sir Christopher Cox, Mr. V. L. Griffiths, Mr. Guy Hunter, Prof. Kenneth Kirkwood, Prof. W. J. M. MacKenzie, Dr. S. C. Mukherjee, Dame Margery Perham, Sir Alexander Carr-Saunders. Professor Kenneth Robinson of London University has been a constant source of encouragement, and Mr. William Clark

PREFACE

and Dr. Tom Soper of the Overseas Development Institute have given skilled guidance amidst the wealth of experience which exists in Britain on many of the questions which have been treated. Professor A. A. J. Van Bilsen in Brussels and M. Sylvain Lourié in Paris have helped greatly both with their own advice and in facilitating discussions with others. Friends from whose experience and hospitality I have benefited while travelling in West, Central and East Africa during vacations from Oxford are too many to mention individually. In some cases the acknowledgement might embarrass both these and others who have talked freely of their experiences. At a number of points in the text the source of information cannot therefore be attributed.

Thanks to the generosity of the authors, I was able to see in typescript two books which have since been published, *The Civil Service in New African States* by A. L. Adu, and *Military Institutions and Power in the New States* by William Gutteridge. Each is a unique contribution in its field. I also wish to acknowledge the kindness of Mrs. C. J. Bryant for allowing me to see her unpublished London University thesis on *Some Problems of Public Administration in Uganda* and of Miss Christine Dobbin for access to her unpublished Oxford University thesis on *The Ilbert Bill*.

Miss Margaret Robins, the Librarian of the Institute of Commonwealth Studies in Oxford, and Mr. H. J. Stook, Librarian of the Indian Institute in Oxford, have been the kindest of guides in the considerable documentation which exists on localization. Finally, I wish to acknowledge that but for my wife this book could never have appeared.

Institute of Commonwealth Studies
Oxford
1965

A Note on Terminology

T hough the pattern of administration was generally similar throughout the British territories, the terminology varied. The district officer, who was the pivot of the administration in the field, was known in some parts of India as District Magistrate and Collector and in others as Deputy Commissioner. In Ceylon he was called Government Agent and in most parts of Africa, District Commissioner.

Above the district officer in India, except in Madras, was a Commissioner in charge of a Division, who was responsible to the Governor of the Province, which towards the end of British rule had a Premier and Council of Ministers. Below the district officer was the Subdivisional Officer. The Provincial Commissioner also existed in Africa, though sometimes he was called Resident and was in charge of a Province instead of a Division. The Indian units of administration were much larger than those of Africa. The Mymensingh District of Bengal, for example, contained a population as large as that of the Gold Coast or Uganda.

In the Government of India and those of the Indian Provinces a Secretary served as permanent head of each Ministry or Department. In colonial territories he usually was designated as Permanent Secretary or sometimes Principal Secretary. Either under a political Minister, or directly responsible to the Governor if there was no ministerial government, the Permanent Secretary was usually an administrative officer, and the heads of technical services reported through him to the Minister.

In India the head of the government under the East India Company was the Governor General. After Crown rule was established, the office was combined with that of Viceroy. The headquarters of the Government of India was Calcutta until it moved to Delhi in 1912. Simla was the summer capital.

British civil service terms may also need clarification for the non-British reader. The British Civil Service contains administrative, executive and clerical classes. The administrative class in Britain and in its colonies were the elite, generally recruited directly from the universities, though in Britain itself promotion between the classes was also possible. Throughout this book the term 'administrative officer' is used in the British sense.

Some educational terms may need explanation. 'Primary' and 'elementary' education were used interchangeably throughout the period studied, though they sometimes had different connotations in particular territories. Until 1948 the British schoolboy and his colonial counterpart took the School Certificate examination as a qualification for entering university, though each university might also hold an additional entrance examination. Two years after School Certificate, immediately before leaving school, he might take the Higher Certificate which had no direct relevance to Oxford and Cambridge entry but was equivalent to the intermediate examination of London University. After 1948, the School Certificate was redesignated as the General Certificate of Education, Ordinary Level (G.C.E., 'O' level) and the Higher Certificate as G.C.E., Advanced or 'A' level. The English universities now raised their entry standards and required passes at the 'A' level. The terms 'School Certificate' and 'O level' continued to be used side by side in some colonial territories, as did 'A level' and 'Higher Certificate'.

Finally, two words may need definition. 'Localization' is an indispensable term invented by the Colonial Office to describe the process by which expatriates in the government services were replaced by local people anywhere in the world, from Adenization to Zanzibarization. A puzzling word for those unfamiliar with India may be 'Babu' or 'Baboo'. Correctly used this is the polite form of address for a Hindu Bengali gentleman. The British, however, generally used it to refer, often in a derogatory sense, to the clerical or intellectual classes.

Introduction

The subject of this book is the succession to the British in the government services which they established in Asia and in Africa. This, of course, is only one aspect, inseparable from others, of the process which the French call 'decolonization'. The pace of localization[1] of the services was evidently related to that of the transfer of political power, and the services could not continue to operate effectively without political stability. The extent to which trained local people were available to replace the British depended on the educational policies which had been followed over the previous ten or twenty years: and in turn the adequacy of the educational structure was dependent upon the development of the territories' economic resources, for until about 1940 each colony was expected to pay for its own social services.

Yet it was equally true that progress in the political, economic and educational fields depended on the maintenance of order and of an administrative machine capable of implementing the development programmes which were impatiently demanded by the new electorates, and for which funds often suddenly became available from fairy godmothers who attended the birthday celebrations at independence. As the Union Jack was lowered at midnight therefore perhaps the principal question which the departing British asked themselves was what they had done to leave behind a stable framework of law and order and services which could provide the essential needs of the population in agriculture, health, education and communications.

It is at first sight surprising that rather little has been written on this subject in Britain and that most of the major works which have appeared on the administration of the new states since independence have been by American scholars. Perhaps this is because the British have not seen the problems with which they lived so long with the same freshness as the Americans, some of whom have been fascinated

13

as well as shocked by the traditions of 'omnicompetent generalism'[2] which the I.C.S. and Colonial Service left behind them.

Yet the question of the succession in the services is one of some importance in British history. Once the stage of company rule was over, the British had governed their dependent territories mainly through civil servants. There were exceptions; the Viceroyalty of India was a political appointment and the Governorships of the Presidencies of Bombay, Madras and Bengal were often given to junior ministers or party whips; sometimes too the governors of colonial territories were retired generals and occasionally politicians. But the normal pattern was one in which political as well as administrative authority was concentrated in the hands of British civil servants of the I.C.S. or Colonial Service in a chain of command which ran down from the Governor, through the Chief Secretary or Colonial Secretary, to the Provincial Commissioner and District Officer. The District Officer was a magistrate, a collector of revenue and sometimes also a judge. 'Such a power as that which Collectors in India have over the people,' said Macaulay, 'is not found in any other part of the world possessed by any class of functionary.'[3] And at headquarters the Secretary would draft legislation in his department: he would sit on the Executive Council, where it was considered in detail, would pilot it through the legislature, where it was debated in general; and finally he would be responsible for its implementation.

To Asians and Africans therefore it appeared that real power lay as much in the civil service as with political parties; and the demand for Indianization and Africanization of the services was one of the earliest and most emphatic to be made by the nationalist parties. As the new English-educated classes emerged, the question became almost an obsession, so that Morley in 1906 believed that the Indians cared far more about access to higher administrative posts than about political reforms,[4] and Lord Hailey thirty-five years later maintained that West Africans judged the seriousness of Britain's intentions in promising self-government by the extent to which Africans were admitted into the administrative service.[5]

The response to the demand was affected by several factors. The attitude of the politicians and of their advisers in London was often a reflection of their views on broader issues. Thus in the early 19th century arguments in favour of Indianization on grounds of natural justice were sometimes used as weapons in the attack on the powers of patronage of the East India Company. In the middle of the century Africanization appealed to Little Englanders and Free Traders who wished to limit colonial expansion and, still more, colonial expenditure. The need for economy was indeed the argument most frequently used in favour of localization in despatches on the subject from London to the Viceroy and to the colonial governors. At the end of the century, the Conservative and Liberal Unionist imperialists who had the upper hand believed that British rule would and should last indefinitely, and were unenthusiastic about using Indians and Africans in senior positions, while the anti-imperialist wing of the Liberal Party, which was simultaneously championing Irish independence, favoured Indianization of the services. In the next generation the Labour Party took up a similar position against the Conservatives in relation to Africa. Behind the Liberal and Labour members, supplying them with questions and facts, were groups such as the Indian Parliamentary Committee, organized by Dadabhai Naoroji and Sir William Wedderburn, and later Krishna Menon's India League; while the Aborigines Protection Society lobbied for the wider use of West Africans in the services. On the other side, Conservative predictions of the disasters which Indianization would bring about were supported by groups in which retired Indian Army and I.C.S. officers were prominent.

The influence of the missionary organizations was indirect but important, particularly in relation to Africa. In most territories priests were ordained long before Africans were appointed to senior posts by the government. The example of the appointment of the Nigerian, Samuel Crowther, as an Anglican Bishop in the 19th century was a powerful symbol of African achievement, as was the appointment of a Tanganyikan Cardinal in East Africa in the 1950s. Missionary organizations were also usually ahead of the government in their advocacy of secondary and higher education. On the other hand in the middle and late 19th century their reports of the sinful character of native society contributed to the change of policy by which Africans were replaced by British officers on the West Coast; nor were they unaffected by the current pseudo-scientific racial theories.

From time to time the British universities exercised a significant influence. Jowett succeeded in linking recruitment and training of the I.C.S. to Oxford and Cambridge, and the Colonial Service mainly used the same sources, though with a different method of selection. Later the Successors themselves came as probationers to be trained at Oxford and Cambridge. In the period after the Second World War the British universities, with London now in the lead, played an enthusiastic part in establishing new universities overseas in their own image and in the debate on 'standards'. The influence of individual university teachers was sometimes considerable. In the middle of the 19th century at Oxford Horace Hayman Wilson and Max Müller challenged the contemptuous attitude of James Mill towards the Indian character and that of Macaulay towards Indian culture. Later, Ruskin, Freeman and others helped to encourage the spirit of racial pride which among other results was temporarily to impede localization. In the next century, Harold Laski at the London School of Economics not only taught socialist planning to Indian probationers but questioned the narrow basis of recruitment to the colonial service. Margery Perham in Oxford by the late forties was emphasizing that the most important British task in Africa was now not so much to administer as to train Africans to administer.

The attitude of the 'Guardians', of the British civil servants themselves, in India and Africa towards the Successors was of the greatest importance. For though London gave an occasional prod to the Viceroy on the question, in the colonies the pace of localization was left very largely to the Governor. It is hard to find a common approach even within the Indian Civil Service, which always contained elements who thought the British should remain as long as possible, but yet produced A. O. Hume, Henry Cotton and Penderel Moon. It would be even more pointless to seek a consensus in the colonial service, whose officers were living among peoples at every level of development from Cyprus and Malta to Borneo and the Gilbert and Ellis Islands. Yet despite differences in local conditions and occasional variations, recognizable characteristics emerged from the similarity of their background. The great majority came from upper middle class but not aristocratic families. The tough boarding school life, with its system of fagging and compulsory games, was followed by studies in classics or the arts at a residential university. There seems wide agreement that this produced a type of district officer who compared favourably with his counterpart in any other colonial system – patient, adaptable and particularly successful with primitive peoples; just and incorruptible. The obverse was often a difficulty in getting on with a rising educated middle class and perhaps the absence of a will to do so. The background also brought to bear what Americans in particular have characterized as an atti-

tude of spirited amateurism towards administration and of technological illiteracy in relation to the problems of economic development, both of which characteristics were often transmitted to the
Successors.

The extreme views on the succession would of course have been
either that on the one hand British imperial rule was so permanent
that the question would never arise, or on the other that it would
settle itself by a process of total assimilation between the local people
and the British. Neither of these positions was really tenable within
the non-white Empire. Though there was often talk about the natives
being 'children' and 'permanent wards', sheer budgetary considerations prevented their total exclusion from the government services.
The colonies could not possibly afford to staff all the posts with
British officers. Once the local people were admitted and trained, the
question became one of degree rather than of principle, as to how far
they should be allowed to rise; though the position was complicated
when, as in East Africa, a third element such as the Asians was introduced into the middle levels of the services. Few believed that a policy
of permanent assimilation was feasible except in the white colonies.
Joseph Hume indeed proposed that the Reform Bill of 1832 should
provide seats in the British Parliament for India and the West Indian
islands,[6] and in 1904 the Indian National Congress asked that India
should be given seats in Parliament.[7] These proposals however
represented temporary phases of enthusiasm and were not pressed:
nor was Mintoff's suggestion in the 1950s that Malta should be
integrated with the United Kingdom, which might have provided a
precedent for the solution to the problems of viability for the very
small dependencies.

Within these theoretical extremes, most of those who looked forward towards the succession on the British side saw it broadly in one
of two ways, which might be described as that of the Anglicizers and
the Conservationists. Of the Anglicizers, Macaulay was the most
eloquent exponent in his great speeches in the Commons on the East
India Company Charter Bill in 1833, and on competitive entry to the
civil service twenty years later, and in his Minute on Education. To
Macaulay the main object of British educational policy was 'to form
a class of interpreters between us and the natives we govern, a class
of persons Indian in blood and colour but English in tastes, in
opinions, in morals and in intellect'.[8] That this class might compete
for posts in the government services on equal terms with the British

and might ultimately even displace them, Macaulay accepted with equanimity. On the most selfish view of the case, it was better for the Indians to have their own rulers 'but wearing our broadcloth and working with our cutlery, than that they were performing their salaams to English Collectors and Magistrates, but were too ignorant to value or too poor to buy English manufactures'.[9] But he went on to sweep into a peroration which was to be recited by generations of Indian schoolboys.

'Are we to keep the people of India ignorant in order that we may keep them submissive? Or do we think that we can give them knowledge without awakening ambition? Or do we mean to awaken ambition and to provide it with no legitimate vent? Who will answer any of these questions in the affirmative? Yet one of them must be answered affirmatively by every person who maintains that we ought to exclude the natives from high office.' And he ended by asserting that the day when India demanded British institutions would be the 'proudest day in English history'.[10]

When the 'proudest day' came, some observers may have wished, on contemplating the kind of government services which had been evolved, like Lord Melbourne, that they were as sure of anything as Macaulay was of everything.[11] Macaulay's contempt for Oriental culture was a major factor in creating a system of examinations and of education which produced a class of 'interpreters' who often lost touch with their own roots and wandered unhappily between two worlds. He was not only ignorant of Eastern learning. As Mark Pattison observed, 'of the marvellous discoveries of science which were succeeding each other day by day he took no note'.[12] This complacent ignorance was to be transferred to the civil service and then to the Successors themselves through the weighted system of competitive examinations which Macaulay and his friends devised.

Yet to generations of Indians, and later of Africans, the patronizing insularity of Macaulay was of far less importance than his assertion, written into the statute book, of the right of men of all races to compete on equal terms for posts in the government service. To this they could cling, often to the embarrassment of the British, when by the end of the century the latter had come to view their rule as much more permanent than Macaulay had done and when it had become fashionable to believe that the levels of potential attainment of different races were irrevocably determined by God and by science.

18

The Conservationists looked at the succession in a quite different way. Elphinstone and Munro in India in the early 19th century regarded the natural successors as those whom the British had displaced, the feudal leaders whom they urged the Government, with little success, to take into its service. In the next century those who developed indirect rule in Africa had the same concept and opposed the recruitment of educated middle class Africans into the British service because this might weaken the influence of the Chiefs. Though there were to be exceptions, as in Northern Nigeria and to some extent in Uganda, this school of thought did not in the end prevail. In India Queen Victoria's great-grandson, as the last Viceroy, was to confront the princes with the brutal necessity of coming to terms with the Congress or the Muslim League, and in most of Africa it was the nationalist party and the civil service rather than the chiefs who shared in the succession.

Similar differences can be observed in the attitudes towards the succession of those who led public opinion in the dependent territories. The feudal aristocracy was often nervous about the development of an educated middle class which might replace the British District Officers, though sometimes, as in Ceylon, they came to terms and sent their own sons into the services. The attitude of the nationalist parties, which were usually controlled by the educated middle class, could be ambivalent. For thirty years, Indianization of the services was demanded at every annual meeting of the Congress; but later Indians were urged to withdraw from the services in order to paralyse the Government. In such a situation the local people in the services faced a conflict of loyalties before independence and a difficult adjustment afterwards. As independence drew near, competition for posts in the services often became a powerful factor in arousing jealousy between different communities or tribes. The replacement of the British by then often ceased to be the main point at issue for the politicians; instead attention became focused on the proportions of Muslims in the Indian services, of Tamils in those of Ceylon, or of Asians in the East African services.

This study attempts to trace the results of the interplay of these different influences and attitudes on the development of the government services in the dependent territories. This cannot be done comprehensively: entire books of considerable value have indeed been devoted to the history of individual services in particular territories. The history of the Indian Forest Service alone fills four volumes.

Some explanation may be therefore needed of the method which has been adopted.

India is the natural starting point, for this was by far the most populous British territory and with almost the longest connection. Here the issues of localization were debated over a hundred years. By the 1860s it was clear that on equal terms Hindus and Parsees could compete successfully in open examinations with British candidates. From then on the British saw themselves as faced with two dilemmas; how to reconcile their own rule with the principle of equal opportunity in the services which had been laid down by Parliament; and how on the other hand to safeguard the position of the less intellectual and often martial communities of India.

Ceylon provides an interesting parallel over the same period. Here it was the minority communities which were capable of defeating the majority, and also very possibly the British, in open examinations. The administration was however separate from that of India and the Government's attitude to localization was somewhat more advanced than that of India, though it was less active in the encouragement of higher education.

The experience of the British in India, and in particular their disillusionment with the results of their educational policies, considerably affected their attitudes in West Africa, particularly at the end of the 19th century when Africans were replaced in senior positions by Europeans. By this time however the mission schools were well established and were already producing a small elite, a number of whom went on to be educated in England and returned to demand posts in the services.

The experience in West Africa in turn had an important influence both on British policy and on the attitudes of African nationalists in East Africa. Unenthusiastic about the results of mission education, the British concentrated in East Africa on vocational education. Though this policy was reversed in 1945, the East African Governments were overtaken by the acceleration towards independence long before they had formed the cadres which were necessary to replace the Europeans in the Government services. Yet the position might have been even more critical at independence had it not been possible to call on the services of some of those who had carried out localization programmes in West Africa.

While the debate on Indianization and Africanization was centred on the administrative services, localization of the armed forces was

20

also an important issue, particularly in India: its significance was vividly demonstrated in East Africa as well as the Congo and is discussed in the chapters on each area. The issues which arose regarding standards in the professional services are also interesting and relatively unexplored and are considered generally in Chapter XII as well as in the chapters on the different regions.

Not only did the development of the government services depend on progress in education, but in turn the qualifications demanded for entry to the services did much to shape the educational system in territories where the government was the principal employer. Educational policy therefore has to be examined as a background to localization in each of the areas which are studied.

Although it is too early to attempt even provisional evaluations, the question inevitably arises of how and with what results the British approach to the succession differed from that of other colonial powers. The attitudes of the French, Belgians, Americans and Dutch to localization in certain of their territories are considered in Chapter XI.

In order to keep the book within manageable length many omissions have been necessary. Thus in West Africa the small territory of The Gambia and in East Africa that of Zanzibar have not been included. Little has been said on the Indian Princely States, and the whole study has been concentrated on the central rather than local government services. Nor has it been possible to deal with South East Asia, where the problems of minorities were of considerable interest, or the West Indies, where localization became an issue at a very early stage.

Much of the documentation on localization is still unavailable under the fifty year rule which restricts access to official papers in the United Kingdom. Future historians may be able to make a more informed appraisal of this aspect of the last stage of empire. The main justification for writing on it meanwhile is that many of those, both on the British and colonial side, who debated localization and educational policies or who carried them out, though willing now to discuss their experiences, will be too modest, too busy or too disillusioned to write their memoirs.

INTRODUCTION

REFERENCES

[1] 'Localization' is a convenient Colonial Office word which comprehends the transfer of the government services to local people in any territory. See 'Note on Terminology', p. 11.

[2] Ralph Braibanti, *Administration and Economic Development in India*, London, 1963, p. 9.

[3] Hansard, House of Commons debates, 24 June, 1853, Col. 746.

[4] See p. 39 below.

[5] See p. 151 below.

[6] Hansard, House of Commons Debates, 16 August, 1831, Col. 110.

[7] D. Chakrabarty, *Congress in Evolution*, Calcutta, 1958, p. 9.

[8] Minute on Education, Selections from Educational Records, Calcutta, 1920, Part I, p. 116.

[9] Hansard, House of Commons Debates, 10 July, 1833, Col. 535.

[10] ibid. Col. 536.

[11] Mark Pattison, article on 'Macaulay', *Encyclopaedia Britannica*, 1951 ed.

[12] ibid.

PART ONE

India and Ceylon

The former Dominion of India was divided into the independent states of India and Pakistan in 1947 with populations of about 357 million and 76 million respectively. Ceylon became independent in 1948 with a population of about 8 million.

CHAPTER I

The Debate on the Indian Civil Service

'And be it enacted that no native of the said Territories, nor any natural-born subject of His Majesty resident therein, shall by reason only of his Religion, Place of Birth, Descent, Colour or any of them, be disabled from holding any Place, Office or Employment under the said Company.'

CLAUSE 87 OF THE EAST INDIA CHARTER
ACT OF 1833

The debate on Indianization lasted almost throughout the period of British rule. It was most keenly focussed on what was until 1858 the covenanted civil service of the East India Company and later became the Indian Civil Service. This was a relatively small service, with never more than 1,200 officers, to whom most of the highest posts in the administration were assured by law. In the world's greatest bureaucracy its members could govern provinces with twenty or thirty million inhabitants or as members of the Viceroy's Council hold cabinet portfolios in the administration of a country of three or four hundred millions. The emoluments, at least in the 19th century, were considerable. As a *Guide to the I.C.S.* pointed out in 1870, 'in addition to the very lucrative appointments which the Indian Civil Service holds out as an inducement to its servants, it possesses another great advantage in the plan of frequently uniting several appointments in the hands of one official'.[1] John Bright told Parliament in 1859 that the I.C.S. were 'more grossly overpaid than anyone except bishops' and received salaries fifty to one hundred per cent higher than those in Ceylon.[2] Its prestige was enormous. Years after independence a Pakistan Government publication could still take it for granted that the I.C.S. had been 'the most distinguished civil service in the world'.[3]

25

The way in which the I.C.S. came to occupy this privileged position may be rapidly traced. The British East India Company's relationship with India from the earliest contacts until the Battle of Plassey in 1757 was that of a trader. Its officials were called 'factors' and 'writers', and it exercised no administrative authority outside its own factories at Calcutta, Bombay and Madras. The earliest Indians in its service were the interpreters and brokers whom it needed in its commercial undertakings and in negotiations with Indian rulers. In 1772 the Company took over administrative and revenue functions from the Nawab of Bengal. It had been the policy of the Mogul Government to employ Indians of all races and religions in senior positions in order to avoid the risk of creating dangerously powerful classes of hereditary officials. Thus Rajputs as well as Muslims were found in military and administrative posts, and, though Muslims predominated in judicial positions, Hindus usually ran the Revenue departments. At first the Company continued to use the services of former imperial officials, but in 1793 Cornwallis, as Governor General, replaced them by Europeans in all senior posts. There were two main reasons for this. Firstly, the corruption both of British and Indian officials in the plundering which followed the acquisition of Bengal caused Cornwallis to see the only remedy as their replacement by officials trained in and brought out from Britain. Secondly, the substitution of English for Muhammedan criminal law had made it virtually impossible to continue to use Muslim judges who neither understood nor could approve of the new procedures.

Henceforward, under the Charter Act of 1793, all posts of over £500 a year were reserved for the Company's new 'covenanted' service. The Covenant which was signed by the officers of the service was an agreement not to trade on their own account; in return for this undertaking they were paid salaries substantial enough to make private trading unnecessary. Vacancies to the service were filled by nomination by each of the Directors of the Company in rotation. Under this system of patronage strong family traditions were established; and the intimacy of the service was fostered by the training given to its cadets at the Company's College, which was established at Haileybury, near London in 1805.

The exclusion of Indians from responsibility was strongly criticized by several of the most prominent of the Company's officials in India in the early 19th century. Men such as Elphinstone and Malcolm, successive Governors of Bombay, and Munro, Governor of Madras, had come out to India in their early teens and were more profoundly influenced and attracted by Indian culture than were their Haileyburian and evangelical successors: they found the Company's policy of exclusion dangerous, unjust and even inefficient. As Munro wrote in 1817: 'It is from men who either hold or are eligible for public office that nations take their character: where no such men exist, there can be no energy in any other class of the community. No elevation can be expected from men who in the military line cannot attain to any rank above that of Subedar, where they are as much below the ensign as the ensign is below the Commander-in-Chief; or who in the civil line can hope for nothing beyond some petty and revenue office in which they may by corrupt means make up for their slender salary. Foreign conquerors,' he added, 'have treated the natives with violence but none with such scorn as we'.[4] Malcolm went so far as to assert 'We must, or we cannot last, associate Indians with us'.[5] These were not by nature social or religious reformers. Malcolm's policy was 'to alter nothing that can be tolerated'[6] and Elphinstone wrote that 'to the mixture of religion with our plans I greatly object'.[7]

Munro and Elphinstone wished to make use of the existing Indian aristocracy and to build on Indian institutions. A very different approach was that of the Utilitarians and Evangelicals in England. The most influential of the Evangelicals were Charles Grant, who was one of the Directors of the Board of the East India Company from 1794 to 1823, and William Wilberforce, the Emancipator of the Slaves, whose second great ambition was the conversion of India. The effect on Indian education of Grant's *Observations on the State of Asia*, which depicted the degradation of Indian life and advocated the extended use of the English language as a medium which would 'silently undermine the fabric of error',[8] will be examined in the next chapter. The Evangelicals were prepared to welcome Indian collaborators, but on their own terms; they must be educated in English, 'civilized' and if possible Christianized.

Of the Utilitarians, James Mill's influence was the most important both through his massive *History of British India* and his work as Chief Examiner at the India House, where he was the principal civil servant of the East India Company. Mill's contempt for the culture and society of India, which he never visited, was even more vehemently expressed than that of Grant. Indians were generally characterized in his *History* as dissembling, treacherous, mendacious, cowardly and unfeeling and disgustingly unclean.[9] He was much less optimistic than the Evangelicals as to the results of education. To him the paramount consideration was the establishment and maintenance of good laws: these, with light taxes, would in time lead to the eradication of poverty which was necessary before education could be productive.

Both the Evangelical and Utilitarian influences affected the attitude to Indians of the generation of the Company's civil servants who passed through Haileybury. Wilberforce regarded the establishment of the College as 'a preliminary step to the evangelization of India' and the Archbishop of Canterbury told the last class to graduate in 1858 that they were just as much missionaries as were the men sent out by the Church.[10] Mill's *History* was Haileybury's most important textbook, and Max Müller considered that it had been responsible for some of India's greatest misfortunes, in teaching the Company's civil servants to despise Indian civilization and character.[11]

When Parliament conducted its twenty-year review of the renewal of the East India Company's Charter in 1830–31, the admission of Indians to higher employment was one of the questions considered by its Select Committee. Elphinstone, now in retirement, gave evidence that it was desirable to admit Indians to all ranks of civil and military employment, as a partial compensation for the lack of popular institutions. John Sullivan, who had spent thirty years in the Company's service in Bengal, supported him, stating that it was universally admitted that there were Indians qualified by their talents and industry for all the offices in the administration, though there was not the same unanimity as to their moral fitness. 'By permitting the natives to fill a few of the high situations,' he maintained, 'we shall gradually raise a native aristocracy of our own, who would consider the security of their own fortunes identified with the safety of the government'. Two other retired officers from India, Holt MacKenzie and Charles Lushington, gave evidence in a similar sense.[12]

James Mill on the other hand considered that 'the mere employment of natives in itself does not appear to me to be a matter of so much importance as it does to some other persons. It appears to me 10,000 times more important with respect to the good of the population in general that the business should be well done than that it should be done by any class of person'.[13]

The Select Committee reported to Parliament that they had received evidence that Indians were alive to the grievance of being excluded from higher employment and that their exclusion was not warranted by their lack of capacity for business. They added that it had been contended that 'their admission, under European control, into the higher offices would have a beneficial effect in correcting the moral obliquities of their general character; would strengthen their attachment to British dominion; would conduce to the better administration of Justice; and would be productive of a great saving in the Expenses of the Indian Government'.[14] Macaulay, who was Secretary of the Board of Control, seized upon this reference as a basis for the inclusion in the Charter Act of 1833 of the famous Clause 87, by which it became illegal for anyone to be excluded from holding office under the Company by reason of religion, birth, descent or colour.

Macaulay declared that to the last days of his life he would be proud of his part in obtaining Parliament's approval of this clause. He and his brother-in-law, Sir Charles Trevelyan, were the most confident of the Anglicizers. Macaulay wrote in his Minute on Education that 'a single shelf of a good European library is worth the whole native literature of India and Arabia'.[15] He made no attempt in his five years in India to study Indian art, philosophy or literature, but in this 'exile' devoted his leisure to reading the Greek classics. Trevelyan was even more confident than Macaulay of the necessity of forming a 'class of interpreters, Indian in blood and colour but Englishmen in tastes, in opinions, in morals and intellect'. 'The Spirit of English literature,' he wrote, 'cannot but be favourable to the connection . . . Indians educated in it will become more English than Hindu, just as the Roman provincials became more Romans than Gauls or Italians'.[16]

The instructions of the Court of Directors of the Company to the Governor General on the Charter Act of 1833 were probably drafted by James Mill, and reflected his lack of enthusiasm for Clause 87. 'To this altered rule,' the despatch stated, 'it will be necessary that you should both in your acts and your language conform; practically, perhaps, no very marked difference of results will be occasioned. The distinction between situations allotted to the covenanted service and all other situations of an official or public nature will remain generally as at present.'[17]

Twenty years later, when the Company's Charter again came up for review, John Bright pointed out to the House of Commons that

Clause 87 had had no practical effect whatever.[18] The company found it necessary to appoint Indians as deputy magistrates and deputy collectors to deal with revenue surveys in newly acquired territories and with the great increase in litigation which arose from the establishment of the courts and from the complexity of their land settlements. But they never appointed an Indian to the covenanted service, to which the top posts were reserved. When an exceptionally well-qualified Indian candidate was proposed, Ram Mohan Roy's adopted son, who had studied in England, they indicated that he would be unhappy at Haileybury, where chapel attendance was compulsory.[19]

After the Indian Mutiny of 1857, however, the Company surrendered responsibility for the rule of India to the British Government and Queen Victoria declared in her initial proclamation of 1858 that 'colour, religion or birth were not to be disqualifications for any office in India under the Crown'. It is from this declaration, 'the Magna Carta of our rights' as Surendranath Banerjea called it, that Indians began to participate in a debate which had previously been conducted between the British of various opinions. It concentrated particularly on the Indian Civil Service, the successor to the covenanted service of the Company.

One of the reforms to which Bentham and the Utilitarians attached great importance was the substitution of competitive written examinations for patronage as a means of entry to the public services. After a long struggle, the Company in 1854 was obliged by Parliament to adopt this method of recruitment to its covenanted service and it was continued when the Crown took over responsibility for India. Macaulay was Chairman of a committee which prepared the syllabus for the competitive examination, and it is not surprising therefore that while 700 marks each were awarded for papers in Latin and Greek, only 375 each could be gained by candidates who took papers in Arabic and Sanskrit. A further discouragement to Indian candidates was that the examination was held in London at a time when a Hindu risked social ostracism on his return if he travelled overseas. On the Committee's recommendation the maximum age of the candidates was established at twenty-three years in order to enable university graduates to compete.

To the Indian middle class not only did it appear that the scales were heavily weighted against Indian candidates, but that the British Government was always prepared to weight them further if there were a danger of a substantial number of Indian candidates passing.

At first sight, the chronology seems to justify this view. In 1859, under some pressure from the British Indian Association and other Indian bodies, the Government raised the marks for Sanskrit and Arabic from 375 to 500 each. In 1864, the first Indian, Satyendranath Tagore, passed the examination. In 1865, the marks allowed for Sanskrit and Arabic were reduced again and the maximum age limit of candidates was lowered to twenty-one. Despite these changes, four more Indians were successful in 1868 and several more in the next few years. In 1876, the Secretary of State for India, Lord Salisbury, against the advice of the Viceroy, Lord Northbrook, reduced the maximum age to nineteen, thus allowing Indian candidates an almost impossibly short time in which to prepare themselves for an examination which was mainly related to classical European culture.

The correspondence between successive Viceroys and Secretaries of State does not however suggest that at this stage the deliberate exclusion of Indians was a primary consideration. The Mutiny of 1857, though the English-speaking Indian middle class was hardly involved, had indeed caused what John Lawrence in 1867 described as a distrust and hatred between the two races which perhaps might never subside.[20] But in lowering the age limits of the I.C.S. examination the government were mainly concerned with getting British officers out to India at a younger age, with more years of active and healthy service ahead of them. They were also confused by characteristically conflicting advice from the various authorities of Oxford and Cambridge Universities.[21] Once the issue was raised in terms of its effect on Indianization however, the Government showed a recurrent uncertainty as to how to reconcile the declarations of racial equality of 1833 and 1858 with the security of British rule. At times the Secretary of State or Viceroy– and occasionally both–were prepared to make a cautious advance. In 1861 Parliament enacted that some posts hitherto reserved for covenanted civil servants might be opened to uncovenanted officers; and in 1867 a Conservative Secretary of State, Sir Stafford Northcote, asked the Viceroy, Lord Lawrence, to review what was being done to open higher posts to Indians in light of the development of education.[22]

Lawrence, who was the only member of the I.C.S. ever to become Viceroy, admitted in his reply that the Act of 1861 had been used to provide posts for Europeans who had distinguished themselves in the Mutiny rather than for Indians.[23] While he emphasized the difficulties of entrusting Indians with administrative duties which might

31

affect Europeans, he proposed to institute nine scholarships a year to enable Indians to study in England for the civil service examination. Some of these scholarships would be awarded by competition, but he considered that it was also 'of great social and political importance to give to the sons of Native gentlemen of rank and position a larger share of the advantages now offered than they would be likely to obtain under such a system'. Some of the proposed scholarships would therefore be awarded by nomination.[24]

The Duke of Argyll, who succeeded Northcote in the Liberal Government of 1868, disallowed the scholarship scheme. While he agreed that personal acquaintanceship with British institutions would be a valuable element in the education of Indian administrators, he believed that on the whole wider employment of Indians should be through promotion from the uncovenanted to the covenanted service. 'It should never be forgotten,' he wrote, 'and there should never be any hesitation in laying down the principle, that it is one of our first duties towards the people of India to guard the safety of our own dominions. For this purpose we must proceed gradually, employing only such Natives as we can trust, and these only in such offices as in the condition of things the Government of India may determine to be really suited to them.'[25]

Argyll's solution to the dilemma was the Act of 1870 by which Indians were enabled to occupy any post previously held by the covenanted service, subject to rules prescribed by the Governor General. The Government of India operated the act with little enthusiasm. Eight years after it was passed, Lord Lytton as Viceroy found that its provisions had not been used at all in Bombay and Madras. Instead this had been a period of general expansion of the British personnel in the services. Lytton admitted privately to the Secretary of State that 'the application to Natives of the competitive system in England and the recent reduction in the age at which candidates can compete are so many deliberate and transparent subterfuges for stultifying the Act [of 1833] and reducing it to a dead letter'.[26]

As he saw it the problem was to reconcile three principles; the first was Parliament's declarations of equal opportunity for Indians, the second the need to maintain British rule, and the third the legitimate claims to senior posts of the officers who had joined the I.C.S. on the expectation that these would be reserved for the Service. Lytton followed up an argument which had first been put forward by John

Stuart Mill, that it was hardly fair to admit Indians to the I.C.S. if it was tacitly understood that they could not be appointed to its higher posts; he suggested that recruitment from England to the covenanted service should be greatly reduced and that it should be closed to Indians. On the other hand, a new native civil service would be established to which appointments would be made by the Viceroy by nomination. Lytton referred to the 'utter impossibility of getting European officers of position and education to serve cheerfully under Natives', which he regarded as an insuperable difficulty in the executive work of a district.[27]

The Secretary of State, Lord Cranbrook, in his reply informed the Viceroy that an application to Parliament to close the covenanted civil service to Indians would have no chance of success. He authorized Lytton, however, to appoint Indians by nomination to a so-called 'statutory service'.[28]

Lytton was succeeded by Lord Ripon, the most popular in articulate Indian circles of all Britain's Viceroys, who considered that Lytton's preference for a statutory civil service, nominated from men of good families, had reflected his hatred of Indian intellectuals.[29] His own sympathies were with the new middle class. 'We have been turning out year by year from our universities streams of men with the best education that the English Government could give them,' he said, '. . . Is it possible to turn round on these men and say to them "we will not give you any openings for those aspirations with which we have inspired you".'[30] By now the admission of Indians to the covenanted service had become a lively issue among the Bengal middle class, and Surendranath Banerjea's all-India political campaign had obtained resolutions in Northern, Western and Southern India, as well as Bengal, in support of fairer conditions for the entry of Indians to the services.* Demands for raising the age limits, for holding simultaneous examinations in India and in England, and for increasing the marks for Sanskrit and Arabic were made in resolutions at the first session of the Indian National Congress in 1885. Ripon warmly supported these demands, writing to the Secretary of State that the change in the age limit had 'practically deprived Indians of the right of admission to the Covenanted Civil Service on equal terms with the rest of Her Majesty's subjects . . . and affected by indirect means a change which would have had no chance of success in Parliament'.[31] He would probably have tried to do more to

* See also Chapter IV

facilitate Indian entry to the covenanted service if he had not had a simultaneous fight on his hands with the European community over the Ilbert Bill. This controversy was itself related to the wider issue of Indianization, for the bill proposed that Indian magistrates should be enabled to try Europeans. Ripon eventually had to concede that in such cases there should be European jurors.

Under mounting Indian criticism, the Government of India in 1886 appointed a Commission on the Public Service to inquire into the employment of Indians in the administration: this was to be the first of many 'localization' commissions within the Empire and Commonwealth. The Chairman, Sir Charles Aitchison, and five others were members of the covenanted civil service, but there were also six Indian members including Sir R. C. Mitter, who had once acted as Chief Justice of India, and Sir Syed Ahmad Khan, the leader of the Muslim educational revival.

The Commission, whose proposals were adopted by the Government, responded to S. N. Banerjea's campaign by recommending that the age limits for the I.C.S. examination should again be raised to twenty-three. It was a great blow to Indian nationalists however when the Muslim members as well as the Hindu Raja Pertab Singh joined the majority in rejecting the demand for simultaneous competitive examinations to be held in India, on the grounds that this procedure would unduly favour certain communities. The Commission also refused to recommend that more marks be awarded for Sanskrit and Arabic, basing their decision on Macaulay's thesis that the education to be tested in the examination should be European rather than Oriental.

The Commission recommended the abolition of Lytton's statutory service which men of ability had proved reluctant to enter because its members were only eligible for a limited number of posts. While Indians would continue to be recruited by competition into the I.C.S., this should be reduced in numbers to an elite service and some of its posts should be thrown open to the provincial administrative services. The members of the latter, entirely Indian, were to be recruited by each province separately, either by competition or by examination according to its needs. The effects of similar recommendations when applied in the professional services will be seen in Chapter III.[32]

In the British Parliament there were always Liberal members who were prepared to harry the Government on its failure to fulfil the pledges of 1833 and 1858. One of the earliest was John Bright who regarded the covenanted system as 'most objectionable and offensive' and suggested that the whole competitive system was a bar to the wider employment of the most intelligent and able Indians.[33] But it was Henry Fawcett who in the 1860s and 70s became known as 'the M.P. for India'. Fawcett was a Professor of Political Economy at Cambridge, one of whose main interests was in Indian finance. He pressed for Indianization of the services in order to save money on the Indian budget and to lessen the outflow of currency from India. But he was equally insistent on 'fair play': because the Indians were not enfranchised he believed that British M.P.s had a special duty to look after their interests.

Fawcett introduced a resolution into the House of Commons in 1868 asking that the competitive examinations for the Indian Civil Service should be held simultaneously in India and in Britain. An amendment was proposed by the young G. O. Trevelyan, Macaulay's nephew, in a speech as full of self-confident aphorisms as those of his uncle. 'Hindus are strong in intellect and confessedly weak in morals. We as a race are far superior to them in force of character ... We are there [in India] because we, as a nation, speak the truth and never take bribes'. Unfortunately, he admitted, there was a real danger that in an open competition the clever Bengali would defeat the Englishman, in spite of the latter's superior character. Recognizing, however, some responsibility to fulfil the promises of 1833 and 1858, Trevelyan proposed that instead of holding competitive examinations locally the Indian Government should be enabled to promote experienced Indians from the subordinate services and from the Bar to posts which were previously reserved for covenanted civil servants.[34]

Sir Stafford Northcote, the Secretary of State, accepted the amendment, which was carried, although he did not 'close the door forever' on simultaneous examinations and expressed himself in favour of the award of scholarships to enable Indians to study in England.

The tradition of Bright and Fawcett was continued in the eighties and nineties by a number of radical M.P.s, of whom two, Sir William Wedderburn and Sir Henry Cotton, had served in the I.C.S. In 1892, Dadabhai Naoroji, one of the principal Congress leaders, won a London seat by a narrow margin, assisted by a remark of the Prime Minister, Lord Salisbury, that 'we had not got to the point where a British constituency would elect a black man'.[35] Dadabhai in 1887

described the institution of simultaneous competitions for all departments of the civil administration as 'the chief aim of my life' and in
1893 he at last succeeded in obtaining a resolution of the House of
Commons in favour of simultaneous competitions for entry to the
I.C.S. and other services. After the overwhelming Liberal victory of
1906 Radical pressure on the Secretary of State, John Morley, was
supported from the benches of the Labour Party whose successive
leaders, Keir Hardie and Ramsay MacDonald, both visited and
wrote about India.

On the other hand there was a formidable body of retired civil
servants and army officers in Britain whose influence was strongly
opposed to Indianization; some of the most influential, such as Sir
John Strachey, were members of the Secretary of State's Council.
Others were members of Parliament like General Sir George Chesney
who, in the debate of 1893, asserted that 'among 70 million Bengalis
not one successful administrator had been produced'.[36]

By the 1890s, the liberalism of Bright and John Stuart Mill had
been eclipsed by the authority of imperialists such as Strachey, who
wrote in his widely read book *India*, 'There never was a country and
never will be in which the government of foreigners is really popular.
It will be the beginning of the end of our empire when we forget this
elementary fact and entrust the greater executive powers to the
hands of natives on the assumption that they will always be faithful
and strong supporters of our government. . . . Our Governors of
Provinces, the chief officers of our army, our magistrates of districts
and their principal subordinates ought to be Englishmen under all
the circumstances that we can now foresee'.[37] Strachey's friend 'the
philosopher of the I.C.S.', Sir Fitzjames Stephen, who was also a
former member of the Viceroy's Council, wrote a number of articles
in which he emphasized that India had 'essentially an absolute
government, founded not on consent but on conquest'.[38] The British
he asserted, had won their position by a great competitive examination which lasted for one hundred years, and of which the first paper
was set upon the field of Plassey and the last (for the present) under
the walls of Delhi and Lucknow.[39]

Fitzjames Stephen was an informal adviser to Lytton to whom
he suggested that 'in the proper solution of the question of introduction of the natives into civil administration lies the fate of the
Empire', urging that those of superior class rather than the de-
nationalized should be employed. His influence was even more

effective on Curzon,[40] who while a schoolboy at Eton heard him speak of 'an empire more populous, more amazing, more beneficent than that of Rome'.[41] Curzon while Viceroy complained privately to the Secretary of State, Lord George Hamilton, who himself regretted Queen Victoria's Proclamation of 1858,[42] that 'an increasing number of the 900 and odd higher posts that were meant for and ought to have been exclusively and specifically reserved for Europeans are being filched away by the superior wits of the native in the English examinations'.[43]

Publicly Curzon stated that 'The highest ranks of civil employment in India, those of the I.C.S., though open to such Indians as proceed to England and pass the requisite tests, must nevertheless be held by Englishmen, for the reason that they possess, partly by heredity, partly by upbringing, and partly by education, the knowledge of the principles of government, the habits of mind and vigour, of character which are essential for the task; and the rule of India being a British rule, and any other rule being in the circumstances of the case impossible, the tone and standard should be set by those who have created and are indeed responsible for it'.[44]

Curzon's assertion that the British must occupy the highest posts, though made with a characteristic lack of regard for Indian sensibilities, was in fact only a reiteration of that made earlier by Argyll: and on the premise that British rule should continue indefinitely it had considerable validity, even if it was hard to reconcile with Parliament's declarations. But the objection more frequently made to free competition was that this would cause the services to be swamped by intellectuals who would be incapable of governing the martial races of Northern India from which the army was mainly recruited since the mutiny. After the Parliamentary resolution of 1893 in favour of simultaneous examinations, the Liberal Secretary of State, Sir Henry Fowler, finding himself in a delicate position in relation to his party, consulted the Viceroy as to what should be done. The Viceroy in turn consulted his Governors who were strongly opposed to implementing Parliament's proposal. The Governor of the Central Provinces said that it would result in the services being flooded by Mahratta Brahmins. The Governor of the Punjab pointed out that no Rajputs or Pathans, and few Sikhs or Muslims, had passed the B.A. or M.A. examination; and the Governor of Bengal indicated that between 1884 and 1893 the Muslims, who comprised half the population of the Provinces had only accounted for three out of the sixty-six candidates who had entered the written examination for entry to the provincial service. Fowler concluded that 'an adequate proportion of the members of the I.C.S. must always be Europeans' and that a reasonable proportion of posts should be filled by Muslims and Sikhs 'who have evinced a large capacity for the practical work of administration but little or no aptitude for passing examinations with success'. Neither the necessary minimum of Europeans nor of minority races could, he considered, be maintained if the examinations were held in India.[45]

How much validity there was in this line of argument, or how far it served to mask the classic device of 'divide and rule' are questions over which historians are likely to continue to argue. It is, of course, true that the Muslims, who had provided most of the military officers, district administrators and judges under the Mogul Emperor, had lost more when the British took over the administration than the Hindus, who in any case returned as revenue officers and as subordinate judges. At first, Syed Ahmed, the leader of the Muslim revival, supported the Congress demands for Indianization of the I.C.S. Some Indian historians maintain that it was the British Principals of the Aligarh College, the centre of the Muslim cultural renaissance, who influenced Muslim educated opinion in a contrary direction. At all events by 1882 Ameer Ali, on behalf of the Central Mohammedan Association, was asking Ripon to preserve a balance in the services by 'selection' of Muslims. 'Up to 1865,' he said, 'the Government maintained a fair balance. . . . A sharp digression then took place and the Muslims found themselves gradually ousted from the public services by their more adaptive compatriots'.[46] As we have seen, Syed Ahmed, together with the other Muslim member of the Public Service Commission of 1886, opposed the principle of simultaneous competitions for the I.C.S. in England and India. The Muslim League's deputation to the Viceroy in 1906, which successfully claimed communal electorates, also asked for separate Muslim representation in the services. After 1917, the claim was supported by Jinnah, the leader of the Muslim League and founder of Pakistan. In fact, statistics show that for most of the period of British rule, though Muslims were seriously under-represented in Bengal, they were over-represented in the government services in the United Provinces and substantially over-represented in the army.

It is significant that the issues of communal representation in the new legislatures and in the services were bracketed together by Syed

Ahmed, by the Muslim League deputation, and eventually by Jinnah. An important motive in insisting on reservation of seats in the legislatures was the belief that the legislators would influence the distribution of government posts between the communities.

But if the British faced genuine Muslim protests against any system of entry which would lead to Hindu predominance in the services, this does not entirely account for their widespread antipathy to Hindu intellectuals and in particular to the Bengalis. Lord Salisbury could 'envisage no more terrible fate for India than that of being governed by competition baboos'.[47] Lord Lytton, who in private life wrote romantic poems, lamented a situation in which 'the only political representatives of native opinion are the Baboos, whom we have educated to write semi-seditious articles and who represent nothing but the social anomaly of their own position. . . . To secure completely and efficiently utilize the Indian aristocracy is, I am convinced, the most important problem before us'.[48] Sir Henry Cotton, whose advocacy of Indianization on economic grounds was untypical of his service, wrote in 1886 that the I.C.S. as a body had no sympathy whatsoever for the aspirations of the educated Indian. 'The more anglicized a native is the more he is disliked by Englishmen'.[49] The European community of Calcutta, unlike that of Bombay, showed a strong and arrogant racial opposition to the policy which the Government adopted in the eighties of replacing Europeans by Indians in middle level posts on grounds of economy. The I.C.S., though less immediately threatened by competition, took an active part in opposing the Ilbert Bill in Bengal.[50]

By the turn of the century, the lack of consistency in British policy, broadly distinguishable under Liberal and Conservative party labels, became marked. The Partition of Bengal by the Conservatives, which among other results led to Muslims obtaining a substantial number of posts in the newly created Province of East Bengal, was reversed under a Liberal Government. Morley, the Liberal Secretary of State, who previously in opposition had close contacts with Dadabhai and the radical Indian group, wrote to the Viceroy, Lord Minto, in 1906. 'I believe that what they really want a million times beyond political reforms is access to the higher administrative posts of all sorts',[51] and he set up a Royal Commission on the Public Services which was headed by Lord Islington, the Governor General of New Zealand and included H. A. L. Fisher and Ramsay MacDonald. The Commission's report in six volumes is primarily of value to historians, for its publication was delayed by the 1914 War: by then its recommendations were outdated by the Montagu-Chelmsford Reforms of 1917–1919, which not only recognized responsible government within the Empire as India's goal but that the success of the new policy must very largely depend on the extent to which it was found possible to introduce Indians into every branch of the administration. Thirty-three per cent of the posts in the I.C.S. were now reserved for Indians, who in 1922 were at last enabled to take the competition in London. 'We are no longer seeking,' said the Montagu-Chelmsford Report, 'to govern a subject race by means of the services; we are seeking to make the Indian people self governing. It will henceforth be accepted as the duty of the European officers in the service of India to do all that lies in their power to fit Indians to take their places beside them'.[52] The Secretary to the Home Department of the Government of India, reflecting on these words, circularized the provincial governments to ask whether perhaps European recruitment might now be stopped completely.[53] This brought a storm of Conservative protest on the head of Lloyd George in the last weeks of his shaky coalition. He made one of his then rare appearances in the House of Commons and more than redressed the balance, declaring of the I.C.S. – 'Their every word is a command, every sentence a decree, accepted by the people, accepted willingly, with trust in their judgement and confidence in their justice and their fairness which might be the pride of our race . . . I can see no period when the Indians can dispense with the assistance of this small nucleus of the British race. . . . They are the steel frame of the whole structure. . . . There is one institution which we will not cripple; there is one institution which we will not deprive of its functions or its privileges, and that is the institution which built up the British Raj – the British Civil Service in India'. The representative of the Labour Party, Col. Wedgwood, in his reply, seems almost to be speaking in another century. 'The best of the British officers,' he said, 'realize that they are doing their finest service to the Mother Country when they assist to forward the process of their own extinction'.[54]

The times were with Wedgwood rather than Lloyd George. In 1924, on the proposal of the Lee Commission, it was agreed that fifty per cent of the posts in the I.C.S. should be Indianized over the next fifteen years. After this time, Congress devoted little further attention to the question of Indianization of the I.C.S. It was clear that Indianization of the very top and security posts had to await the capture of political power. By 1939, the proportion of Indians had risen from five per cent in 1913 to forty per cent, and when the British left in 1947 it was about fifty per cent. But the Muslims also gained their point: in 1934, twenty-five per cent of the posts in the All India services were reserved for them, to be filled by nomination if they did not win sufficient places by competition. In the closing stages of British rule, the I.C.S. lost much of its popularity in England, and at times British candidates had to be appointed by nomination in order to maintain the ratio.

The British remained in India for thirty years after the Montagu-Chelmsford declaration. The period was not a very happy one in the Services, where by now there were Indians ready and impatient to take over from them. For a hundred years, the inconsistencies in British policy towards Indianization had reflected the basic uncertainty as to how long it was intended to continue the British rule of India. In the end perhaps the tail wagged the dog: for in February 1947 Sir Stafford Cripps told the House of Commons that a main reason for the early transfer of power was the impracticability on the one hand of recruiting new British officers and on the other hand of retaining the undivided loyalties of the Indian officers.[55]

Now the Successors come to the centre of the stage. But before turning to them, it may be useful to examine the relationship between higher education and the services under British rule as well as the development of some of the other Central and All India Services.

REFERENCES

[1] A. C. Ewald, *Guide to the I.C.S.*, London, 1870, p. 13.

[2] John Bright, *Speeches*, Vol. I, London, 1868, p. 91.

[3] *Careers in Pakistan Superior Services*, Pakistan Government, Karachi, 1954, quoted in H. F. Goodnow, *Civil Service of Pakistan*, London, 1964.

[4] G. R. Gleig, *Life of Sir T. Munro*, London, 1831, Vol. II, p. 85.

[5] M. Edwardes, *History of India*, London, 1961, p. 259.

[6] P. Woodruff, *The Founders*, London, 1963, p. 210.

[7] ibid. p. 243.

[8] Charles Grant, *Observations on the State of Asia*, in P.P. 1812–13, X, p. 77.

[9] James Mill, *History of British India*, London, 1820, Vol. II, p. 137.

[10] A. Embree, *Charles Grant and British Rule in India*, p. 286, London, 1962.

[11] Max Müller, *India, What Can It Teach Us?*, London, 1883, p. 42.

[12] P.P. 1831–32, Vol. IX, pp. 292–3, p. 66, and appendix, p. 312.

[13] ibid. p. 56.

[14] ibid. p. XIV.

[15] *Selections from Educational Records*, Bureau of Education, Government of India, Calcutta, 1920, Part I, p. 109.

[16] P.P. 1852–53, XXVIII, p. 422. C. E. Trevelyan, 'Education of the People of India'.

[17] A. C. Bannerjee, *Indian Constitutional Documents*, Vol. I, Calcutta, 1948, p. 253.

[18] J. Bright, op. cit., p. 21.

[19] P.P. 1852–53, Vol. XXVIII, p. 96–97.

[20] C. H. Philips, *Select Documents on History of India and Pakistan*, Vol. IV, London, 1962, p. 509.

[21] P.P. 1884–85, Vol. LVIII, p. 117 ff.

[22] P.P. 1878–79, LV, Papers Relating to the Admission of Natives to the Civil Service in India, p. 301.

[23] ibid. p. 302.

[24] ibid. p. 305.

[25] ibid. pp. 7–9.

[26] Hansard, House of Commons Debates, 2 June, 1892, Col. 113, Speech by D. Naoroji.

[27] P.P. 1878–79, Vol. LV, p. 311.

[28] ibid, pp. 317–319.

[29] L. Wolf, *Life of Lord Ripon*, London, 1921, Vol. II, p. 116.

[30] Quoted by Sir Henry Cotton, *New India*, London, 1886, p. 27.

[31] P.P. 1884–85, Vol. LVIII, p. 117 ff.

[32] *Report of the Public Service Commission* (Aitchison Report), Calcutta 1888.

[33] J. Bright, op. cit., p. 6.

[34] Hansard, House of Commons Debates, 5 May 1868, Col. 1843 ff.

[35] R. P. Masani, *Dadabhai Naoroji*, London, 1939, p. 263.

[36] Hansard, House of Commons Debates, 2 June, 1893, Col. 120.

[37] Sir John Strachey, *India*, London, 1888, p. 359.

[38] Letter to *The Times*, 1878, quoted in M. Edwardes, *History of India*, London, 1961, p. 306.

[39] ibid. p. 312.

[40] See E. Stokes, *English Utilitarians and India*, London, 1959, for the transmission of ideas from James Mill through J. F. Stephen to Curzon.

[41] T. Raleigh, *Lord Curzon in India*, London, 1906, p. 3.

[42] H. L. Singh, *Problems and Policies of the British in India*, London, 1963, p. 73.

[43] C. H. Philips, *Select Documents on History of India and Pakistan*, Vol. IV, London, 1962, p. 564.

[44] Quoted in N. C. Roy, *Civil Service in India*, Calcutta, 1958, p. 134.

[45] P.P. 1893–94, Vol. LXIV, p. 871 ff.

[46] Ram Gopal, *The Indian Muslims*, Bombay, 1959, p. 54.

[47] Lady G. Cecil, *Life of Lord Salisbury*, London, 1921, Vol. II, p. 68.

[48] Lady Betty Balfour, *Lord Lytton's Indian Administration*, London, 1899, p. 109.

[49] Sir Henry Cotton, op. cit., p. 40.
[50] Christine Dobbin, 'The Ilbert Bill', unpublished B.Phil. thesis, Oxford 1964.
[51] Lady Minto, *India, Morley and Minto*, London, 1934, p. 100.
[52] *Report on Indian Constitutional Reforms*, CD 9109 1918, p. 5 and p. 258.
[53] N. C. Roy, op. cit., p. 149.
[54] Hansard, House of Commons Debates, 2.8.22, Col. 1507.
[55] Hansard, House of Commons Debates, 5.3.47, Col. 497.

CHAPTER II

Competitive Examinations and Indian Education

'As soon as any young native . . . should by the cultivation of English literature . . . have enabled himself to be victorious over European candidates . . . he would obtain access to the Service.'

MACAULAY, 1853

W hen an open competition for entry to the covenanted civil service was instituted in 1854, those responsible for the decision were not greatly concerned with its effect on Indian education. Macaulay and Sir Charles Trevelyan saw this mainly as a victory in the campaign for reform of the civil service in Britain itself which was still recruited by patronage. Jowett, later Master of Balliol College, Oxford, who served on Macaulay's Committee, was primarily interested in the stimulus which would be given to the English universities. 'I cannot conceive,' he wrote, 'a greater boon which could be conferred on the University than a share in the Indian appointments'. This would provide, he believed, 'an answer to the dreary question which a college tutor so often hears "what line of life shall I choose, with no calling to take orders and no taste for the Bar, and no connections who are able to put me forward in life?" '[1]

The report on the Examination for Candidates for the Indian Civil Service, drafted by Macaulay and accepted by the Government, had however an incalculable influence on Indian education over the next 100 years. It recommended that candidates should be examined in European rather than Indian studies. They should be able 'to show the extent of their knowledge of our poets, wits and philosophers and their skill in Greek and Latin verses'. Sanskrit and Arabic were only included 'reluctantly' and with few marks. The examination was entirely written, except for the viva voce tests for modern languages.

44

What the Committee had in mind was a competition intended to select graduates from the British universities. 'Skill in Greek and Latin versification,' they admitted, 'has indeed no direct tendency to form a judge, a financier or a diplomatist. But the youth who does best what all the ablest and most ambitious youths about him are trying to do well will generally prove a superior man'.[2] Or as Macaulay told the House of Commons, 'The general rule is beyond doubt that the men who were first in the competition of the schools have been first in the competition of the world'.[3]

As for what probably seemed the fairly remote question of Indian candidacies, Macaulay claimed that 'under the proposed system it would depend on the natives and upon them alone at what time they should enter into the civil service. As soon as any young native of distinguished parts should, by the cultivation of English literature, have enabled himself to be victorious over European candidates he would in the most honourable manner, by conquest, as a matter of right and not a mere eleemosynary donation, obtain access to the service. It would then be utterly impossible for his European fellows to look down upon him.'[4]

Before the arrival of the British, written examinations were unknown in India, as they were in Britain until the 19th century. There was indeed an ancient Indian civilization: as Burke observed, 'They were cultivated by all the arts of polished life while we were yet in the woods'.[5] Public instruction, however, was not the business of the state but was rather a religious responsibility. Sanskrit and Arabic schools were founded by wealthy men and supported by the offerings of the pupils. When the British came on the scene many of these schools had fallen into decay in the disorders of the last stages of the Mogul empire.

In the late 18th century Warren Hastings, who believed that if the East India Company was to survive it would be as an Indian power, founded a Muslim Madrasa in Calcutta, one of whose objects was to produce judges and assessors for Criminal and Civil courts. His successor as Governor General, Cornwallis, established a Sanskrit College at Benares at which the Resident hoped both to endear the government to the Hindus by helping to collect a library of treatises on their laws and also to train doctors of law to assist European judges. By the early 19th century however the influence of the Evangelicals began to be felt. The most influential of them, Charles Grant, who had spent some years in India, wrote a pamphlet entitled, 'Observations on the State of Society among the Asiatic subjects of Great Britain, particularly with respect to morals; and the means of improving it'. His thesis was that Indian society was utterly depraved. 'In Bengal a man of real veracity and integrity is a great phenomenon. . . . Patriotism is absolutely unknown in Hindoostan. . . . Power entrusted to a native of Hindoostan seldom fails of being exercised tyrannically.'[6] The causes were ignorance and want of a proper religion. The remedy was to introduce the English language as a medium of instruction which would lead to conversion to Christianity and general enlightenment.

The British Parliament, which was jealous of the powers of patronage of the East India Company, took a keener interest in Indian administration while it was still the responsibility of the Company than it did after 1858, when the Indian budget was usually discussed in an almost empty House of Commons. Every twenty years an intensive investigation of Indian policy was made when the Company's Charter came up for renewal. Grant and Wilberforce tried to take advantage of this opportunity in 1793 in order to attach a clause to the Charter renewal bill by which the Company would be required to send out missionaries and schoolmasters to India. News of this proposal was unfavourably received by a meeting of the Court of the Company which had assembled to consider the more congenial subject of raising the salaries of the directors. One member pointed out that it was the founding of colleges and establishment of seminars for education which had led to the loss of the American colonies; another 'hoped that the age was become too enlightened for an attempt to make proselytes'.[7] Outside the meeting Grant was told that his schools would produce Jacobins;[8] and the directors managed to bring about the rejection of the proposal.

Twenty years later in 1813 Grant and Wilberforce, who were both in Parliament, succeeded in having a clause included in the Charter bill which enabled, but did not oblige, the Governor General to spend 100,000 rupees a year on the revival of literature and the introduction of knowledge of the sciences in India. The Governor General, Lord Hastings, did not however take advantage of this authorization. We have seen that the next Charter Act of 1833 declared that no native of India would in future be debarred from office by reason of his religion or colour. The Charter Act of 1813 had enabled British subjects, including missionaries, to enter India without authorization by the Company or Board of Control. The Governor General was now instructed to provide educational facilities which would enable Indians to enter the public services, and the missionaries were available to staff such schools. Macaulay, who had been mainly responsible for piloting the Charter Act of 1833 through Parliament, went out to India immediately afterwards as Legal member of the Governor General's Council. His famous 'Minute on Education' of 1835, vivid and self-confident as it is, was not the only factor in the decision that the 100,000 rupees available to the Governor General should be used to support education in English rather than in oriental languages. The influence of Ram Mohan Roy, whose evidence had greatly impressed the Select Committee of Parliament on the Charter; pressure from the missionaries; the needs of the government services; and the views of the Governor General, Bentinck, all contributed to the decision. Indeed as early as 1824 the Court of Directors had described Hindu and Mohammedan literature as 'frivolous, if not mischievous'.[9]

The policy of 'filtration' which was now adopted was described in 1838 by Sir Charles Trevelyan. 'The rich, the learned, the men of business will first be gained; a new class of teachers will be trained; books in the vernacular language will be multiplied; and with these accumulated means we shall in due time proceed to extend our operations from town to country . . . until every hamlet shall be provided with its elementary school.'[10] Under this theory, the leaders who were to be educated would in turn educate the masses. It took little account of caste; and those who took advantage of the new education turned out to have no desire to return to the villages as school-masters. Trevelyan was proved over-optimistic. 110 years after he wrote, when the British left India, 85% of the population was still illiterate.

The first English language school, the Hindu College in Calcutta, was established not by the missionaries, but by David Hare, the rationalist watchmaker, and Ram Mohan Roy, the Hindu social reformer. But after 1833 the missionaries became increasingly active in education, and the government supplemented their work by establishing a secondary school at each district headquarters in 1835. The close and perhaps disastrous association of education with government service can be traced from the resolution of the Council of the Governor General, Lord Hardinge, in 1844 that a preference would be given in government service to those educated in the English schools: to qualify, the students were required to have a critical acquaintance with the works of Bacon, Johnson, Milton and Shakespeare.[11]

The last Charter Act in 1853 brought about the most thorough consideration by a Select Committee of Parliament which was ever given to Indian education. The instructions embodied in the despatch of Sir Charles Wood to the Governor General in 1854 were perhaps the only attempt made under British rule to devise a comprehensive educational policy, at least until the Sargent Report of 1944 which was published just before the British departure. Wood's despatch imposed upon the government the task of 'creating a properly articulated scheme of education, from the primary school to the university'. This was to be done through establishing vernacular schools for primary education, and middle and high schools and colleges and universities, in which instruction was in English. Grants in aid were to be based on perfect religious neutrality. To the Court of Directors the whole educational system described in this despatch had as an important object the provision of educated entrants to the public service. They also believed that 'this knowledge will teach the natives of India the marvellous results of the employment of labour and capital, rouse them to emulate us in the development of the vast resources of the country . . . and at the same time secure to us a longer and more certain supply of many articles necessary for our manufactures . . . as well as an almost inexhaustible demand for the product of British labour'.[12]

The enthusiasm of the Hindu middle class for English education and for the universities which were established in 1857 was intense, and the expansion of the latter rapid, particularly in the arts faculties. By 1882, there were over 5,000 arts students, 20,000 by 1902, and 50,000 by 1922. At the end of British rule, Calcutta and Bombay Universities each had over 40,000 students. The expansion was accompanied by enormous wastage. By 1900, only 32% were passing the intermediate B.A. examination in arts and only 19% in the final B.A. examination.

The commissions which reviewed Indian education in the last 50 years of British rule were unanimous on the effects of the examination system. 'The greatest evil from which the system of university education in India suffers,' wrote the University Commission of 1902, 'is that teaching is subordinated to examination and not examination to teaching.'[13] The Calcutta University Commission of 1919 concluded that the examination system had become 'a vast machine of which those who operate it have become the slaves rather than the masters, a machine turning out much that is of inferior quality and gravely damaging, intellectually and physically, some of the best human material with which it deals'.[14] The University Education Commission of 1949, which was set up immediately after independence, reported 'In our visits to the universities we heard from teachers and students alike the endless tale of how examinations have become the aim and end of education, how all instruction is subordinated to them, how they kill all initiative in the teacher and the student, how capricious, invalid, unreliable and inadequate they are, and how they tend to corrupt the moral standards of university life . . . we are convinced that if we are to suggest one single reform in university education it should be that of examinations.'[15]

The examiner, as the Calcutta University Commission of 1919 found, had become 'more a recorder of mistakes in memory than a judge of mental calibre'.[16] Students devoted their time not to studying their literary textbooks but to memorizing commentaries on them, even longer than the originals, which contained specimen essays on each major character and situation. The efforts of the university teachers were limited to the preparation and dictation of notes to be memorized. If they departed from this procedure, their lectures would be deserted, for the students were unwilling to give their attention at lectures to any remarks or explanations except those bearing on likely examination questions. Indeed, as the Principal of Bethune College explained to the Commission, 'good teaching would result in most cases in a failure of the students so taught to pass the examinations'.[17] The Commission's report gave examples of instructions to examiners which were 'so devised as to encourage the memorizing of absolutely useless, because unexplained, facts and actually to discourage an intelligent treatment of the question asked'.[18] The effort required to memorize the enormous content of meaningless information often led to serious deterioration of health and indeed, as it was alleged, to an early intellectual decline. 'The system breeds a positive distaste for learning. . . . Books are done with and banished on the proud day of graduation.'[19]

The wastage continued to be very great. At the time of independence, in the first B.A. examination 59% of candidates failed in Madras and 44% in Bombay, even though only 33 marks out of a hundred were required for a pass. Of the graduates it was estimated even in 1944, when the war had brought new openings for the middle class, that 20% were unemployed. The fate of the failed B.A.s was far worse.

There were several explanations for the lamentable situation in which the universities and their graduates found themselves in the last fifty years of British rule. As Lord Curzon said in 1904, 'by making education the sole avenue to employment in the State, we have unconsciously made examinations the sole test of education'.[20] From 1837 English replaced Persian as the language of government. Although initially in 1857 the Calcutta University allowed entrance papers to be answered in the vernacular language, in 1864 it was decided that papers must be answered in English only. English however was poorly taught in the High Schools: in government schools teachers' posts were Indianized at an early stage in order to save money and provide employment. The university student was therefore usually incapable of understanding lectures in English, and had to proceed by memorizing notes. The examiner himself had passed through the same system. If he had the enterprise to attempt to diverge from it, he came under great pressure and even physical danger, for it was vital for the students to pass. While the first Indians to take advantage of English education had come from wealthy Calcutta families, by the end of the century two-thirds of the students in the city came from small landholding or trading families in the rural areas whose investment in the student's education was expected to be made good with heavy interest as soon as his B.A. secured him a government appointment.

For those who obtained the B.A. in Arts, which was being studied by 22,000 out of 26,000 students at Calcutta in 1917, there were three openings: government service, teaching and law. But for the majority, those who failed either at the intermediate or final stage, the years of memorization of notes on the 'Merchant of Venice' and 'Paradise Lost' were wasted. They were fitted for no employment and did not often even prove very efficient as revolutionaries.

Indian higher education has been described as 'an attempt to realize western dreams on an eastern budget'.[21] The Indian universities were modelled on London University because that was the cheapest model. Those of Calcutta, Madras and Bombay were founded in the year of the Mutiny, when there was little money to spare. The universities were until 1919 purely examining and affiliating bodies and even after that time the only teaching which they organized was post-graduate. It became a principle of the government in the second part of the 19th century that higher education, because it benefited the few, should become as far as possible self-supporting. But where the government gave no financial support, it could not exercise control. Many of the colleges affiliated to the universities were privately owned, profit-making concerns. The universities were not equipped to inspect the colleges, and had an interest in their expansion, whether they were properly staffed or not, since the university had to derive its income from the fees of students at matriculation and subsequent examinations. It was beyond the capacity of Calcutta University, which had become by 1917 the largest examining university in the world, to arrange viva voce tests for language candidates or laboratory tests for the intermediate science candidates. All was on paper.

The dangers of the development of a class of unemployed graduates with a purely literary education were foreseen by British officials at an early stage. The Hunter Commission of 1882 recommended the development of a 'modern' side in high schools, and courses were subsequently offered as a preparation for commercial, engineering and even agricultural careers. They had little success. The University of Calcutta was not prepared to adapt its entrance examination to the proposed bifurcation.

Lord Lansdowne in 1889 drew attention to the danger of graduate unemployment. Lord Curzon, who was Viceroy from 1898 to 1905, made a vigorous assault on the system of higher education which he described as 'a huge system of active but often misdirected effort, over which, like some evil phantom, seemed to hover the monstrous and maleficent spirit of CRAM'.[22] Curzon's political unpopularity prejudiced the chances of reform, for he had been less than sympathetic to the aspirations of the middle classes and in particular those of Bengal; but he did at least succeed in introducing the teaching of science in the universities.

Reports on Indian education, particularly those written by the British, are full of references to the lack of 'character building' in Indian schools, colleges and universities. The Government of India confirmed the Company's policy of religious neutrality, though this had been bitterly attacked by the missionaries as 'a blot upon the Honourable Company's record involving the most awful guilt before Almighty God'.[23] The Hunter Commission of 1882 recommended that 'a moral textbook, based upon the fundamental principles of natural religion, should be used in all schools, and the Principal is

51

everywhere to be required to deliver sessional lectures on the duties of a man and a citizen',[24] but this suggestion was received with apprehension or derision by those who would have had to implement it.

The comparison which was often made with the English public schools and older universities was not, it might seem, very useful. In England, as Lord Curzon pointed out in 1902, an undergraduate was not greatly concerned with passing university examinations as a test for the public service. 'He goes to a college in many cases less for the sake of the academic standards to which he is required to conform than of the social and moral influences which result from a university career and which are entirely lacking in this country.'[25] To compare Curzon's Oxford with the Calcutta University was hardly meaningful without also comparing the earlier formation given by Curzon's Eton with that of colleges where hungry country boys were huddled together without recreation or exercise in the slums of Calcutta, memorizing texts in an inadequately comprehended language and supervised by miserably paid failed B.A.s. To Curzon it came as a shock to be petitioned to commemorate the memory of Queen Victoria by a general lowering of examination standards.[26]

It was not only the British officials and the Christian missionaries who were critical of the universities. Rabindranath Tagore's private Santiniketan University was a protest against a system which had turned India's students into 'eternal rag-pickers at other people's dustbins';[27] the Anglo-Mohammedan College which Sir Syed Ahmed founded, and which later became Aligarh University, was also residential and gave religious and moral instruction. No observations of the British were harsher than those of Gandhi who maintained that the educated class had been maimed mentally for life, made strangers in their own land, were rendered almost unfit for productive work and harmed physically.[28]

Under the 1919 reforms education became the responsibility of elected ministers in the Provinces who were under popular pressure to do nothing which would make examinations more difficult or which would raise standards and lower the number of students. There was some advance in technical education, but even in 1931 it was found that over the previous twenty years the number of law students equalled that of students of medicine, engineering and teacher training combined. While this lack of balance caused unemployment of lawyers, it probably did not indicate a general shortage of professionals in relation to the employment possibilities. A survey at independence which took into account the greatly expanded manpower needs of the 5-year development plan showed that India would have a surplus of mathematicians and statisticians and would produce 2,200 out of 3,800 chemists required and 1,000 out of 2,700 physicists.[29]

The hopes of the 1854 Despatch had been far too optimistic. Indians had not been educated in 'the marvellous results of capital and labour to develop the vast resources of their country'. Government service had remained the one great industry, and examinations geared to the requirements of government service had deformed the whole educational system.

Immediately after independence, the Indian Government set up a University Education Commission headed by Dr. Radhakrishnan and including British and American as well as Indian educationists. They found the standards so low that one college principal maintained that an Indian university graduate was not very much superior to a matriculate at a British university. The teaching staff were demoralized by low salaries and by the indiscipline of the students, which had been fostered by years of non-co-operation under the national independence movement. There was a huge failure rate and some universities and colleges contained five or ten times the number of students who could be adequately taught. The main reason for this deplorable situation was the weakness of secondary education; and at the bottom, the primary level, there was 85% illiteracy.[30]

There was another side to the picture, a Calcutta University in whose postgraduate departments research was carried out by scientists of the brilliance of P. C. Ray and J. C. Bose; there were doctors, veterinarians, agriculturalists and statisticians who had survived the educational system, specialized in England, and after years in government service could hold their own with specialists of any country in the world. The tragedy was the colossal wastage, the path strewn with 'failed matrics', 'failed intermediates', 'failed B.A.s and M.A.s', which took these few to the top.

In 1828 Malcolm had urged that Indian officials should be more widely employed by the government in place of Europeans on grounds of economy, and that they should be educated for this purpose. He had added presciently however 'I must deem the instruction we are giving them dangerous instead of useful unless the road is open wide on those who receive it to every prospect of honest ambition and honourable distinction'.[31]

Before British rule was established India had bureaucratic castes, a respect for learning and a tradition of using learned men in the administration. It was predominantly the higher castes which made use of the new education when the M.A., B.A., and Intermediate examinations became required for admission to the various grades of the provincial as well as the Central and All-India services. There were not places in government service for all who passed and no alternative outlet for these castes. Those who remained unemployed felt the government to be responsible for their predicament. In their bitterness the question of admissions to the I.C.S. and the other 'Imperial' services came to have a symbolic importance. Had the British agreed to hold the competitive examinations in India this would hardly have affected graduate unemployment, for the places involved were few. But the Indianization of the higher services became, as a recent Indian historian has recognized, an obsession with all Indian nationalists until 1920, whilst those who regarded themselves as the cream of the universities were excluded from the higher posts in the administration.[32]

The lesson which the British drew from this experience in India was to have a profound effect on their approach to higher education in Africa.

REFERENCES

[1] R. J. Moore, 'Abolition of Patronage in the ICS' in *Historical Journal*, 1964, VII, 2, p. 246.

[2] P.P. 1854–55, XL, p. 112.

[3] Hansard, House of Commons Debates, 24 June, 1853, Col. 751.

[4] ibid, Col. 758.

[5] Edmund Burke, *Collected Works*, London, 1894, Vol. II, Speech on East India Bill 1783, p. 182.

[6] P.P., 1812, Vol. X, p. 25 ff.

[7] Woodfall, *Debate at East India House, 23 May 1793*, p. 128 ff.

[8] A. Embree, *Charles Grant and British Rule in India*, London, 1962, p. 3.

[9] *Selections from Educational Records*, Government Press, Calcutta, 1930, Vol. I, p. 92.

[10] P.P. 1852–53, XXVIII, p. 422.

[11] *Selections from Educational Records*, Part II, p. 91.

[12] 'Education Despatch of 1854', reprinted as Appendix III, Calcutta *University Commission Report*, Vol. VI, p. 18.

[13] Quoted in *Calcutta University Commission Report*, Calcutta, 1919, Vol. II, p. 142.

[14] *Calcutta University Commission Report*, Vol. II, p. 224.

[15] *University Education Commission Report*, Delhi, 1949, Vol. I, p. 328.

[16] *Calcutta University Commission Report*, Vol. II, p. 151.

[17] ibid., Vol. II, p. 147.

[18] ibid., Vol. II, p. 171.

[19] ibid., Vol. II, p. 152.

[20] C. H. Philips, *Select Documents on History of India and Pakistan*, Vol. IV, London, 1962, p. 742.

[21] J. J. Cunningham in *Modern India and the West*, ed. L. S. O'Malley, Oxford, 1941, p. 163.

[22] T. Raleigh, *Lord Curzon in India*, London, 1906, p. 352.

[23] T. N. Siquiera, *Modern Indian Education*, Calcutta, 1960, p. 53.

[24] *Report of the Indian Education Commission* (Hunter Commission), Calcutta, 1883, p. 312.

[25] T. Raleigh, op. cit., p. 326.

[26] ibid., p. 326.

[27] K. Kripalani, *Rabindranath Tagore*, London, 1962, p. 268.

[28] S. Nurallah and J. P. Naik, *History of Education in India*, Bombay, 1951, p. 801.

[29] Scientific Manpower Committee's Report, quoted in *University Education Commission Report*, Delhi, 1949, Vol. I, p. 156.

[30] *University Education Commission Report*, Delhi, 1949, Chapter IV.

[31] *Selections from Educational Records*, Part I, p. 144.

[32] V. Subramaniam, 'Graduates in the Public Services' in *Public Administration*, XXXVI, 1958, p. 376.

CHAPTER III

The Army and Some other Services

THE ARMY – THE INDIAN STATES AND THE
INDIAN POLITICAL SERVICE – PROVINCIAL
AND SUBORDINATE SERVICES – THE ALL INDIA
AND CENTRAL SERVICES – MEDICAL – ENGI-
NEERING – FORESTRY AND AGRICULTURE –
EDUCATIONAL – POLICE AND JUDICIARY

'We must either trust the Indian or not trust him . . .
There is no half way house.'
LORD RAWLINSON, COMMANDER-IN-CHIEF, INDIA,
1922

The debate on Indianization of the officers of the Indian Army was conducted with almost equal intensity to that on the I.C.S. though at a somewhat later period.

The armies with which Clive had defeated the French in the 18th century had Indian and Eurasian battalion commanders. We have seen how Munro in 1817 had deplored the exclusion of Indians from higher military as well as civil employment. Thirty years later, Henry Lawrence pointed out that while 'for the lower orders our service is a splendid one, it offers no inducement to superior intellects or more shining spirits. Men so endowed . . . leave us in disgust and rise to rank in foreign services. There are many commandants in Mahratta and Sikh service who were privates in our army'.[1] Kaye, writing shortly after the Mutiny of 1857 and trying to analyse its causes, also showed that the founders of the East India Company's native armies had intended to employ Indian officers of high social position but that 'it was the inevitable tendency of our increasing power in India to oust the native functionary from his seat or to lift him from his saddle, so that the white man might fix himself thereto'. The class which was ousted played an important part in the Mutiny. Kaye added the generalization that 'an Englishman believes that he can do all things better than his neighbours and therefore it was doubtless with a sincere conviction of our own good that we gradually took into our own hands the reins of office . . . and left only the drudgery and dirty work to be done by the people of the soil'.[2]

The Mutiny of 1857 was largely led by Indian N.C.O.s. For the next thirty years the British military authorities were usually more worried by the dangers of revolt within their army than of attack from outside their frontiers. The proportion of British troops was increased; all artillery was placed in British hands; and until the end of the century the Queen's Commission was reserved for British officers. An inferior Commission was given by the Viceroy to Indian officers, who were hardly more than glorified warrant officers.[3] By the 1880s, however, a number of senior British officials became concerned by the possible effect in India of the example set by the Russians in their newly acquired Asian territories, where natives were able to rise to the highest ranks in the army.[4] A more important argument for Indianization appears to have been a desire to build up an aristocratic Indian officer class as a counterpoise to the disaffected intellectuals. As Lord George Hamilton, the Secretary of State, wrote in 1897 'If we can keep the affection of the fighting races and higher orders of society in India, we can ignore the dislike and disaffection of intellectual non-fighting classes, the baboos, students and pleaders'.[5]

One of those who drew attention to the Russian example was General Chesney, the military member of the Viceroy's Council. 'So far as the Army is concerned,' he wrote, 'Queen Victoria's proclamation on assuming the Government of India is a dead letter.'[6] Chesney suggested that it would be 'safer to have Indians with talent and ambition within us than to alienate them'. The Commander-in-Chief, Lord Roberts, who had won his V.C. in the Mutiny, maintained however that it was 'the consciousness of the inherent superiority of the European that has won for us India', and that it was dangerous to have highly trained Indian commanders who could be used against the British.[7] Chesney persuaded the Viceroy in 1885 to suggest to the Secretary of State that two regiments should be formed with entirely Indian officers, but the latter rejected the proposal on the advice of his Council, mainly composed of retired I.C.S. and Indian Army officers. Twenty years later Kitchener as Commander-in-Chief, revived Chesney's proposal. Lord Curzon, however, characteristically considered that 'military education should be confined to the small class of nobility or gentry'[8] and was more interested in recruiting from the sons of the Indian aristocracy an Imperial Cadet Corps, to be attached to his court.

Indianization of the officers of the armed services really dates from 1917 when the Montagu-Chelmsford constitutional reforms included a declaration that Indians would be trained at the Royal Military College, Sandhurst, and the Royal Flying Corps College at Cranwell; in the 1914–1918 War, Indians were commissioned both in the Army and R.F.C.

There was considerable opposition to Indianization of the army after that War in Conservative British circles, inspired mainly by retired Indian Army and I.C.S. officers. This was partly due to the difficulty of finding employment for demobilized British officers but some of the other arguments advanced now read somewhat quaintly, such as that of Sir O'Moore Creagh, a former Commander-in-Chief of the Indian Army, in 1919 that social integration within a regiment would be prevented by the fact that 'English ladies do not care to associate with Indian ladies whose social position they do not know'.[9] A fairer appreciation of the difficulties was made by Lord Rawlinson who was Commander-in-Chief immediately after the First War. In some ways Rawlinson was more realistic than the British Government and was prepared to go further and faster with Indianization.

'The Home Government,' he wrote in 1922, 'having introduced the Reform schemes, are now afraid they are going too fast. . . . But we must either trust the Indian or not trust him. The schemes have got to be carried out honestly in their entirety, with a view to eventual self-government, or else we must return to the old method of ruling India with the sword. There is no half way house."[10]

To Rawlinson the two great obstacles to Indianization were the difficulty of persuading British officers to serve under Indian officers, and that of getting troops of 'the martial races' to obey the orders of Indian intellectuals.

On the first point, he wrote 'old officers say they won't send their sons out to serve under natives. . . . If it [Indianization] is rushed the supply of British officers will dry up long before India is in any degree ready to do without them'. His solution to this problem was to introduce a scheme characterized by Indian nationalists as 'segregation': complete units were Indianized, so that no British officer had to serve under an Indian.

Rawlinson's other difficulty we have already seen arise in the argument over the I.C.S. 'Will we ever get the young educated Indians,' he asked, 'to lead a charge of veteran Sikhs against a Senghar held by Mahsuds, and if he did so would the Sikhs follow him? Will we ever get the sons of the landowners of the fighting races, who are brought up to despise the Babu, just as our feudal chiefs despised the clerks, sufficiently educated to be trusted with the lives of men in modern war?'[11]

Rawlinson, in spite of these difficulties, considered in 1922 that the Army could be Indianized in thirty years, an estimate which turned out to be fairly realistic in relation to the date at which Indian independence came. In 1928 the Commander-in-Chief committed the Government to a policy of establishing a national army by stages corresponding to the development of self-government.

Indian nationalists took a keener interest in the localization of the armed services than did the political parties in most other countries before independence, and Motilal Nehru and M. A. Jinnah served on the Indian Sandhurst Committee of 1926 which visited military colleges abroad. Indian politicians were particularly scornful of the argument that the martial races would not follow educated Indian officers; indeed some British spokesmen played into their hands by pressing this point so crudely as to appear to suggest that there was an intrinsic conflict between the qualities of leadership on the one hand and those of education and intelligence on the other. Indians pointed out with considerable historical justification that the 'martial races' were a British invention of the late 19th century and that the Company had conquered India with troops recruited in Bombay, Madras and the United Provinces. Only after the Mutiny had the British turned instead to recruitment from the loyal Punjab. Later they had found it convenient to continue to recruit from this area because it was adjacent to the North West Frontier, which was the main field of the army's actual operations against tribesmen and of potential operations against Afghanistan and Russia.

Indians were also amused by the argument that officers recruited from Bengal and Madras could never adapt themselves to the harsh climate of the Frontier. In that case, they asked, what were the pink-skinned British themselves doing in India?[12] The Indian Legislative Assembly adopted a resolution in 1921 'that every encouragement should be given to Indians – *including the educated middle class* – to enter the commissioned ranks of the army'.[13]

The failure rate of the first Indian cadets at Sandhurst was much higher than that of the British. Rawlinson therefore opened the Prince of Wales Royal Military College at Dehra Dun which provided an education on English public school lines in order to prepare boys for entry to Sandhurst. His successor, Sir Philip Chetwode, saw this preparation as the core of the Indianization problem.

'It is the preliminary training of the boy between 9 and 18 that counts. What we require in military officers is not only education but the qualities of character, leadership and a sense of responsibility; these can be developed only by a regular system of discipline in schools. Such a system exists in British public schools and we have done our best to introduce it into Dehra Dun and the King George's schools.'[14]

In 1923, the principle of complete Indianization of eight army units was adopted. The government justified this as an 'experiment' which would test the capacity of the Indians. Indian political parties attacked the policy bitterly, maintaining that 'segregation' provided too severe a test and that the government was afraid of the loss of its prestige with the ranks if British officers were seen to be subordinated to Indians in mixed units. It was, they suggested, strangely inconsistent to stress the benefits which the Indians experienced at Sandhurst from mixing with English cadets while refusing them thereafter the opportunities of mixing with British officers.

Steady progress was now made. After the Report of the Indian Sandhurst Commission and further discussions at the Round Table Conference, an Indian Military Academy was set up in 1932. By 1939 about 10% of the officers in the Army were Indians, and the normal peacetime recruitment was one-third Indian and two-thirds British.

The War of 1939 brought about a sharp change of roles. Hitherto Congress had been pressing for a more rapid Indianization than the British considered practicable. Now Congress urged Indians not to enlist in a war to which it had refused co-operation, while the Government engaged in a massive recruitment campaign. The latter was successful. Whereas there had been about 400 Indians with King's Commissions at the beginning of the War, there were 8,000 at the end, representing about 20% of the total number of Indian Army officers.[15] There were also over 1,000 Indian officers each in the Navy and Air Force. After demobilization of the expanded Army, India and Pakistan in 1947 had no great difficulty in providing a sufficient number of officers for their peacetime needs, though their senior officers were inexperienced. The wartime expansion had also lessened the preponderance of the so-called martial races.

Successive British Commanders-in-Chief had insisted that the training of the Indian officers should be exactly the same as that of the British. It has, however, been suggested that a policy which purported to avoid the creation of a 'double standard' in fact imposed one; for, as was shown by the Sandhurst failure rates, a considerable strain was imposed on Indians in carrying out their duties in an alien language, environment and climate.[16] The Sandhurst fees, together with those of the preliminary training at Dehra Dun, were too high for all but wealthy Indian families to afford; others were discouraged by the failure rate from sending their boys to acquire an education which would be of no economic value should they not pass the final examination.

But they went, some sons of officers on government scholarships, more privately financed, always in sufficient numbers to fill the vacancies. What they acquired perhaps as much as the quality of leadership at those English modelled public schools and at Sandhurst were the English characteristics of understatement and repression of the emotions. In the chaos of the Punjab after the partition of India in 1947 and in the following year when they were skirmishing against each other in Kashmir, the officers of the Indian and Pakistan armies appeared the least excited elements on the scene.

Though the issue was to be complicated by the creation of two successor states instead of one, the prediction of many British officers and officials that the Indian intellectual middle class would not be able to control the army did not turn out to be true. On the contrary, the Bengali former Congress President Subhas Bose succeeded during the War in recruiting Indian prisoners of war in Singapore into an Indian National Army. The increasing complexity of the instruments of war both in the Army and Air Force came to give wider scope to the young Bengali and Madrasi intellectuals and mathematicians whose earlier ambitions had not been aroused by the prospect of footslogging: thus the old distinction between 'martial' and 'non-martial' races became less sharp.

The British tradition of non-involvement of the army in politics continued in India after independence. In Pakistan in 1958 the Army deposed a civilian government. No tribal or class issue was involved and the background of the new leaders was not very different from that of the old. It was an unflamboyant and reluctant military regime compared with those of the Middle East and Latin America. In one of his first speeches, General Ayub Khan promised to 'build a true national army *free from politics* . . . our major task is to give cover to the country behind which it could build a sound democratic foundation'[17] and a year later he claimed that *'while keeping severely aloof from politics* the armed forces went about the difficult and arduous job of cleaning the mess . . . we are not there to perpetuate ourselves or to exercise power for its own sake'.[18] Sandhurst did not perhaps inculcate a great respect for politicians among its graduates, but its traditions probably left them also with the feeling that military dictatorships were not quite respectable.

THE INDIAN STATES AND THE INDIAN POLITICAL SERVICE

Since this study is generally concerned with the succession to the British, it deals with British India rather than with the Indian Princely States. It should be remembered, however, that the latter before independence contained a quarter of India's territory and a fifth of its population. The size of the States and the degree of efficiency of their administrations and of the benevolence of their rulers varied greatly. Two States in particular, Mysore in the south and Baroda in the west, had advanced constitutions and attracted able Indians from outside their borders to their service. A few Indian administrators, such as Sir Mirza Ismail and Sir V. T. Krishnamachariar, made successful careers as Prime Minister of several States consecutively, with perhaps greater scope than their contemporaries found in the Indian Civil Service.

It is difficult to find any measure of agreement about the government services in the States. The Congress tended to characterize them all as despotic and backward; many British officers agreed in general with this impression but found the court atmosphere congenial. Some of the larger States, such as Hyderabad, sent their administrative and professional officers for training in British India, but in most of them selection depended on connections. Even in Hyderabad, which had a civil service examination, the top posts were usually held by the Muslim minority.

The Viceroy maintained contact with the States through the Indian Political Service, 25% of which consisted of officers seconded from

THE ARMY AND SOME OTHER SERVICES

the I.C.S. and 75% from the Army. The I.P.S. not only provided the Presidents and Political Agents for this work but on the North West Frontier and in Baluchistan its officers were responsible for the administration of tribal areas. Another function of the I.P.S. was to provide consular staff for the British Foreign Office in neighbouring countries to India.

Understandably in light of its role this was the last service to be Indianized. The official reason was the reluctance of the rulers of the States to receive Indians as Residents. Indianization was introduced cautiously in the early 1930s but of 150 I.P.S. officers at independence, only 16 were Indians. Pakistan used some of these officers to form a nucleus for her Foreign Service.

THE PROVINCIAL AND SUBORDINATE SERVICES

The long controversy over the Indianization of the I.C.S. should not obscure the fact that apart from the key posts at the top the rest of the administration had been Indianized fifty or sixty years before independence. Indians had been appointed as Deputy Collectors and Deputy Magistrates from 1833–43. In 1879 appointments in most departments to posts carrying a salary of more than 200 rupees were restricted to Indians, exceptions having to be approved by the Governor General in Council. Ripon believed that it was largely indignation against this policy which subsequently caused the Europeans of Bengal to react so strongly against the Ilbert Bill. As a result of the recommendations of the Aitchison Commission of 1887, while the former 'covenanted officers' became the I.C.S., the uncovenanted officers were organized into the Provincial and Subordinate Services which were reserved for Indians. Sir George Chesney in 1891 described a typical district of a million inhabitants as having at most six European officials – the District Magistrate who was also Collector, the Joint and Assistant Magistrates, two police officers and the District Judge. Below these, Indians served as Deputy Collectors of the Provincial Service, tehsildars or sub-deputy magistrates of the Subordinate Service, subordinate judges and police officers. There were at that time only 750 I.C.S. officers in India, or one to every quarter million of the population. Besides these, the higher judicial and executive service had about 2,600 officers, of whom only 30 were British officers not domiciled in India. The subordinate civil service had 110,000 officers of whom 97% were

Indian. Chesney described the civil administration of India as 'carried on by native agency supervised by a small body of Englishmen'.[19]

By this time, most of the uncovenanted officers had studied at universities. Some, such as Bankim Chandra Chatterjee, the Bengali novelist, were men of considerable distinction who had not wished to go to England for the I.C.S. examination. Although the very top posts were reserved for the I.C.S., there was a considerable overlap between the functions of each service. A provincial service officer could rise to be a district officer, and frequently did so towards the end of British rule, when the needs of the new departments set up to meet the war situation removed many I.C.S. officers to headquarters posts. Provincial service officers also fulfilled an essential middle level role in the secretariats as Assistant Secretaries who disposed of routine business, while policy issues were referred to the Secretary or Deputy Secretary who was usually an I.C.S. officer.

The Aitchison Committee of 1887, faced with very conflicting advice on methods of recruitment offered by witnesses from different provinces and communities, prudently recommended that each Province should be allowed to adopt its own procedures, whether by written competition, nomination, or a combination of both, for entry to the provincial service. Only the Punjab Government decided to hold written competitive examinations at that time. Later, the provincial and subordinate services were recruited by open competition in several of the Provinces; in others this was combined with a system of nomination in order to secure a balance between the communities. There was considerable mobility between the provincial and subordinate service. In Bengal, 50% of the places in the former were reserved for promotion from the latter, and before 1905 and after 1923 recruitment to both services was undertaken through the same written competitive examination from among candidates of the same educational background.

Thus when the British departed and the I.C.S. lost half its numbers in 1947 the successor services in India and Pakistan were able to promote provincial service officers to assume greater, but not unfamiliar, responsibilities.

THE ALL INDIA AND CENTRAL SERVICES

In addition to the I.C.S., there were a number of All India and Central Services. The All India Services were organized on the same lines as the I.C.S. Their European members were recruited by the Secretary of State as members of a single service, but were seconded for the whole of their career to a provincial government unless recalled to the Government of India. The Central Services on the other hand, such as railways, customs and posts and telegraphs, were unitary, and their members were not responsible to the provincial government.

Indianization of these services was considered by the same series of Commissions which reviewed the position in the I.C.S. The first was the Aitchison Commission of 1887 which laid down the principle that 'policy and economy alike require that so far as is consistent with the ends of good government the recruitment of the official staff in England should be curtailed and advantage taken of qualified agency available in India'.[20] Ironically however the measures which they recommended and which were accepted by the government to bring this about increased the exasperation of the Indian nationalists. A general pattern was established by which each service was divided into an imperial service and a provincial service. The former was recruited in Britain, often by nomination, and was almost entirely and sometimes completely British; the provincial service was entirely Indian and was recruited in India by competition. Every year from 1885 to 1913 resolutions of the Indian National Congress protested in general and in particular as to these arrangements which prevented the promotion of Indians to senior posts in the professional departments.[21]

The Islington Commission in 1917 recommended that the services should be divided into three groups; the I.C.S. and Imperial Police would continue to be recruited preponderantly in Europe; the imperial education, medical and engineering services would be recruited partly in Britain and partly in India; and the imperial agricultural and veterinary services would eventually be recruited entirely in India.[22]

The Montagu-Chelmsford Reforms of the following year, however, led to more drastic changes. On the one hand quotas were established by which 33% to 50% of the posts in each of the imperial services were reserved for Indians, who were to be appointed in India:[23] for some services the Indian quotas were increased by the Lee Commission of 1924.[24] On the other hand under the reforms a number of subjects were 'transferred' and became the responsibility of Indian elected ministers in the Provinces. The Provincial Governments under the 1935 reforms became almost autonomous, except for the Governor's reserved powers in the field of law and order. The only All India services which remained in existence at independence therefore were the 'security services' (as the I.C.S. and the Indian Police were significantly called) together with irrigation and forestry. The Indian Medical Service was disbanded just before independence. Agricultural, veterinary, educational and engineering services had by then become a purely provincial responsibility, and it was for the provincial governments to determine how many Europeans were recruited to them. The reforms made no change on the other hand in the structure of the central services, such as the railways and post office, although a continuous and more or less successful pressure was exercised by the Congress to Indianize these at higher levels. An interesting feature of both the imperial and central services, as well as of several of the technical services in the Provinces, is that the highest posts were often held by I.C.S. rather than by professional officers.

After 1919—and indeed from the outbreak of the War of 1914—Indianization of most of the services was accelerated by a shortage of British candidates, who were discouraged after the war by the political uncertainty of India's future. There was also a considerable exodus of British officers, who were allowed to resign on proportionate pensions when the reforms of 1919 were introduced; the All India services lost 345 officers between 1920 and 1924.[25] The problem had become one of filling the British quotas: the question was no longer 'How many Indians should be admitted?' but 'What is the minimum number of British officers who still need to be recruited?'[26] After 1924 salaries were raised and the British quotas were maintained in most services by nomination.

THE MEDICAL SERVICES

Doctors were among the first professionals to obtain Western training. Indian ayurvedic practitioners had treated the Portuguese in the 17th century, though they appear to have known nothing of surgery. Medical schools on western lines were established by the Company in the 1820s. Medicine was involved in the subsequent language controversy and its development was greatly influenced by the decision that English should be the language of secondary and university education. A medical college was founded in 1835 in

66

Calcutta whose students, after a three and a half years' course, were appointed as sub-assistant surgeons. In 1844 some of these students were taken by one of their professors to complete their training in England, and one of them, Dr. Chuckerbutty, after serving as an uncovenanted officer for several years passed top into the Indian Medical Service in 1855.[27]

From 1857 medical degrees were granted by the new universities of Calcutta, Bombay and Madras. Unlike the Indian engineering degrees, Indian medical degrees were recognized in Britain. Full recognition by the British General Medical Council was given in 1891. Calcutta lost this recognition from 1922 to 1926 because its midwifery teaching did not satisfy the G.M.C., and after a prolonged period of controversy India set up its own medical council in 1931.

The Indian Medical Service had a unique status. Its members were recruited by competitive examination in England by the Army and held military rank, but the majority of them were seconded to civilian duties from which they might be recalled in wartime. The service was responsible for remarkable achievements, notably in the fight against malaria, cholera, amoebic dysentery and plague. Its prestige was high. When emergency commissions were granted in the Second War almost every Indian graduate doctor of appropriate age volunteered.[28] The service was unpopular, however, in Indian political circles who alleged that Indians were discriminated against in it. A particular cause of irritation was the argument that the numbers of Indians in the service must be limited because European officials and their families insisted on being treated by European doctors. This point was raised before the British Parliament as early as 1852 and as late as 1922.[29] The Lee Commission in 1924 stated that 'the almost universally expressed anxiety of British members of the services in India to have access to British medical advice for themselves and their families is intelligible and in our opinion is vital to their contentment'.[30] The Commission recommended that a sufficient proportion of the I.M.S. should remain British in order to meet this situation, but this principle was flatly rejected by the Round Table Conference Sub-committee on the Services in 1931.[31]

Indianization of the service proceeded slowly. Though between 1855 and 1913, 105 Indians entered the I.M.S., by the latter year they represented only 7% of its strength and none had ever risen to the rank of Colonel.[32] It became increasingly difficult, however, to recruit British officers towards the end and, as in the I.C.S., they had to be appointed by nomination instead of by competition. As late as 1937, ratios were established by which the majority of posts in the service would remain British.

Indian nationalists were critical of a system by which the government's senior medical officers were on secondment from the army, which could and did withdraw them in time of war. Congress passed resolutions almost annually from 1893 demanding the separation of the military from the civilian medical services in order to encourage the development of the Indian medical profession. The Indian Army on the other hand resisted any change which would deprive them of a convenient reserve which was paid for on the civil budget. Two other questions which were disputed for many years were whether the I.M.S. should be merged with the Royal Army Medical Corps, and whether members of the I.M.S. should be allowed to conduct private practices. During the Second World War, the military side of the I.M.S. was incorporated in the Indian Army Medical Corps. In 1945 the service ceased to recruit, and before independence it anticipated its demise by placing its regular officers on leave preparatory to retirement.

The greatest achievement of the I.M.S., as Attlee said when it was dissolved in 1947, had been in the training of medical practitioners, of whom India had 50,000 at independence.[33] There was about one doctor per 6,000 of the population in British India, a ratio which, though comparing unfavourably with that of Britain (1 per 1,000), was one of the highest in Asia. There had been much less success in training of nurses, of which there was 1 per 43,000 of the population, compared with 1 per 300 in the U.K.[34]

Indian and Pakistani former officers of the I.M.S., like those of the I.C.S., achieved considerable international recognition after independence and served as President of the World Health Assembly, President of the W.H.O. Executive Board and Director of the W.H.O. Regional Office in South East Asia.

ENGINEERING

Professional and technical education was mainly developed to meet the needs of government. The British needed craftsmen and artisans for construction and maintenance of roads, public buildings, ports and canals. Industrial schools were therefore established early in the 19th century, at which reading, writing, arithmetic, geometry and mechanics were taught. In 1847 the first engineering college was established at Roorkee to produce civil engineers for the construction of the Grand Trunk Road. Engineering colleges were also included in the Universities of Bombay, Madras and Calcutta by 1860.

General Chesney, who had been an army engineer, pointed out in 1879 that although Roorkee had been set up to train Indians, it had in fact turned out more Europeans and Eurasians, whose services had at first been needed at a time when Indians spoke inadequate English. Now that English-speaking Indians were available, Chesney urged that they should replace the Europeans in subordinate engineering posts. Among other advantages, this would restore the morale of the Europeans in the service by removing the bottleneck in promotions which had come about when the Indian empire had ceased to expand.[35] The Government of India subsequently proposed to reserve for Indians the posts which were guaranteed for graduates from Roorkee: the suggestion was greeted with consternation in British and Eurasian circles and was withdrawn, but entry of Indians to the college was facilitated by reducing the educational qualification. In 1883 quotas for the superior posts in the Public Works Department were established at 15 from the Coopers Hill College in England, 9 from the Indian Colleges and 6 from the Royal Engineers. On the recommendation of the Aitchison Commission of 1887, however, an Imperial Service, recruited in England, was created. Ten per cent of the posts in this were reserved for Indians who had studied in England, while the provincial services were recruited from the Indian colleges.[36]

The effect of this step was to depress the status of the Indian colleges, although their graduates believed that their knowledge of local conditions and languages made them more useful than those of the English colleges. It was also a grievance that whereas recruitment in India was by competition, in England it was by nomination. After the Islington Commission's report the Imperial and Provincial engineering services were merged, except for the Irrigation Department, which was responsible for one of Britain's proudest achievements in the great canal system of the Punjab.

For the earlier British engineers their Indian colleagues had felt the natural respect of the student for his teacher. These had been men who spoke the local language, made inspections on horseback, and knew the country. By the 1920s the Englishmen who came out were no longer the best in their profession and sometimes had to be instructed by the Indians in local problems. A Punjabi, in his memoirs of this period, wrote 'For an ordinary engineering graduate, with no training in irrigation engineering or building work, to start ahead of the highly trained talent of Roorkee in the name of a "ratio" seemed indefensible. . . . In the beginning, it had been accepted that Indians could only go so far; later frustration was avoided by the barriers being successfully lowered; but now with plenty of able Indians crowding at the penultimate post there was growing bitterness at being deprived of the goal'.[37]

India's Commission on National Education, which was set up at independence, found that while engineering education had been started in India almost as early as in England it had subsequently stagnated. Indian engineers, even of the highest grades, also had little background of general education and consequently exercised little initiative. The Commission attributed their lack of influence to the historical evolution of the engineer from the craftsman, in whose opinions nobody had been interested, and to the fact that engineers even from the educated classes went straight to engineering college after matriculation.[38] Perhaps the social status of the engineer was also relevant. As Jinnah told the Pakistan Conference on Education a few months after independence, 'One of our greatest weaknesses as a people is our unwillingness to use our hands, and a misconception of the true nature of manual work.'[39]

The same Commission criticized the system of teaching as providing a less effective association between research and its application than would have been found if the German or American pattern had been adopted. By independence about 1,100 engineers a year were graduating and this appeared to represent about half the rate needed for India's needs. But under British rule, the design and research of major waterworks, bridges and factories had been carried out abroad or by foreign consultants. The departure of the British, therefore, according to the Commission 'produced a decapitation in our engineering and technological set-up'.[40]

FORESTRY AND AGRICULTURE

A remarkable characteristic of the Forest Service was that for many years it was headed by foreigners. In the mid-19th century, Indian teak was required to replace England's exhausted stocks of oak for naval construction, and the Viceroy, Lord Dalhousie, in 1855 pointed out the great importance of setting up an organization which would ensure the scientific management of India's forests. Britain had little experience in this field and from 1864–1900 the first three Inspectors General of Forests in India, Brandis, Ribbentrop and Schlich, were Germans.

Under them the first forest officers were British, selected from the police, army, Public Works and Survey Departments, and were sent to France and Germany for training. One Indian was included in the group who went out in 1867. Later, from 1885 to 1926, the basic training was carried out in Britain in schools which were generally headed by men with Indian experience. Until 1922, all recruitment to the Imperial Forest Service was undertaken in Britain and there were then only two Indians in it.

It is remarkable that there were any at all. In order to enter the Imperial School of Forestry at Oxford, Sir William Schlich still insisted in 1913 that Latin was essential.[41] A degree in science from a British university was also required; those from Indian universities were not recognized. Part of the training was still carried out in France and Germany, whilst, as Indian witnesses pointed out to the Islington Commission, French and German were not taught in Indian schools and colleges.[42]

In 1922 40% of the vacancies in the service were reserved for Indians and a Forestry School was set up at Dehra Dun to train them. At this period the Service was not very popular and there were sometimes insufficient candidates to fill the vacancies. This situation was ascribed by a British member of the Islington Commission to the Indians' 'dislike of the conditions of work, which involve a life of isolation, often in unhealthy tracts, combined with hard physical exercise'.[43] The implication that educated Indians did not like to work in the forestry department because of the rough life is found in most of the reports and became something of a legend. In fact the salaries offered in the provincial services do not seem to have been sufficient to cover the expenses of an officer who had had to maintain two establishments and put his children in boarding school. During the economic depression of the 1930s recruiting to the Imperial Service ceased for several years and in 1935 forestry became a Provincial subject. At independence two-thirds of the members of the service remained in India, while one-third returned to England or went to Pakistan.

The history of the Indian Forest Service illustrates several problems. The slow development of the department was attributed by its historian to the fact that 'the administrators of India were trained on the Public School Standard of the times by which science and scientific knowledge were of little account'.[44] The vested interests of the public schools in England, he maintained, also prevented candidates for the service being examined in botany and geology which these schools did not teach, just as later Oxford with its classical tradition for long opposed the establishment of a degree in forestry and only awarded a diploma.[45] Schlich, in his efforts to establish equality of status for his officers with those of the I.C.S., insisted on a level of classical knowledge which excluded the Indians. In many ways this was the least insular of the services, sending its forest officers to be trained in France and Germany in the 19th century and its forest engineers to the U.S.A. and Canada in the 20th. But despite this breadth of vision, there was at times a blindness to the obvious point nearer home, which Brandis, the first Inspector General, had made, that the Department could not possibly be adequately staffed to bear even a remote resemblance in efficiency to those of the Continent, except by Indians.[46]

Agriculture was mainly treated as a provincial subject. The Imperial Agricultural Service was very small and concerned only with research. The University Commission of 1949 suggested that research had been concentrated on those market crops whose industries could pay the expenses, notably cotton, jute, sugar, coconuts, tea and tobacco. Crops in which an organized industry did not take a direct interest, on the other hand, such as wheat and rice, though involving the welfare of far more of the population, had little help from research.[47]

At independence there were twenty agricultural colleges in India, admitting 1,500 students a year. On the assumption that one-half of them would graduate, it was calculated that this would provide only three agricultural graduates per million of the farming population.[48] The University Commission considered that only a bare beginning had been made at meeting the needs of agriculture at the university level, and that India would profit by trying out the methods of the American Land Grant Colleges.

THE ARMY AND SOME OTHER SERVICES

THE INDIAN EDUCATIONAL SERVICE

In no department did the Aitchison Commission's principle of the creation of 'Imperial' and 'Provincial' services cause more bitterness than in Education. Before this time there had usually been a warm professional relationship between British and Indian members of the service who were teaching at the same institutions. Now that the British officers were recruited into the Imperial Service in London and the Indians into the Provincial Services in India, the most senior man in the Provincial Service, even if he were a Fellow of the Royal Society, was treated as junior to the latest recruit to the I.E.S. who might be teaching in the same college. Widespread indignation was aroused by the case of the brilliant Bengali chemist, P. C. Ray, who had a doctorate from Edinburgh and whose experiments won him considerable esteem in France and Germany, but who was not admitted into the Imperial service. Ashutosh Mukerjee, who became Calcutta's most distinguished Vice-Chancellor, was another notorious example. It was a particular source of disgust to the Indian professors that recruitment in England was by nomination while it was by examination in India. Sir J. C. Bose complained to the Islington Commission in 1913 that while scientific education was the crying need of India, the government was discouraging Indians from reading science by reserving for the British not only the top posts in the education department, but also in those of geology, meteorology, agriculture and forestry.[49]

Under the Montagu-Chelmsford reforms education was a 'transferred subject' which became the responsibility of the Indian ministers of the provinces, and after 1924 there was thus no further recruitment to the I.E.S.

THE POLICE AND JUDICIARY

Under the Mogul Empire the zemindars, or landlords, had been responsible for maintaining law and order, ultimately through the village headmen. Warren Hastings continued this system but Cornwallis in 1792 entrusted the British magistrates with responsibility for the police and authorized them to recruit their own superintendents. The change had the effect of losing the co-operation of the villagers, and in 1814, village watchmen, mostly hereditary, were once more entrusted with police functions. In 1860 a regular police force was established whose officers were mostly recruited from army veterans of the Mutiny. Subsequently, according to the Aitchison Commission, recruitment was by nomination 'of youths who have failed to succeed in examinations held in England and who came to India in the hope of securing a nomination in the police by influence brought to bear on the nominating authority'.[50]

Curzon in 1902 appointed a Commission under Sir Andrew Fraser to inquire into the administration of the police. Its report was scathing. The British officers were described as having an 'imperfect knowledge of the vernacular, being out of touch with the people, especially the respectable classes, and paying insufficient attention to public opinion'. Of all branches of the public service, according to a subsequent Resolution of the Government of India, the police was the most backward. It had never escaped from the traditions and reputation of its feudal origins.[51] Under Curzon's reforms an Imperial Police Service was created, whose officers were recruited in Britain between the age of 18 and 20: only Europeans were admitted and strict steps were taken to exclude Eurasians.

The Islington Commission cautiously recommended that Indians should be allowed to sit for the Imperial Service examination provided they had spent five years in England, and also that they might become eligible for promotion to the I.P. from the provincial service. The Montagu-Chelmsford Reforms established the principle that Indians should be admitted to the Imperial service, and the Lee Commission in 1924 fixed the proportion of admission at 50% British and 30% Indian by competition and 20% Indians by promotion. Indianization was thus slower in the police than in the I.C.S. By 1929 there were 564 European and 128 Indians, but the Simon Commission did not recommend an acceleration of the pace of Indianization in the 'security services'.

The police was not a service in which the British took much pride. The subordinate ranks throughout British rule were almost universally regarded as corrupt and oppressive. The British officers were recruited at a younger age than the I.C.S. and had no university education, with the curious result that they were often less well educated than the Indian graduates who served under them and ultimately succeeded them. The one branch of the police whose efficiency won a healthy respect from Indian nationalists was the C.I.D.

Indians were appointed as subordinate judges from the first half of the 19th century; in the second half of the century they were appointed members of the High Courts and during Lord Ripon's Vice royalty R. C. Mitter acted as Chief Justice of Bengal. The early Indians who entered the I.C.S. also tended to be employed on the judicial rather than on the administrative side.

A controversy which continued for almost a hundred years centred on the question as to whether I.C.S. officers, who were of course mainly British, should exercise judicial functions at all or whether, alternatively, judges should be recruited from the Bar. Minor criminal and civil cases were heard by the District and Sessions Judges, who were also I.C.S. officers. These had no legal degrees and entered the judicial line after six to twelve years of administrative work. Thus when they first sat as judges they had very little legal experience. A Government of India Despatch of 1907 gave a pathetic picture of I.C.S. judges being flurried by experienced Indian lawyers into making all sorts of errors and subsequently being pilloried in the press, which was largely controlled by the legal profession.[52]

Most I.C.S. officers preferred administrative work and Indian critics argued that the judiciary thus became the dumping ground for the incompetent. They also suggested that quite apart from their ignorance of the law the I.C.S. judges were prejudiced by the membership of their service and by their administrative experience, and were unlikely to give judgements which would embarrass the Government.

The British argument, from Sir Thomas Munro in 1831 to the Home Member of the Government of India 100 years later, was that the experience which a revenue officer obtained of local life and conditions as he moved round the villages was a better qualification for a judge than reading books or sitting in a court. The argument was easier to sustain in the early days, when rough and ready justice was appropriate to unsettled times. It was much less convincing later when the I.C.S. judges were reviewing judgements of the subordinate judges in the provincial services who were law graduates. Congress demands that all judges should be recruited from the Indian Bar were given impetus not only by a desire for more professional judgements but by the existence of a great number of unemployed lawyers. Some barristers were recruited as District Judges on the recommendation of the Islington Commission, and I.C.S. officers were given opportunities to be called to the Bar while on leave. But to the end the grievance remained; I.C.S. officers continued to occupy most of the positions of district sessions judges, and one-third of the posts of judges of the High Courts were reserved for them by law.

At independence the question settled itself. India was so short of I.C.S. officers to staff senior posts in the new Indian Administrative Service that the government was glad to transfer all judicial work to former barristers. Ten years after independence, when the issue could be considered dispassionately, the Indian historian N. C. Roy cautiously conceded that there was something to be said for the British point of view. The niceties of the law, he said, fitted in well with Indian intellectual traditions and many Indian lawyers enjoyed hair-splitting decisions between one case and another–'In a lawyer and a judge training in such matters is important. But equally important is the capacity to grasp the spirit of the law and its applicability to a particular case. We cannot say that all civilian judges were very much outdistanced in this regard by the Indian lawyers'.[53]

G. K. Gokhale spoke with great effect in the Imperial Legislative Council in 1911 on the question of the employment of Indians in the public service. With characteristic fairness he recognized the difficulties of the British and the good intentions of Aitchison, but pointed out that the position of the Indians had deteriorated in several departments since the Aitchison Report, illustrating this by the position of P. C. Ray in the Education Department and of the Indian engineers in the Public Works Department. He did not ask for a sudden withdrawal of British personnel but for continuous progress. He closed with a devastating extract from a report by Col. Dupree, who had been Surveyor-General of the Government of India from 1881–86. Col. Dupree had noticed that some of the European surveyors had been allowing their Indian assistants to do the drawing. 'It is suicidal,' he told them, 'for the Europeans to admit that Natives can do any one thing better than themselves. They should claim to be superior in *everything* and only allow Natives to take a secondary or subordinate part. In my old parties I never permitted a Native to touch a theodolite or an original computation, on the principle that the triangulation or scientific work was the prerogative of the highly paid European and this reservation of the scientific work was the only way by which I could keep a distinction so as to justify the different figures respectively drawn by the two classes – the European in office time and the Native who ran him so close in all the office duties as well as in field duties.'[54]

That the British should retain the top posts in the I.C.S., Army and Police was perhaps a political necessity. The segregation of

76

THE ARMY AND SOME OTHER SERVICES

British and Indians into 'Imperial' and 'Provincial' branches of the professional services, however, was a clumsy and unnecessary affront to Indian feelings. At independence there were hardly any fields in which trained Indian staff were not available to take over from the British. In some of them the successors had waited too long, and years of frustration had clouded the genuine friendship which earlier British teachers and colleagues had won.

REFERENCES

[1] Sir Henry Lawrence, *Essays Military and Political*, London, 1859, p. 27.

[2] J. W. Kaye, *History of Sepoy War in India*, London, 1880, Vol. I, p. 211.

[3] W. F. Gutteridge, *Military Institutions and Power in the New States*, London, 1964, p. 86.

[4] e.g. General Chesney, *Indian Polity*, London, 1894, p. 271 and Lord G. Hamilton, cited by H. L. Singh, *Problems and Policies of the British in India*, London, 1963, p. 173.

[5] H. L. Singh, op. cit., p. 173.

[6] Chesney, op. cit., p. 268.

[7] Sir George Arthur, *Life of Lord Kitchener*, London, 1920, Vol. II, p. 179.

[8] C. H. Philips, *Select Documents on India and Pakistan*, Vol. IV, London, 1962, p. 518.

[9] O'Moore Creagh, *Indian Studies*, London, 1918, p. 274.

[10] F. Maurice, *Life of Lord Rawlinson*, London, 1928, p. 307.

[11] ibid. p. 284 and p. 296.

[12] Many of these general arguments are summarized in the Minute of Sir P. S. Sivaswamy Aiyer and Major General Rajwade in the *Report of the Indian Military College Committee*, HMSO, 1931.

[13] *Gutteridge*, op. cit., p. 89.

[14] *Report of Indian Military College Committee*, op. cit., p. 24.

[15] *Official History of Indian Armed Forces in World War II*, Volume on 'Expansion of the Armed Forces,' Calcutta, 1956, Chapter XI.

[16] W. Gutteridge, 'Indianization of the Indian Army', in *Race*, May, 1963, p. 43.

[17] M. Ayub Khan, *Speeches*, Karachi, 1959, Vol. I, p. 3.

[18] ibid. Vol. II, p. 45.

[19] Chesney, op. cit., p. 173 and p. 195.

[20] *Report of the Public Service Commission* (Aitchison Report), Calcutta, 1888, p. 152.

[21] D. Chakrabarty publishes the Congress Resolutions in *Congress in Evolution*, Calcutta, 1958.

[22] *Royal Commission on Public Services in India* (Islington Report), London, Cmd 8382, 1917, p. 60 ff.

[23] *Report on Indian Constitutional Reforms*, London Cd 9109, 1918, Chapter XI.

[24] *Report of Royal Commission on the Superior Civil Services in India* (Lee Report), London Cmd 2128, 1924, Chapter V.

[25] *Report of Indian Statutory Commission*, (Simon Report,) London, 1930, Vol. I, p. 267.

[26] *Report of Royal Commission on the Superior Civil Services in India* (Lee Report), London, 1924, p. 18.

[27] Donald MacDonald, *Surgeons Two and a Barber*, London, 1950, p. 138.

[28] MacDonald, op. cit., p. 247.

[29] Sir W. Joynson Hicks, Hansard House of Commons Debates, August 2, 1922, Col. 1495.

[30] op. cit., Chapter III.

[31] *Indian Round Table Conference*, Cmd 3778, 1931, p. 405.

[32] *Islington Report*, op. cit., Annexe XII.

[33] Hansard, House of Commons Debates, August 7, 1947, Col. 1650.

[34] *Report of Health Survey and Development Committee* (Bhore Committee), Delhi, 1946, Vol. II, p. 387.

[35] G. Chesney, 'The Indian Services' in *Nineteenth Century*, Vol. V, 1879, p. 1040.

[36] *Aitchison Report*, Proceedings of Sub-committee on Public Works Department, pp. 3–4.

[37] P. Tandon, *Punjabi Centenary*, London, 1961, p. 198.

[38] *University Education Commission Report*, Delhi, 1949, Vol. I, p. 235.

[39] *Report of the Commission on National Education*, Karachi, 1959, p. 12.

[40] *University Education Commission Report*, Vol. I, p. 240.

[41] *Islington Report* op., cit., Vol. XV, p. 98.

[42] ibid., Vol. XV, p. 28.

[43] ibid., Vol. I, p. 154.

[44] E. P. Stebbing, *The Forests of India*, London, 1923, Vol. II, p. 462.

[45] ibid., Vol. III, p. 313.

[46] ibid., Vol. II, p. 509.

[47] *University Education Commission Report*, Vol. I, p. 181.

[48] ibid., Vol. I, p. 181.

[49] *Islington Report*, Vol. XX, p. 140.

[50] *Aitchison Report*, p. 120.

[51] Published in *Islington Report*, Vol. XIII, p. 160.

[52] Quoted in *Islington Report*, Vol. I, p. 167, footnote.

[53] N. C. Roy, op. cit., p. 196. His chapter on 'The I.C.S. and the Judiciary' is the main source for these observations on the subject.

[54] *Speeches of G. K. Gokhale*, Madras, 1920, p. 452–453.

CHAPTER IV

Successors and Collaborators

'No new order can be built up in India so long as the
spirit of the I.C.S. pervades our administration and our
public services.'

JAWARHARLAL NEHRU, 1936

One evening in March, 1868, three nineteen-year-old boys
slipped out of Calcutta to spend the night in a friend's
house in the suburbs before boarding the steamer for
England. All were Bengali Hindus, Surendranath Banerjea, Romesh
Chunder Dutt and Bihari Lal Gupta, making their way to London
to attempt to pass the competitive examination for the I.C.S., a feat
achieved only once before, in 1864, by Satyendranath Tagore, the
elder brother of the poet. A Hindu who travelled overseas at this
time faced social ostracism on his return, and neither Dutt nor
Gupta had dared to inform his parents of his intentions. Banerjea
had the sympathy of his father, but the secret had been kept from his
mother.

These were exceptional young men. Banerjea came from a Brahmin
family, but his father was a medical practitioner who had been a
favourite pupil of David Hare at the Hindu College. Surendranath
grew up in a home in which there was constant conflict between
father and grandfather, between Hindu orthodoxy and Western
ideas. In his teens, he was active in the Hindu reformist Brahmo
Samaj, the temperance movement, and the campaign to allow re-
marriage of widows. He attended an Anglo-Indian school and had a
brilliant career at Calcutta University, where it was the Principal
of his college, John Sime of St. Andrews, who urged him to go to
England to compete for the I.C.S.

Dutt's family had a background of government service. His

father was a deputy collector who had been drowned in 1861 whilst on duty. Romesh Chunder was brought up by his uncle who was both a head assistant in the Bengal Secretariat and a professor of English. The boy's favourite studies were the English poets; his cousin, Toru Dutt, at the age of 19 published poems in English and French which were reviewed with admiration by Edmund Gosse. But his was a more orthodox family than that of Banerjea. Romesh Chunder was married at 15, before he matriculated, and he left two children behind when he sailed for England.

In his first letter home from the steamer, Dutt spoke of the risks which he and his friends were taking. 'Against the voice of experience and reason we have set out on this difficult undertaking – stealthily leaving our homes – recklessly staking everything on an almost impossible success. Shall we achieve that success or shall we come back to our country impoverished, socially cut off from our countrymen ... to face the reproaches of advisers and regrets of our friends?'[1]

In London the students found lodgings with Mr. Talfourd Ely, a teacher of Latin at University College, whose happy middle class home impressed them with its air of discipline in the family.[2] In the year which they spent in preparing for the examination they not only attended classes at University College but also took private lessons from some of the Professors. Working twelve and fourteen hours a day, they were greatly helped by the kindly Henry Morley, Professor of English, and the eccentric German Professor of Sanskrit, Dr. Goldstucker.

At last the day of the open competition came. For 50 places there were over 300 candidates, many of them coached by the famous crammer, Wren, others from Oxford, Cambridge and London. The examinations lasted a whole month. Dutt did brilliantly on his English papers (What do you think to be the best of Shakespeare's plays? Do you find anything in common between Milton and Wordsworth?) taking second place in this subject with 420 marks out of a possible 500. He did even better in Sanskrit with 430 marks out of 500, but was at a considerable disadvantage against competitors who could score a maximum of 1500 by submitting papers in Latin and Greek. His mathematics and philosophy, however, proved sound, for when the results of the whole examination were announced, he held third place. Banerjea and Gupta were also successful, as well as a fourth Indian, S. B. Thakur, from Bombay.

The enthusiasm with which this success was greeted in Calcutta was suddenly dispelled by the news that Banerjea and Thakur had been disqualified for being above the maximum age limit by the Civil Service Commissioners, who had been urged to examine their matriculation certificates by a disappointed Indian candidate. In vain the candidates tried to explain that in India a child's age was reckoned from the moment of conception, so that by English calculation they were within the age limits.

In this crisis Banerjea and Thakur received encouragement not only from their indignant friends in India but in England. Professor Morley sent a spirited letter to the Press, and enlisted the sympathies of Charles Dickens, who wrote a strong article in his journal *Household Words*. 'Banerjea,' said Morley, 'one day they will yet raise a statue to you for the fight you are putting up.'[3] John Bell, a retired barrister from the Calcutta High Court, took their case to the Court of Queen's bench without accepting a fee 'for', as he said, 'it was a just cause, and he had eaten the salt of India'.[4] The Lord Chief Justice ruled in the candidates' favour, and they were reinstated.

During their two-year probationary training period in England, which involved four further examinations, Dutt and Gupta found time to be called to the Bar. The friends listened to Gladstone and Disraeli in the House of Commons, chatted with John Bright, and attended readings by Charles Dickens. Banerjea had lost a year in his fight for reinstatement, but managed to complete the two year probationer's course in one.

A great garden party was given for the three I.C.S. probationers on their return to Calcutta by Keshab Chunder Sen and other progressive Bengalis, at which Dutt urged the organizers 'to send as many young men as possible to England, for there they would imbibe ideas of liberty and equality between men and women'.[5] All three were taken back into their homes, but the general attitude of Hindu society was disapproving. Banerjea's family were among the highest of Brahmins and many of those who used to eat and drink with them ceased to visit or invite them after his return.

Gupta, like Tagore, the only previous Indian to enter the I.C.S., now went into the judicial line and had a successful, but not spectacular career. Those of Dutt and Banerjea, who both went into the executive or revenue line, were a striking contrast.

Dutt indeed combined several successful careers. In the I.C.S., he was the first Indian to be appointed as a District Magistrate and as such was congratulated personally by the Viceroy on the diminution of crime and rioting in his District of Backerganj, a notoriously difficult one with a predominantly Muslim population. He was given the C.I.E. in 1892 and in 1894 became the first Indian to be appointed as a Commissioner of Division. In 1897, he retired after twenty-six years' service. He did not entirely avoid racial difficulties. Whilst Joint Magistrate in Dacca, he was transferred to another district when the new railway began to bring European businessmen to Dacca as residents. His appointment as Commissioner was also rudely attacked by the Calcutta *Englishman*. But he was not inhibited by such criticism from standing up stoutly to the irascible Mr. Hallward, Principal of Cuttack College, when the latter publicly caned two young chiefs, who were the wards of government, because they had failed to salute him as they rode by whilst he was playing golf.[6] Dutt was never passed over in the regular line of promotion and on two occasions was even promoted above the heads of his British seniors. His retirement appears to have been due to his desire to concentrate on literature and to work for social and political reforms, as well as to ill health.

It is probably as an historian and novelist that R. C. Dutt is mainly remembered. For seven years after his retirement, he was Professor of History at the University College of London. At the same time he took an active part in political controversies, notably in the struggle against the Government's proposal to limit the powers of the Calcutta Corporation and on the tariff question. He became President of the Indian National Congress in 1899 and engaged in a celebrated debate with Lord Curzon on agrarian policy. But he ended his life as Revenue Minister to the Maharaja of Baroda, where his friend B. L. Gupta was Legal Adviser: and there were many who saw significance in the fact that it was only outside British India that these earliest Indian I.C.S. officers found their highest fulfilment. Dutt always remained loyal to the British connection. He said that there was no finer body of administrators in the world than the I.C.S. 'We identify ourselves with the British rule,' he wrote after his retirement from the I.C.S., 'and pledge our support to that rule at every sacrifice: and we demand under the British rule a larger share in the administration of our own concerns'.[7] He had few illusions however. 'I know the India Office,' he once wrote privately to B. L. Gupta. 'Considerations of race are paramount there. They want to shut us out, not because we are critics but because we are natives, and their policy is rule by Englishmen. Licking the dust off their feet will not

82

move them from this policy: unsparing criticism and persistent fighting can and will do it. Englishmen understand fighting and they will yield to persistent fighting, not begging'.[8]

Sir Stewart Bayley, the Lieutenant Governor of Bengal, described Dutt as the most capable executive officer of his time.[9] His biographer, J. N. Gupta, a fellow Bengali officer in the I.C.S., claimed with justice that his career as an administrator indicated once and for all the capacity of an Indian to be entrusted with the highest responsibilities in the administration of the country.[10]

Very different was the life of S. N. Banerjea, who suffered disaster in his first post. The District Magistrate to whom he was responsible was an Anglo-Indian, and there was evidently little sympathy between them. About a year after his posting, Banerjea's clerk entered on a list of absconding prisoners a case which in fact had been postponed owing to heavy work. Banerjea signed the order 'along with a heap of other papers'[11] although the man had not absconded. The District Magistrate made an unfavourable report on Banerjea; a Commission of Inquiry was held, and he was dismissed from the service. A number of civil servants who have looked into the incident in later years have felt that he was treated with great harshness and that a reprimand would have been sufficient.

This was not the end of his troubles. Always a fighter, he went back to London to attempt to persuade the India Office to reverse the recommendation of the Government of India for his dismissal. When this failed, he decided to stay on to complete the studies for the Bar which he had started whilst an I.C.S. probationer. He continued to eat his dinners, but, when he came to apply, the Benchers of the Middle Temple decided that his dismissal from the Civil Service was a fatal objection to his admission. An old English barrister, Mr. Cochrane, formerly of Calcutta, 'though tottering with the weight of years', took up the case: but all his efforts were in vain. 'From the civil service I had been dismissed. From the Bar I was shut out. Thus were closed to me all avenues to the realization of an honourable ambition'. Some friends suggested that he change his name and go to Australia; but instead when the numbness of his grievance wore off, he decided to enter politics. 'I felt that I had suffered because I was an Indian, a member of a community that lay disorganized, had no public opinion, and no voice in the counsels of their Government. The personal wrong done to me was an illustration of the helpless impotency of our people.'[12]

Banerjea now determined to devote his life to 'the service of my fallen country' and after a year of further general reading in London returned to Calcutta to accept a Professorship of English: this not only left plenty of time for political activities but placed him in a position of considerable influence with the student community of Bengal who were to become the spearhead of the nationalist movement. Shortly after his return he helped in 1876 to found the Indian Association, which was to represent the views of the educated Indian middle class, since the existing British Indian Association was felt to be essentially an association of landowners. To Banerjea the decision of Lord Salisbury at this point to reduce the age limits for candidates to the I.C.S. came as 'the first great opportunity to realize some of those ideals that had given birth to the Association. Reactionary rulers are often the creators of great public movements. . . . The agitation was the means, the raising of the maximum limit of age for the open competitive examination and the holding of simultaneous examinations were among the ends; but the underlying conception, and the true aim and purpose of the Civil Service agitation was the awakening of a spirit of unity and solidarity among the people of India'.[13]

A mass meeting was held in Calcutta. Banerjea was appointed as Special Delegate and toured the United Provinces, the Punjab, Bombay and Madras, addressing meetings and obtaining resolutions. It was, as Sir Henry Cotton noted, the first time that under British rule India, with its varied races and religions, had been brought upon the same platform for a common and united effort.[14] The agitation accelerated the introduction by the Government of India of the Statutory Civil Service, but this was not sufficient to quell it.

Banerjea consolidated his influence as editor of the *Hindoo Patriot*, in which capacity he served a brief jail sentence for contempt of court. He was for many years a leader of the Indian National Congress, of which he was twice President. He played a leading part in the fight against the Bengal partition and in the Swadeshi movements and became known as the 'Uncrowned King of Bengal'. He never lost an opportunity to press for Indianization of the services. At the age of seventy, under the Montagu-Chelmsford reforms, he became Minister of Local Government in Bengal and was knighted. Now at last he was able to practise what he had preached. Yet it was a moderate policy. Efficiency came first – 'other things being equal,' he wrote in his memoirs, 'the Indian was preferred'.[15]

The British were fortunate in this gentle rebel. As Sir Edward Baker, Lieutenant Governor of Bengal, said many years after Banerjea's dismissal from the I.C.S. – 'We have done him a grievous wrong; but he bears no malice'.[16]

The career of the very first of the Successors in the I.C.S. is less well known than those of Dutt and Banerjea. Satyendranath Tagore, who passed the I.C.S. examination in 1862, wrote his memoirs in Bengali over fifty years later. Tagore's whole career had been spent as a judge in Western India. He had preferred the judicial to the administrative side because it enabled him to lead a quiet family life. For himself he had few complaints. Western India was more cosmopolitan than Calcutta. His British colleagues had invited him to tennis and to dinner at home and even to the Club. Only once did he have serious difficulties with them when he had been transferred by the Government because he had dismissed a case, but he had been vindicated by the High Court.

Satyendranath, in his old age, looked back with pleasure to his studies and his holidays in England. He could understand the British reserve in their dealings with Indians in India, which he compared with the attitude of Aryans to non-Aryans in India's earlier history. Though he considered the British civil servants to be arrogant and haughty in their general conduct towards Indians, he was enthusiastic about the exceptional Civilians such as A. O. Hume who had overcome their prejudices. But he could not help admitting that as communications with England had improved the British civil servants retained less affection for India and made less effort to be sociable. And this to him was a tragedy. There was such a wealth of potential friendship for the British on the Indian side waiting to be released: if only the British could bring themselves to make one step forward the Indians, he said, would advance ten, and much good might still come of their association.[17]

The dislike and contempt for the Bengali intellectuals, which had been growing amongst the British over the past thirty years, had by the 1890s created a tradition of Bengali ineffectiveness which disregarded inconvenient facts such as Dutt's distinguished career. As we have seen, General Chesney in 1893 told the House of Commons that there never had been a capable Bengali administrator,[18] and Kipling in his short story, 'The Head of the District', published in 1891, painted an unpleasing picture of the typical Bengali I.C.S. officer as arrogant, timorous and nepotistic.

85

The Islington Commission in 1913, with a singular disregard for the esprit de corps of the service, included in their questionnaire to witnesses a question as to whether Indians had proved as efficient as Europeans in the I.C.S. Several British I.C.S. officers in Bengal who gave evidence replied that the Indians had been less efficient. This provoked J. N. Gupta, an Indian I.C.S. officer of twenty years' standing, to protest against vague allegations that British officers were superior in pluck and daring, and to challenge evidence to be produced to prove that man for man, Indian officers had done less to break up gangs of dacoits and to quell riots, or in the constructive work of building schools and roads and tanks. He pointed out that since Dutt's retirement seventeen years earlier no Indian had been appointed as a Commissioner or to a Secretariat post. This had caused Indian I.C.S. officers to prefer the judicial side where their chances of promotion were better.[19]

After 1922 Indians began to enter the service in substantial numbers and the position changed. A. D. Gorwala, who served in the I.C.S. in Bombay, has left a vivid picture of this period.

The successful candidate, selected after examination in India, would spend a year or two at Oxford or Cambridge studying Indian history, language and law. On his return, once he had passed his qualifying examinations, he would be posted to a district to work with a subdivisional officer. After two more examinations and a period at the Survey School, he would be given charge of a subdivision. More important than formal instruction, says Gorwala, was the informal part of his training. 'This unofficial training was often administered quite imperceptibly. . . The Collector . . . might ask the new Magistrate to come and have tea with him one evening a week. Almost in passing he would suggest that it would perhaps be a a good thing if he brought along any particular cases in which he had written judgements or in which points of evidence were perplexing him. . . . Plied with good tea and excellent home-made cake, the touchiness and arrogance so characteristic of the intelligent inexperienced young prize-winner, to whom for some period at least all the world seems inferior, would fall off like an old garment. Differences of kind or race would sink to insignificance and the young man would, sometimes to his own surprise, find himself talking freely, listening with attention, proffering his work for examination, pleased at the praise, not hurt at the warning and advice.'[20]

There is of course a less pleasing side to Gorwala's generous picture. There was the racial exclusiveness which prevented Indian members of the I.C.S. even from being members of the United Services Club in Calcutta: and until within a few years of Independence the very top jobs most Secretaryships of Ministries and all Governorships were kept in European hands. As late as 1945 when the Governor of Bengal took over direct rule of the Province from his ministers he appointed European officers exclusively as his senior advisers.

Philip Woodruff, in his history of the I.C.S., leaves a sketch of some of the men who took over the top posts. 'Among the Indians of the I.C.S. were men of the highest calibre. No civil service in the world could hope for abler men than Bajpai, Hydari, Trivedi, H. M. Patel, Gorwala and others. . . . Whether in the districts or anywhere else there was nothing at all between the best English and the best Indians: there was more difference in the tail on both sides. Whereas the Englishman whom no one could call brilliant would sometimes become a picturesque eccentric or a conscientious plodder, there had been many more Indians who were definitely misfits'.[21] Woodruff attributes this to the system of selection. Many men who were up to I.C.S. standard, he felt, had been relegated to the provincial service and would thus take twenty-five years to reach a position which a more fortunate schoolfellow might hold in his second year of service.

S. K. Chettur of the Madras I.C.S. in his autobiography has more mixed memories than Gorwala of his relationship with the British. There was a Commissioner who transferred him on account of his 'impudence'; to one of young Chettur's remarks, he told him 'not to teach his grandmother to suck eggs', at which Chettur replied that she was a vegetarian. The eccentricity of the British I.C.S. officers impressed him. There was one who made his subordinates climb trees and another who, when a tehsildar jailed his cook for burning the curry, made that tehsildar enter himself in the common pound as a donkey . . . Chettur learned to live with the eccentrics but remained sensitive about his own dignity. He would insist that British army officers put their hats on so that they would have to salute him when they came into his office.[22]

Chettur had to put two future Prime Ministers of his Province in jail. In his morning coat and striped trousers, presenting the King-Emperor's birthday honours while the ladies' choir sang patriotic songs, he may well have wondered what the future had in store for him. For in many ways the position of the Indian officer was more difficult than that of his British colleague. The latter might be tired and disillusioned but, in the end when the British flag came down, he could count on a proportionate pension and compensation. The Indian was balanced between the present and the future. Congress, which in the 19th century had clamoured for Indianization of the services, in the 20th century called on the Indian administrators to resign in order to paralyse the British Government. To many of these Indian administrators the attitude and tactics of Congress seemed misguided and imprudent. While non-co-operation could easily deteriorate into anarchy, co-operation they felt would have provided a quicker and safer way to accelerate the transfer of power. So very few had resigned; many more, like Chettur, had at one time or another put Congressmen in jail.

Jawarharlal Nehru, who was to become Independent India's first Prime Minister, had made his views on the I.C.S. very clear. He had accused them of being 'self-satisfied and self-sufficient, narrow, with fixed minds, static in a changing world and wholly unsuited to a progressive environment. . . . Of one thing, I am quite sure, that no new order can be built up in India so long as the spirit of the I.C.S. pervades our administration. . . . It seems to me quite essential that the I.C.S. and similar services must disappear completely as such, before we can start real work on a new order'.[23]

In 1947, when India and Pakistan became independent, 52% of the I.C.S. officers were British. Virtually none of these stayed on in India, though some remained for several years in Pakistan. Of the remaining 48% of the officers who were Indian, about 500 continued to serve in India and 100 in Pakistan.

The reconciliation between the I.C.S. and Congress, when the latter came into power in independent India, was largely the work of Sardar Patel, the first Home Minister. Patel retained the I.C.S., renamed the 'Indian Administrative Service', as an all India service and insisted that 50% of the I.A.S. officers serving in any 'State', as the old provinces were now called, must come from outside that State. The jealousy of the exclusiveness of the Service was diminished by promoting into it officers from the State civil services. By 1960 less than half the Service had been admitted directly by the competitive examination which was held at the age of 21 to 24:[24] the remainder had mostly come from the State civil services and the army. The I.A.S. probationers were no longer sent to England. They were trained at the Civil Service Academy in India where in the first four months of their course they worked together with the probationers of other central services, such as Audit and Accounts, Income Tax and the Post Office. The salaries of the former members of the I.C.S., which had been criticized by Congress, were not reduced, but they did not keep up with inflation and were thus no longer better than those paid in commerce and in industry. The new I.A.S. scale was established at a more modest level.

The background of the officers had not greatly changed. 44% of them were sons of government officials; 95% were M.A.s and two-thirds of these had arts degrees. Their ambitions were perhaps different from those of the old I.C.S. An American visitor who interviewed probationers between 1959 and 1962 found none who wished to work in a district: all hoped to obtain posts in the Secretariats or in planning boards or public corporations.[25]

The proportion of I.A.S. officers serving as district officers had fallen. Yet the district officer, so long a target of Congress, still remained the pivot of the administration, retaining his powers as a magistrate and his responsibility for collecting revenue. More of his time since independence was occupied with development schemes and to reviving the village panchayats than with maintenance of law and order. More often too he might now find himself acting as an adviser to an elected body or as an executive who carried out its decisions instead of imposing the orders of government, and he had to listen patiently to the criticisms of local politicians.

The value of the experience of the senior Indian officers of the old I.C.S. was immediately recognized by the new government. They not only became Secretaries of ministries but were appointed as ambassadors and even in occasional emergencies as Cabinet Ministers. Some went on to the top positions in international organizations, such as B. R. Sen who became Director General of F.A.O. and C. V. Narasimhan, who was first Executive Secretary of ECAFE and then Chef de Cabinet in the United Nations.

Some criticism continued and an occasional whiff of gunpowder still drifted across the field from old battles, as when the Vice-President of India, Dr. Zakir Hussein, a veteran Congressman, told the Indian School of Public Administration in 1962 that 'The present administration has inherited some of that exclusive, forbidding, touch-me-not attitude, some of that lack of sympathetic understanding, which was associated with the past.'[26] An American scholar, too, in 1963 found that 'the familiar pattern remained unchanged, recruitment at an early age, followed by successive postings in district administration, central or provincial secretariats and in varying substantial fields. The shadow of an omnicompetent generalism cast by Macaulay, Wellesley and the whole I.C.S. tradition, whilst perhaps not lengthened, is fading slowly'.[27]

Pakistan's administrative problems at independence were greater than India's. She had to create a complete central government machinery, and her territory consisted of two wings separated by a thousand miles of India. On the other hand, there had been no tradition of hostility between the Muslim League and the I.C.S. Some of the relatively few Pakistani officers inherited from the I.C.S. and from other central Indian services were therefore given, or acquired, great responsibilities. Iskander Mirza of the Political Service became President of Pakistan; Choudhury Mohamed Ali, who had served in the Audit and Accounts Service, became Prime Minister; Ghulam Muhammad, who had started in the same Service, became Governor General.

The new Central Service of Pakistan retained even more of the traditions and procedures of the I.C.S. than did the I.A.S. in India. It continued to recruit entirely by written competitive examination. The first 20% of places were awarded each year on merit; the remaining 80% were divided equally between the West and East. The probationers continued until 1959 to go to Oxford and Cambridge for training. 75% of the posts of Secretaries to Government and of District Officer were reserved for the C.S.P. by law.

Of the hundred Pakistani I.C.S. officers at independence one third were Punjabis and the others came from homes which were now in India. None were natives of East Pakistan where the level of Muslim education was low. The British and Hindu officers in the East thus had to be replaced by Western Pakistanis, and local jealousy of these outsiders contributed to the bad relations between the two wings which bedevilled Pakistan's early years. The C.S.P. also inherited the hostility which other services had felt towards the I.C.S. An American observer in 1959 noticed that a C.S.P. probationer with a bachelor's degree started with a salary almost twice that of an agricultural officer with equivalent qualifications. He found 'intense animosity towards the C.S.P. felt by engineers and others trained abroad, where they had experience of the adulation of scientist and technocrat'.[28] In addition, an old criticism was revived by lawyer-politicians that the District Officer, having judicial as well as magisterial powers, could be at once prosecutor and judge in the same case.

An analysis by a Pakistani writer of the functions of the District Officer in West Pakistan in 1957 seemed to indicate that the Deputy Commissioner had as wide powers as ever. He was responsible for assessing and collecting revenue and maintaining law and order. He heard appeals from junior magistrates and approved transfers of police officers. No municipal or District Board tax could be imposed without his consent. The criticisms also were familiar: that because he had too much paper work, his clerks became too influential; decisions were delayed, and he had insufficient time to tour his district.[29]

In fact, however, in the unsettled political period between the death of Liaquat Ali in 1951 and the assumption of power by General Ayub Khan in 1958, the position of the C.S.P. officer, except for those who became politicians, was less strong than it appeared. He no longer held his appointment from the Secretary of State in London and was thus more dependent on politicians in a time when the centre of power was constantly shifting. His patronage had been curtailed, and if he did not satisfy politicians he was liable to be transferred. As District Officer he could no longer exercise effective control over the district agriculture, education and other departmental officers, whose parent ministries were involved in a constant manœuvre for power. The Munir report on the disturbances in the Punjab of 1954 accused the local government of subordinating law and order to politics and wistfully recalled 'the days of the Steel Frame, when we saw the erect figure of a district officer in the middle of an excited procession; a soft smile on a firm mouth, determination written on his face'.[30] Some officers yielded to pressures, and one of the first acts of the military government which came into power in 1958 was to purge the civil service: thirteen C.S.P. officers were compulsorily retired for corruption, misconduct or inefficiency.

The purge complete, the C.S.P. appeared to settle down with the military regime in a harmonious collaboration which has been described as reminiscent of the period in the late 19th century when the Viceroy's Council of civil servants ran the world's largest bureaucracy.[31] All the strategic positions in the Provincial administration in 1960 were in the hands of the C.S.P. and at least until President Ayub's 'basic democracy' became a reality the District

Officer would continue to be addressed like his British predecessor as he toured his district as 'Incarnation of Justice', 'Cherisher of the Poor', and 'Father and Mother of the People'.[32]

Before leaving the Successors in India, the varying fortunes may be considered of a community which ultimately had little share in the succession, namely, the Anglo-Indians, known at earlier periods as 'East-Indians' and 'Eurasians'.

The East India Company in the 17th century, like its Portuguese predecessors, encouraged its soldiers to marry Indian women and paid a gratuity for each child. Mixed marriages among senior civil and military officials were common from the time of Job Charnock, the founder of Calcutta, who married a Hindu widow at the end of the 17th century, to that of General Roberts, father of the future Field Marshal, whose first wife was a Rajput princess whom he married early in the 19th century, though Lord Roberts himself was the son of a second marriage by a European wife. The Indian wives lost their caste by their marriage, and their children had therefore to identify themselves with their fathers. The Eurasians held posts at all levels in the Company's service: in the 18th century there were probably more Eurasians than Europeans both in the civil service and in Clive's armies. A number of them held senior positions, particularly on the military side; General Jones who commanded the Madras Army, Colonel Skinner, who raised Skinner's Horse, and the Hearsay family are among the best known.

Between 1791 and 1795, however, the Company took successive steps to exclude the Eurasians from its covenanted civil service, from commissions in the army, and finally from serving in any capacity in the army except as bandsmen. The initiative for this change came from the Court of Directors in London, ostensibly because they were concerned lest the Eurasians might lead mutinies or even rebellions against the Company, as had the mulattoes in Haiti against the French. The argument was supported by the observations of Lord Valentia whose report on a visit made to India in 1806 apprehended that the Eurasians, rapidly increasing in numbers and more energetic and better educated than the Indians, might soon become impossible to control. 'In every country where this intermediate cast has been permitted to rise,' he wrote, 'it has tended to the ruin of the country. Spanish America and San Domingo are examples of this fact.' He recommended that 'every father of half-cast children be obliged to send them to Europe, prohibiting their return in any capacity whatever'.[33] Anglo-Indian writers have possibly exaggerated the influence of this itinerant nobleman,[34] whose evident silliness was indicated in the early pages of his memoirs, which express his indignation at being obliged to sail in convoy from England in wartime and the shock to his European delicacy of encountering fishermen who wore no clothes. The Company's real object in excluding the Eurasians was probably to increase the number of posts which could be filled by patronage from London.

Many of the most enterprising Eurasians now joined the armies of Indian princes, only to be recalled by the Company during the Mahratta Wars. Several of these officers were beheaded by the Maharajah of Holkar when they refused to fight against the British. Most of those who had been recalled were again dismissed by the Company when the war was over. Even the services of Colonel Skinner, whose regiment had achieved remarkable successes, were only retained because the advice of the Commander-in-Chief was ultimately preferred to that of the Governor General.[35]

In 1830 the Eurasians of Calcutta sent one of their number, J. W. Rickett, a customs officer, to London to present their grievances before the Select Committee of Parliament which was considering the renewal of the Company's Charter. The theme of his evidence was that 'we are sometimes recognized as Europeans and sometimes as natives, as it serves the purpose of government'.[36] Though he was overshadowed in these proceedings by the Hindu witness, Ram Mohan Roy, his arguments may have contributed to the insertion of the famous Clause 87 in the Charter Act of 1833. At all events the community benefited by the Clause and entered into a period of prosperity. Even before 1833, because their mother tongue was English and they had founded their own schools, they had obtained many of the clerical posts in Calcutta. After English replaced Persian as the official language of the administration they were in an even stronger position and in 1840 held 90% of the clerical posts in the Company's employment in Calcutta.[37] They had also acquired technical skills which could be privately practised while they were excluded from higher employment. These subsequently enabled them to take a leading part in the surveying and staffing of the new railway and telegraph systems which were established in the middle of the century.

Their high point came in the Mutiny of 1857, when Eurasian telegraph operators saved the Punjab (and, as legend maintained, Calcutta and Bombay also) and when their schoolboys held the La Martinière College at Lucknow against the sepoys. Afterwards there was a steady decline. The Eurasian army units which were formed in the Mutiny were disbanded between 1860 and 1870 as being more expensive than Indian units. More important, the Hindus of Bengal began to overtake them in English education. The Eurasian schools had not been included on the list approved by Lord Hardinge in 1844 to which the Government gave preference in recruitment. For many years Eurasian candidates, on the grounds that English was their mother tongue, continued to be accepted with certificates of secondary education for posts in which university degrees were required from other candidates. The loss of this privilege in 1919 was a severe blow, as few of them had university degrees. One reason for this was that they were educated as 'Europeans', and the curriculum prescribed by the Government for the European schools was not related to that of the Indian Universities. Their treatment in different departments was inconsistent. In 1882 they were excluded from the government appointments which were offered each year to graduates of the Roorkee Engineering College and which were now to be reserved for pure blooded Indians.[38] This order was rescinded under a storm of protest from the European Community which was also affected, but similar orders about this time seem to have contributed to the reduction of the numbers of Eurasians in the subordinate judicial and executive services in Bengal.[39] In the army medical service on the other hand they continued to be given a special status in the 'Indian Medical Department' which was recruited entirely from Anglo-Indians and domiciled Europeans.

The progress of Indian education and of self-government led to a considerable reduction of the numbers of Anglo-Indians, as they now called themselves, in senior posts in the provincial governments. While in 1862 in Bengal they had occupied 67 posts as deputy magistrates and deputy collectors, by 1922 they were only 12; and there was a similar diminution in the number of police officers above the rank of sergeant.[40] They retreated therefore into the All-India services which were still controlled by the British and in which it was essential for the Government to be able to rely on the loyalty of its officers during nationalist disturbances. In 1930 of 50,000 Anglo-Indian men of working age, 14,000 were employed on the railways, 2,000 in the Telegraph Department and 2,000 in the Customs.[41] Under the 1935 Government of India Act quotas of places in these departments were reserved for the community.

In the First and Second World Wars 80% of the Anglo-Indian men served in the forces, winning several Victoria Crosses, and their women were the backbone of the nursing and women's auxiliary services.[42] But as independence approached, their leader, Frank Anthony, was given little encouragement that the British could do anything to help the community. Sir Stafford Cripps now gave them advice which was more realistic than that offered by various Viceroys who had interested themselves in their fortunes, namely to come to terms with the Congress.[43] Though the latter had little reason to appreciate a loyalty which had kept the railways running during a Congress rising and had supported a war effort which Congress opposed, they behaved with magnanimity. Under Article 336 of the Indian Constitution of 1949, places continued to be reserved for the Anglo-Indians in the railways, telegraphs and customs, though the quota was reduced progressively and expired after ten years,[44] since when the Anglo-Indians have had to compete on equal terms with other communities.

The response to this provision was poor.[45] Whether because they felt that their promotion would be blocked by prejudice or by their lack of university education, or whether because they now improved their education and were no longer content to be guards and tele-graphists, the Anglo-Indians failed to take up their quota of places. In India some went into expanding trade and industry; many emigrated to Britain and some of the fairer ones to Australia. Most of the community lived in the great cities, Calcutta, Bombay and Madras, which remained in India at partition. A number went over to Karachi at independence to take jobs as clerks or receptionists which had been created by the departure of Hindus. Statistics are unreliable, for at independence a number of Indian Christians who had previously described themselves as Anglo-Indians reverted to their former classification, and the Anglo-Indians who went to Britain were treated as British nationals. It is difficult to estimate the real numbers of the community at any time. Lord Curzon was furnished with figures which ranged between a million and 120,000. Probably they were about 125,000 to 150,000 at independence.[46]

They were thus far fewer in proportion to the population than were the Eurasians of Indonesia and, while the Dutch treated these as their own nationals both before and after independence, the Anglo-

Indians were statutory natives of India, though treated as Europeans for purposes of education and internal security. After the end of the 18th century the one brief moment of recognition of the services of the community came after the Mutiny. A collection was then made to establish schools for their children, but by a refinement of contempt Anglo-Indians were ineligible to teach in those set up by the Protestant missions. Henceforward, as increasing numbers of British women arrived in India by steamship and through the Suez Canal, the Anglo-Indians were allowed even less social contact with the British. In vain they contrasted their treatment with that in French, Dutch, Portuguese and Spanish territories. Pseudo-scientists now spread the idea that 'even a little admixture of native blood seems to result in an individual who possesses the bad qualities of both races'.[47] That this was nonsense was shown by the ease with which the children of Indian fathers and European mothers have been integrated into modern Indian society and by the distinguished positions which they have held; but it was widely propagated by the novelists of the imperialist period, in which Eurasians were almost invariably depicted as cowardly, feeble and treacherous. Their V.C.s, their athletic successes, their pioneering in aviation, never succeeded in changing the legend. The last scornful kick of the race of their fathers as they departed was to produce a best-selling novel, subsequently filmed in Hollywood, which appeared to the Anglo Indians to be a savage mockery of their service to their beloved railways.[48]

REFERENCES

[1] J. N. Gupta, *R. C. Dutt*, London, 1911, p. 18.
[2] S. N. Banerjea, *A Nation in Making*, London, 1925, p. 12.
[3] ibid, p. 21.
[4] ibid., p. 14.
[5] J. N. Gupta, op. cit., p. 38.
[6] ibid.
[7] ibid., p. 318.
[8] ibid., p. 315.
[9] ibid., p. 497.
[10] *Royal Commission on the Public Services in India* (Islington Commission), London, 1914, Vol. 3, p. 457.
[11] S. N. Banerjea, op. cit., p. 28.
[12] ibid., p. 32.
[13] ibid., p. 44.
[14] H. Cotton, *New India*, London, 1886, p. 16.

[15] S. N. Banerjea, op. cit., p. 368.

[16] ibid., p. 30.

[17] Satyendranath Tagore, *My Boyhood and My Life in Bombay*, Calcutta, 1915 (in Bengali).

[18] Hansard, House of Commons Debates, 2 June, 1893, Col. 102.

[19] *Royal Commission on the Public Services in India* (Islington Report), Vol. III, p. 453–475.

[20] A. D. Gorwala, 'Role of the Administrator, Past, Present and Future' (Gokhale Institute Lecture, 1952), p. 9.

[21] P. Woodruff, *The Guardians*, London, 1963, p. 300.

[22] S. K. Chettur, *The Steel Frame and I*, London, 1962.

[23] J. Nehru, *Autobiography*, London, 1938, p. 442–445.

[24] R. Braibanti, *Administration and Economic Development in India*, London, 1963, p. 52.

[25] ibid., p. 63.

[26] Indian Journal of Public Administration, Vol. 8, July 1962, p. 267.

[27] R. Braibanti, *The Civil Service of Pakistan*, Duke University, 1959, p. 9.

[28] ibid., p. 285.

[29] A. H. Aslam, *The Deputy Commissioner*, Lahore, 1957.

[30] Quoted by H. F. Goodnow, *The Civil Service of Pakistan*, Yale, 1964, p. 70.

[31] Ian Stephens, *Pakistan*, London, 1964, p. 304.

[32] K. B. Sayeed, *Pakistan The Formative Phase*, Karachi, 1960, p. 395.

[33] George, Lord Valentia, *Voyages and Travels to India and the Red Sea*, Vol. I, London, 1809, p. 241.

[34] e.g. H. A. Stark, *Hostages to India*, Calcutta, 1936, p. 69.

[35] D. Holman, *Sikander Sahib*, London, 1961, p. 206.

[36] H. A. Stark and E. W. Madge, *East Indian Worthies*, Calcutta, 1892, p. 51. Also P.P. 1830, Vol. VI, p. 190.

[37] *Indian Statutory Commission (Simon) Report*, 1930, Vol. XVI, p. 275.

[38] *Aitchison Report*, Proceedings of Sub-committee on Public Works, p. 3–4.

[39] *Aitchison Report*, Vol. VI, p. 111, evidence of Dr. Chambers.

[40] *Simon Report*, Vol. XVI, p. 275.

[41] ibid., p. 277.

[42] R. J. N. Maher in *Pilot Survey of Socio-Economic Conditions of the Anglo-Indian Community*, Calcutta, 1958, p. xiv.

[43] Reginald Maher, *These are the Anglo-Indians*, Calcutta, 1962, p. 100.

[44] M. V. Pylee, *India's Constitution*, London, 1962, p. 361.

[45] ibid., p. 361.

[46] T. Raleigh, *Lord Curzon in India*, London, 1906, p. 365. J. A. H. Bower in *Ambition Mocked Our Honest Toil*, Madras, 1959, p. 110, and Maher in the two works cited support the figure of about 125,000.

[47] Dr. H. N. Ridley (1895) quoted in R. Maher, op. cit., p. 38.

[48] The Anglo-Indian reaction to 'Bhowani Junction' is described by Maher *These are the Anglo-Indians*, p. 38.

CHAPTER V

Ceylon

'The prospect of future advancement to situations now exclusively held by Europeans will constitute a most powerful inducement with the natives to relinquish many absurd prejudices and to qualify themselves for general employment.'

COLEBROOKE COMMISSION'S REPORT, 1832

The development of the government services in Ceylon was decisively influenced by the separation of its administration under British rule from that of India. The separation was somewhat accidental after the British had acquired most of Ceylon fortuitously from the Dutch. During the wars against revolutionary France the Stadtholder of the Netherlands, who was a refugee in Britain, ordered the Dutch Governor of Colombo to admit a British garrison. The Governor refused, and recognized the revolutionary government in Holland which was collaborating with the French. Troops of the Madras Government of the East India Company then occupied Colombo and coastal Ceylon without difficulty after the Swiss mercenary troops in the Dutch service had been bought over by a British agent.

The Dutch East India Company, which had taken Ceylon from the Portuguese in 1656, had maintained a decentralized form of administration, under which its officers were permitted to trade privately so long as they respected the Company's monopoly of cinnamon. In the districts the traditional Sinhalese chiefs or 'Mudaliyars' retained their authority, providing labour for the plantations and being remunerated with grants of land. The British Company, however, introduced not only its own European officials from Madras but also Madrasi headmen who replaced the local Mudaliyars. Both classes behaved with rapacity and imprudence, and taxes on land and on coconut trees were demanded in place of the customary services. Riots ensued and, partly as a result of these and partly because of the strategic importance of the Island, responsibility for its administration was taken over by the Crown from the Company in 1802. Henceforth, no more officials from Madras, either British or Indian, were employed in Ceylon.

The senior posts, or 'writerships', were filled by the Secretary of State in London, and Ceylon thus became the first British territory to have a career civil service under the Crown. In the early days it was a remarkably well remunerated service. The first batch of writers to come out were aged thirteen; and they were allowed to retire on pension after twelve years' service. The cost of such an administration was a considerable burden on the revenues of the new colony, and when the remainder of the Island was conquered from the King of Kandy in 1818 army officers, part of whose salaries was carried on the military budget, were appointed as Government Agents of the new provinces.

Ceylon when it was conquered by the British contained two principal communities, the Sinhalese, who were Buddhists, and the Tamils, more recent invaders from India, who were Hindus and were mainly concentrated in the North. These 'Ceylon Tamils', who were long established, later came to be distinguished from the 'Indian Tamils', who were brought in to cultivate the tea estates in the 19th century. In addition there were the Burghers, of Dutch or Portuguese origin, and the Moors who were Malayans. A few aboriginals remained in the jungles, and in the course of the 19th century a small but influential group of European planters was established. The proportions of the population at independence in 1948 were about 69% Sinhalese, 11% Ceylon Tamils, 12% Indian Tamils, 6% Moors and 1% Burghers. The population as a whole were known as 'Ceylonese'.

Although Sir Thomas Maitland, the second Governor, took the two Sinhalese de Saram brothers back to be educated in Cambridge in 1811, little serious attention was given to employment of educated Ceylonese in the administration until the arrival of the Colebrooke Commission of 1829–32. This Commission had originally been intended by Parliament to visit not Ceylon but Mauritius and the Cape; as an afterthought it was instructed to inquire into the system of government in Ceylon, mainly because the Island had failed to become financially self-supporting. William Colebrooke had worked with Raffles in Java and his general approach was liberal. The political reforms which he proposed and which Lord Goderich, the Secretary of State, accepted, produced a Legislative Council with Ceylonese as well as European members. Both for reasons of economy and because he was opposed to patronage Colebrooke criticized the selection of the civil service by the Secretary of State in London and recommended that as many posts as possible should be filled by local Europeans and by Ceylonese. He noted with approval that the Ceylonese clerks already employed were usually selected from the higher castes, as this 'fosters the prejudices of the people in favour of a system from which the ascendancy of the privileged classes is derived'. He urged that more should be done to provide English education in order to qualify Ceylonese to occupy senior posts, but suggested that this should take place by setting up a college in Ceylon rather than by sending young men to Europe.[1]

The Secretary of State, Lord Goderich, accepted Colebrooke's proposals enthusiastically and instructed the Governor that 'Employment on the civil situations of the Island will henceforth be open to all classes of the native community, and to such other subjects of His Majesty whose long residence in the Island may have given them a fair claim to participate in the advantages of the colonial service.' He also instructed the Governor to establish a college at Colombo with the object 'of affording to native youths a means of qualifying themselves for different branches of the public service'.[2]

General Sir Edward Barnes, who was Governor of Ceylon during the visit of the Commission, had served on Wellington's staff in the Peninsula and at Waterloo and had little sympathy with Colebrooke, to whom he wrote – 'Whatever Utopian ideas theorists may cherish of universal fraternity without regard to colour, religion or civilization, or whatever notions Levellers may wish to see adopted, I am decidedly of opinion that this people cannot nor ought to have under existing circumstances any greater share in the government than they have at present. I am not one of those persons who think that black and white people can ever be amalgamated in the situations of society, so as to do away with those distinctions which at present exist all over the world. . . . As to the propriety of gradually introducing natives into situations at present held by Europeans, I should be glad to know where you propose to draw the line. Admitted to one situation, they would have an equal claim to another, so that unless you contemplate the supersession of all European administrators, not excepting the Governor, I do not see where you could stop. My opinion is that the line is now well defined, that the natives are perfectly content and that it ought not to be invaded'.[3]

As for the education of the Ceylonese, he continued, 'A college is a high sounding term, at the mention of which one is naturally inclined to turn one's attention to the British universities, but on reverting to the state of civilization, of cultivation, of literature amongst the natives of the island a smile will naturally arise'.[4]

Barnes departed to become Commander-in-Chief in India and the Colebrooke reforms were implemented. On the public service they had disastrous effects. Goderich had decided that it was 'of the first importance to break through the principle of an exclusive civil service'.[5] Pensions were abolished and salaries were reduced to a level which was adequate for local candidates but not for expatriates, with the result that the quality of British entrants deteriorated and officials spent much of their time growing coffee to supplement their incomes. The mismanagement of the Kandyan rebellion of 1848 was attributed to the idleness of the British officers and their failure to learn the Sinhalese language. On the other hand, until the mid-forties, the reforms did not cause any Ceylonese to be taken into the service, for Colebrooke's educational proposals were slow to produce results and there were few Ceylonese with adequate knowledge of English. In 1845 pensions were reintroduced and a new system initiated. The Secretary of State once more appointed the writers to fill vacancies in an exclusive service, but the Governor could recommend local candidates, either Ceylonese or European, to the Secretary of State for appointment. From 1844 a few Ceylonese were appointed as members of the Civil Service; the two earliest were Frederick de Livera, who had been educated in Calcutta and had served as Assistant Government Agent and District Judge, and Casie Chitty, who had been a nominated member of the Legislative Council. Of five Ceylonese admitted in 1845 and 1846, three had been district judges, one was promoted from the clerical service and one from the public works department.

Shortly after Macaulay had succeeded in introducing competitive examinations for entry into the Covenanted Service in India, a petition was sent to the Secretary of State for the Colonies by a Ceylonese association in 1860 to suggest that the same principle should be introduced in Ceylon. The Governor, Sir Henry Ward, viewed this proposal with 'the greatest alarm'. In nine cases out of ten, he feared, the precocious Burgher, Tamil or Low Country Sinhalese would defeat the European candidate. All minor offices in the districts, he told the Secretary of State, were already held by natives, but 'make them masters, not servants, and I do not believe there are four in the whole island in whose hands the government could safely place its authority'.

He apprehended serious trouble with the European planters, whose submission to authority was already difficult to enforce by the Government Agent. 'If the officer were a native he would be accused of partiality and corruption, and in too many cases this charge would be well founded. For there is a laxity of feeling and practice in all orientals which nothing but the strictest surveillance can check.'

Ward was equally apprehensive of the jealousies between communities which would be aroused. To place Ceylonese in charge of districts 'would not only alter the character of British rule, but would amount to a breach of faith with the two million Tamil, Moormen and Sinhalese who have placed themselves under it, not to be governed by each other but by us'. To summarise this long and agitated despatch, he concluded 'The British officer cannot do a corrupt, an ungentlemanlike thing, without exposure and censure. With a native the very reverse of this would occur. Corruption would be the rule'.[6] The Secretary of State, the Duke of Newcastle, replied in due course that he did not agree with the demand for competitive examinations, but the issue was not buried for long.

In 1868 Sir Hercules Robinson as Governor wrote to the Secretary of State to propose that the salaries of the civil service be raised by 30%. The Duke of Buckingham rejected the request, observing in particular that 'the salary of the Governor, which you appear to think that the people of Ceylon would be glad to see increased' was considered 'sufficient and liberal at its present rate of £7,000 a year': but he took the opportunity to suggest that it would be economical, as well as equitable, to introduce Ceylonese into higher civil employment.[7] This counter-proposal was not well received by the Governor's Executive Council, deprived of their expected rise in salary, who resolved that 'the claims of properly qualified natives for employment in the highest appointments of the public services have for years past received from the local government the most liberal consideration'.[8] They attached an annexe showing that of 84 superior appointments, 10 were filled by Sinhalese, Tamils or Burghers and another 32 by Europeans who were sons of former government officials or had been born on the Island.

Despite Ward's apprehensions, from 1870 examinations were held simultaneously in London and Colombo for entry to the civil service, identical papers being set. In practice there proved to be no chance for a Ceylonese to pass unless he had attended a British university. Though Ponnambalam Arunachalam succeeded in this way in 1878, fewer Ceylonese now entered than in the days when they could be nominated by the Governor. From 1880 the competition was held in London only. Sir James Longden, who was Governor at this time, justified the change by explaining to the Secretary of State that it was 'impossible for any young man without leaving the Island to shake himself so free of local ties and local feelings of caste prejudices and insular narrowness as to acquire any independence of thought'. He maintained that he did not wish to exclude Ceylonese from writer-ships, but that in the Ceylon schools, although they taught classics, mathematics and history, the 'moral, physical and social training of an English Public School or University are wholly wanting . . . an almost essential factor for the civil service'. He wanted to abolish the Colombo examinations because of the 'inconvenience that may at any time arise from the admission of gentlemen who may perhaps cram sufficient superficial knowledge to pass successfully an examina-tion but who have never had a chance of emancipating their minds from the narrow views and narrower prejudices incident to the circumstances of the native population'.[9]

Lord Kimberley, the Secretary of State, only agreed with some reluctance to close the Colombo examination and to 'the practical exclusion of able and deserving natives of the colony from all except the lower grades of the government service';[10] as a partial remedy a lower division of the civil service was created in 1891, recruited by competition from candidates nominated by the Governor. Although members of the lower division could rise to senior posts, Sir Solomon West Ridgeway, who was Governor in 1896, found that 'the badge of inferiority affixed to the Ceylonese is far more distasteful than any difference of pay, which can be defended without any imputation of social or official inferiority'.[11] Ridgeway on his arrival was appalled by the spirit of lethargy and indifference in the whole service and proposed to amalgamate the two divisions, but Joseph Chamber-lain, who was Secretary of State, told him that he was trying to apply Indian ideas too soon after his arrival in Ceylon. To this Ridgeway observed tartly that in India and Ceylon conditions were indeed different; 'during my employment in the Military, Diplomatic, Indian and Irish Services, I have known officers to be retired on account of inefficiency, but I doubt whether under the existing regulations of the Colonial service similar measure can be meted out to incompetence pure and simple'.[12] The lower division, however, was not incorporated in the general civil service until 1920, and simultaneous examinations in Colombo and London were not reintroduced until 1924.

One of the most remarkable features of the first decade of the 20th century, according to the Census Commissioner, was 'a passion for education'–a popular clamour for English education which would enable the sons of small landowners and cultivators to pass examinations and obtain posts in offices in the towns.[13] The demand arose as much from a desire to improve the status as the fortunes of the family and was accompanied by an agitation for the Ceylonization of the services. The Ceylon Reform League demanded that all posts below that of Governor be opened to Ceylonese, and Sir Ponnambalam Arunachalam in 1917 reminded the Ceylon National Congress that the progressive Indian State of Mysore had Indians at the head of all the departments of government.[14]

Under this pressure the Government appointed a Committee on Further Employment of Ceylonese in the Public Service in 1919 which found that of 108 posts in the cadre of the Ceylon Civil Service, 18 were filled by lower (now 'local') division officers and 10 by non-European officers recruited in England. They recommended that one-third of the posts should in future be reserved for Ceylonese and that this proportion should progressively be raised to one-half. Presumably on grounds of security, they affirmed, however, that 'the necessity for maintaining at any rate for many years to come a larger proportion of Europeans than would appear prima facie to be unavoidable rests on the fact that there is a certain number of administrative posts in which the employment of Europeans is inevitable'.[15]

From now localization of the civil service proceeded faster in Ceylon than in India. The Donoughmore Constitution of 1931, somewhat surprisingly modelled both on those of the London County Council and of the League of Nations, gave considerable authority to an elected State Council, which voted that no expatriate could in future be appointed to a post without the specific approval of his salary by the Council. Recruitment of British officers to the C.C.S. was suspended and only resumed briefly between 1935 and 1937. By 1940, eight years before independence, the Europeans were already outnumbered by 81 to 47. From about 1930 Ceylonese began to be appointed as Government Agents (equivalent to the Indian District Magistrate or Deputy Commissioner).

The earliest Ceylonese in the Civil Service were Low Country Sinhalese Christians. These held all seven of the posts occupied by Ceylonese in 1870, having entered the service by nomination. By 1907 the position was quite different: there were 6 Burghers, 4 Sinhalese and 2 Tamils. The Sinhalese however gradually improved their position again. In 1925 the numbers were 14 Burghers, 17 Sinhalese and 8 Tamils; and in 1946, 16 Burghers, 69 Sinhalese and 31 Tamils. The Tamils and the Burghers were, however, still considerably over-represented at the time of independence.[16]

Until about 1865, the Government's main concern was with law and order and the improvement of communications. From this time the development of Ceylon's natural resources enabled the expansion of the social services to be financed, and Ceylonese were needed to staff them. The earliest institution of professional education was the medical college, founded in 1870. From 1888 its diplomas were recognized by the British General Medical Council, so that Ceylonese doctors could proceed direct to higher degrees in Britain. Sixty-seven per cent of the surgeons and assistant surgeons were Ceylonese by 1907 and the service was almost completely Ceylonized by 1919. Initially the medical service was dominated by Burghers. By 1925 Sinhalese were in a majority, though even at independence Burghers and Tamils were over-represented and Tamils predominated in the medical profession outside government.[17] At independence Ceylon's health service, the low death rate and the eradication of malaria commanded the admiration of other Asian countries. The Health Department was considerably affected later by the National Language Act, however, and there were more resignations in this department than in any other.

A technical college was founded in 1893. Though the engineering profession had less prestige than that of medicine, nearly a third of the engineers in the Public Works Department were Ceylonese by 1907 and well over half by independence. A high proportion of the engineers in early years were Burghers and later Tamils.[18] Few Ceylonese, however, entered the irrigation department which was unpopular and mainly active in remote and malarious areas. Agricultural education was late to develop. There was no Department of Agriculture in the University College, and even when a Faculty of Agriculture was ultimately established by the University, it was neither strong nor popular.

A country-wide police service was only organized in 1908. Until that time the policing of the rural areas had been the responsibility of the Government Agent through the local headmen. In the Ceylon Police the Inspectors were generally Burghers. At first the Superintendents and Assistants were Europeans, recruited in England by the same examination through which the Indian police officers were selected. By 1919, however, three out of the seven Superintendents were Ceylonese. In that year the Government decided to Ceylonize half of the officer posts. As in the Civil Service, the process was rapidly extended in the 1930s and by independence the force was almost wholly Ceylonized from Inspector General downwards.

As in India, the earliest local civil servants were used on the judicial side, partly because of the difficulties experienced by Europeans in interpretation of the legal systems. From 1856 in Colombo and from 1872 in Kandy, it was government policy that the District Judge should be a barrister and this policy was subsequently extended into other districts. A Law College was established in Kandy and many Ceylonese studied at the Inns of Court in London.

Colebrooke shared Macaulay's contempt for oriental learning. 'The education afforded by the native priesthood in their temples and colleges scarcely merits any notice,' he wrote, and proposed that apart from the government college in Colombo education should be carried out by Christian missions.[19] In this he was as usual in disagreement with Barnes who considered that 'one of the greatest defects of our [English] school system is that it has got too much into the hands of the clergy'.[20] The British had inherited a school system from the Dutch which had developed to meet a situation in which posts in government service were reserved for baptized Christians. Although the British Government, in accordance with Colebrooke's recommendation, established Royal College, Colombo, with this exception the famous secondary schools, such as Trinity College, Kandy, and St. Thomas's, were run by missions: even the Royal College always had a clergyman as principal.

Two parallel systems evolved, the vernacular schools and those which taught in English. The government service was recruited from the latter. Ceylon had no university until the 20th century, but from 1881 the Cambridge senior examination could be taken locally; from 1882 the London matriculation; from 1886 the London intermediate arts; and eventually the external B.A. of London. London University until 1945 made little effort to modify its curriculum for external students, and Ceylonese boys studied English history and English geography. Ormsby-Gore, who visited Ceylon in 1928 while Parliamentary Under-Secretary for the Colonies, found an 'over-emphasis of the purely clerical and literary traditions coupled with a neglect of the life and social conditions of Ceylon'. Public opinion, he said, had demanded that the elementary school must lead to the secondary school and the secondary school to the university, and thereby the whole course and aim of education became controlled by a British university course and a series of examinations designed to lead to that course. This had had the customary denationalizing, demoralizing, and intellectually and socially cramping results, but 'popular opinion hugged the chains because it thought it was getting English "standards" '.

He lamented an education which had concerned itself above all with words, resulting in 'an accumulation of an imposing array of miscellaneous unco-ordinated information, none of it complete or profound, about a large number of subjects'. The fundamental remedy, he thought, would have been to eliminate the external examinations, but this would have made it much more difficult for the few at the top to get to Cambridge.[21]

Twenty-five years later a report of a World Bank Mission was hardly less critical. It described the educational system as dominated by examinations, such as London matriculation, which was intended as a test of fitness for further education but had become a test of educational attainment. The Mission deplored the lack of attention to teaching of science, agriculture and handicrafts, and suggested that the Ceylon schools were still modelled on those of 19th century England.[22]

Yet the differences between Ceylon's education system and that of India were considerable and were to have important effects on the government services. In higher education, in spite of occasional early links with India, Ceylon finally chose association with Britain, firstly through the external degrees of London then, after a somewhat unproductive association with Oxford, by setting up a University College which had a special relationship with London. D. R. Wijeyewardana, the Ceylon newspaper proprietor who played a leading part in the decision that the University should be residential, pointed to the Indian universities as models to be avoided–'factories turning out myriads of anaemic graduates . . . killing the body as well as the soul'.[23] The establishment of the University College was delayed for twenty years by a dispute between the Tamils and Burghers on the one hand who wanted it in Colombo, and the Sinhalese who wanted it to be established, as eventually it was, near Kandy. It became a fully independent university precipitately during the Second War, when the examination papers could no longer penetrate the German–Japanese blockade. But after the War it continued to use outside examiners and its degrees were recognized for admission to higher studies in Britain. Being fully residential its numbers were strictly limited.

At the same time the introduction of adult suffrage and the relative prosperity of Ceylon resulted in primary education becoming compulsory and all education free before independence. There was thus a much higher literacy rate in Ceylon than in India, but whereas government posts were reserved for the 15% who attended English language schools, those who attended the vernacular schools had limited openings. The Tamils, whose lands in the Jaffna peninsula were unsuited to estate cultivation, and whose Hindu caste system often precluded them from working as artisans, entered the English schools, and consequently the government services, in proportionately much greater numbers than the Sinhalese. So did the Burghers, who were urban and English-speaking. Those Sinhalese who occupied senior posts were descendants of the families of Mudaliyars whom the British found and confirmed in office; many of them had become Christians and from about 1910 onwards were often more literate in English than Sinhalese.

Here then was a potentially explosive situation, in which the Buddhist, Sinhalese-speaking majority saw the best jobs going to the English-educated Christian and Hindu minorities. Bandaranaike's election victory in 1956 and the language policy which his government adopted were due as much to the influence of the frustrated Sinhalese lower middle class as to that of Buddhist monks.

The strength of feeling was shown in the Report of the National Education Commission of 1961. The Commission pointed out that, though Buddhists represented 74% of the population, 75% of the bursary holders at the Ceylon University were non-Buddhists.

Whereas only one Sinhalese in every three thousand received a university education, the proportion of Tamils was one to three hundred, almost as high as that in the U.S.A. The Commission maintained that 'the discrimination to which the majority of our people have been subjected' took place 'simply because they have stuck to the religion which binds them to their native soil' and recommended that quotas by religion should be established for admission to the University and public service for the next ten years.[24]

Under British rule, the Ceylon Civil Service, whose members were appointed by the Secretary of State after taking the same examination as the I.C.S., occupied the top administrative posts, as Permanent Secretaries of Ministries, Government Agents in the Provinces, and even as heads of professional services and often of technical departments. For most of the period the Government Agent and Assistant Government Agent in the districts conducted the administration through chief headmen who were men of substance, receiving an honorarium rather than a salary. The village headmen were also selected on grounds of rank or birth. In the 1930s the popularly elected government replaced the headmen by paid Divisional Revenue Officers.

Colebrooke in 1832 had found that there were 25 appointments as heads of civil departments, collectors of districts and judges reserved for the C.C.S., and he did not consider that the Service could fill these effectively when it had only 38 members at various stages of seniority. The number of C.C.S. officers rose to about 100 by the end of the century and 120 by independence in 1948. But during the Second World War there was a far greater, and largely unplanned, expansion of the administrative services outside the C.C.S. Officers were employed on temporary contracts to deal with rationing, to organize civil defence and to run government industries. After independence in 1948, the expansion continued as new development schemes were started. The Commission on Salaries and Cadres in 1961 described the public service as 'expanding like a cancerous growth'.[25] It had doubled in size since 1948 and its cost had trebled. Indeed the first recommendation of the Commission was that an accurate census should be made of government employees, who were believed to be 20% of all wage and salary earners in the country.

The Commission stated that 'it has unfortunately been a feature of our system that administrative officers have been comparatively speaking better paid and have better prospects of advancement than their technical counterparts. This has inevitably led the latter to seek administrative posts in order to obtain some financial benefit'.[26] In fact, however, the highest civil servants received lower salaries than those earned outside by many businessmen, doctors, lawyers and planters. The Vice Chancellor believed that the best brains of the University went into the medical and engineering faculties. Ninety per cent of the C.C.S. between 1945–1959 were graduates in languages, economics and history who had, said the Commission, 'nowhere else to go'.[27] The magic letters, C.C.S., gave status rather than wealth, but as a consequence the young C.C.S. officer attracted a handsome dowry in the marriage market.

N. S. Perera's minority report went further than that of the majority of the Salaries and Cadres Commission in stating that the favoured position of the administrative service was 'a relic of the colonial regime which had as its objective the suppression of our scientific and technical advancement' so that the country would serve the purpose of a colony, namely the production of primary agricultural commodities and a market for the industrial products of the rulers. Ceylon, he suggested, would do better to stop modelling its civil service systems on those of Britain and follow those of America and Russia which 'though poles apart politically are on common ground with regard to the pre-eminent position accorded to their scientists and technicians'.[28] The Commission as a whole was critical of the privileged position of the C.C.S., who had been recruited by competition, over the administrative officers who in recent years had been appointed by interview. To end this 'caste system' they recommended that the C.C.S. should be merged in a general administrative grade. The Government accepted the recommendation, and so after 130 years the aim of the Colebrooke Commission was realized and the monopoly of the C.C.S. was broken.

We have seen how in 1919 Arunachalam, the Tamil who had been Ceylon's most distinguished former civil servant, had agitated through the Ceylon National Congress for localization of the public services, just as R. C. Dutt and Surendranath Banerjea had done in India. But in 1921 Arunachalam and his brother Ramanathan, who had been Solicitor General, resigned from the Congress on the question of separate representation for the Tamils in the legislature. A change of emphasis can also be seen in the reports of the two com-

missions on constitutional reform which the British Government
sent out.

The Donoughmore Commission of 1928 was very much concerned
with the position of the expatriate civil servants, which had already
become difficult under a system in which they could be cross-
examined by an irresponsible legislature. The Commission made proposals by which expatriates could either retire and receive compensation, or remain and have their rights safeguarded by a Public
Service Commission. But they gave little attention to the balance of
the communities in the services. This fitted with their approach to
the legislature, in which communal representation was abolished.[29]

By the 1930s no more expatriates were being recruited except for
professionals on contract. The sharing of posts between the communities now became a more important issue than Ceylonization,
and the Governor, Sir Andrew Caldecote, wrote to the Secretary
of State in 1938 that 'employment under government provides a
social cachet which approaches almost to that of a social caste . . . I
have no doubt that a great part of the communalism that is so unfortunately rampant derives from jealousy about government appointments'.[30]

The Soulbury Commission of 1945 reported that the Tamils and
Burghers had far more than their share of posts in the services. One
attempted remedy had been to omit arithmetic, in which the Tamils
were specially gifted, from the list of compulsory subjects for the
General Clerical Services examination. It is hard to know whether
the Commission was being serious in recalling in this connection that
at one time the Scots, owing to their superior education, had secured
a disproportionate share of administrative posts in the United
Kingdom, but that the English had since made strenuous and not
unsuccessful endeavours to meet the deficiencies of the past.[31] The
Sinhalese were not consoled by the precedent. When the Bandaranaike Government took over in 1956, Sinhalese was declared to be
the official language and government servants were made to pass an
examination in it within a given period or to resign; Tamil doctors
and engineers departed to staff West African government departments, an ironic reflection on the observation of the report of the
Salaries and Cadres Commission of 1961 that 'the present shortage
of engineers and other technologists is a serious obstacle to our
economic development on which our very survival in the future will
depend'.[32]

The Government Agents continued after independence to be the administration's principal representatives in the countryside, but their charges were much reduced in size from Provinces to Districts, and their functions were curtailed by the appointment of departmental officers, directly responsible to Colombo. The relics of the old feudal system through which the British had governed disappeared and even the village headmen were now recruited by competitive examination.

In the senior posts the officials no longer necessarily came from wealthy English-speaking families, as the system of free education from primary school to university began to bring to the top young men of quite humble origins. Yet even this social change and the abolition of the C.C.S. did not satisfy the lower ranks of the civil service, who continued to clamour for the removal of class barriers in the service and the right to share in the administration of every department, while they organized themselves into trade unions and prepared to strike if such demands were not granted.[33]

It may seem paradoxical that while higher education developed later, the services were localized rather earlier in Ceylon than in India. This was mainly due to the earlier development of representative government in Ceylon. The professional services also avoided the sharp differentiation between the 'Imperial' and 'Provincial' Services which took place in India in the 19th century. Later, in contrast to what happened in other colonies, when unified Colonial Services were introduced in the 1930s the advanced constitutional position in Ceylon prevented the promotion of local people being blocked by expatriates transferred from other territories.

There are obvious similarities in the history of localization in Ceylon and in India. The Colebrooke Commission established the principle that local people should be eligible for senior posts at about the same time as Macaulay wrote the same principle into the East India Charter Act of 1833. Later there were the same apprehensions in Colombo as in Calcutta that if civil service competitions were held locally the 'natives' would defeat the European candidates. But while in India the practice of appointment by nomination to the Civil Service was on the whole successsfully opposed by the nationalists, it persisted in Ceylon: candidates could not compete unless they were first selected by the Governor.

Behind this procedural difference was an important social difference. Colebrooke unlike Macaulay had advocated the appointment of members of an anglicized aristocracy rather than of an anglicized middle class to posts in government service. The Ceylonese landed aristocracy responded, sending their sons to Christian schools, modelled on the English public schools, to Cambridge, and finally into the civil service. By contrast in India there was much wider competition for government posts from the greater number of students of high caste but poor families who had received a higher education, even though the base of the educational pyramid was broader in Ceylon than in India.

Macaulay would have been delighted however by the emergence of a class which absorbed English traditions so completely that they became Christians, adopted English as a mother tongue and spoke of Britain as 'home'. In their little island this elite had far less defence against English culture than had either the Hindus or Muslims in India, where even the most senior civil servants would wear Indian dress, eat Indian food and speak the vernacular language at home with their families. The Successors in Ceylon were also more vulnerable to attack from below than were their counterparts in India. British planters in Ceylon had insisted on good roads and communications; first coffee, then tea and rubber had paid not only for roads but for elementary schools. Pressing behind the elite therefore was a literate electorate which read newspapers in which the 'Brown Sahibs' and the 'Black Knights' of the civil service were cruelly caricatured. There was no constituency which could not be reached in a day from Colombo, so that the district officer was much more liable than his opposite number in India to be visited and harassed by members of Parliament. The erosion of the prestige of the C.C.S., Ceylonese as well as British, perhaps began with the Donoughmore Constitution of 1931. It may be significant that the most prominent of all the Successors in Ceylon, Sir Oliver Goonitilleke, K.C.M.G., K.C.V.O., K.B.E., who served as Civil Defence Commissioner, Food Commissioner and finally as Governor General, came not from the C.C.S. but the Audit Department.

For better or worse, the British never faced the communal issue in the services in Ceylon, as they had in India, by establishing quotas for different races or religions in the services. The difference could be accounted for by the fact that a policy of 'divide and rule' was necessary for a colonial power in a large country but not in a small one: or the simpler explanation could be accepted that in Ceylon it was the majority, while in India it was the minorities, who failed to win adequate places in open competition, and that majorities can ultimately safeguard their position through the ballot-box.

REFERENCES

[1] G. C. Mendis, *Colebrooke-Cameron Papers*, London, 1956, Vol. I, pp. 69–75.

[2] ibid., Vol. I, pp. 243–252.

[3] ibid., Vol. II, pp. 25–30.

[4] ibid., Vol. II, p. 31.

[5] ibid., Vol. I, p. 255.

[6] C.O. 54/353, Ward to Newcastle, 23 June, 1860.

[7] C.O. 55/115, Buckingham to Robinson, 17 March, 1868.

[8] C.O. 54/434, Robinson to Buckingham, 23 May, 1868.

[9] C.O. 54/528, Longden to Kimberley, 15 October, 1880.

[10] ibid., Kimberley to Longden, 9 December, 1880.

[11] Ceylon S.P. XXVII, 1897, *Reclassification of the Ceylon Civil Service*, p. 24.

[12] ibid., p. 3.

[13] E. B. Denham, *Ceylon at the Census of 1911*, Colombo, 1912, p. 399.

[14] Sir P. Arunachalam, Address to Ceylon National Association, in *Handbook of Ceylon National Congress*, Colombo, 1928, p. 73.

[15] Ceylon S.P. I, 1919, *Future Employment of Ceylonese in the Public Service*, p. 3.

[16] S. J. Tambiah, 'Ethnic Representation in Ceylon's high administrative services, 1870–1946', in *University of Ceylon Review*, Vol. XIII, April, 1955, pp. 113–134.

[17] ibid.

[18] ibid., p. 123.

[19] *Colebrooke-Cameron Papers*, op. cit., Vol. I, pp. 71–75.

[20] ibid., Vol. II, p. 32.

[21] *Report of Rt. Hon. W. G. M. Ormsby-Gore on his visit to Malaya, Ceylon and Java*. Cmd 3235, 1928.

[22] I.B.R.D. *Economic Development of Ceylon*, Baltimore, 1953, p. 768 ff.

[23] Quoted by Sir Ivor Jennings 'The Foundation of the University of Ceylon' in *University of Ceylon Review*, Vol. IX, 1951, p. 226.

[24] *Final Report of the National Education Committee*, Sessional Paper 7, Colombo, 1961, p. 153. This recommendation was not accepted by the Government.

[25] *Report of Salaries and Cadres Commission*, Ceylon S.P. 3, 1961, Vol. I, p. 16.

[26] ibid., Vol. I, p. 18.

[27] ibid., Vol. I, p. 594.

[28] ibid., Vol. I, pp. 589–599.

[29] *Report of the Special Commission on the Constitution* (Donoughmore Report), London, Cmd 3131, 1928.

[30] *Correspondence relating to the Constitution of Ceylon*, London, Cmd 5910, 1938, p. 20.

[31] *Report of Commission on Constitutional Reform* (Soulbury Report), HMSO, Cmd 6677, 1945, p. 49 ff.

[32] op. cit., Vol. I, p. 189.

[33] *Community*, Colombo, 1963, Vol. 4, No. 3, article on 'The Public Services and the People', p. 47.

PART TWO

West Africa

The Gold Coast became independent as Ghana in 1957 with a population of about 6·7 million. Nigeria became independent in 1960 with a population estimated at 40 million but for which subsequent censuses give a much higher figure. Sierra Leone became independent in 1961 with a population of about 2·4 million and the Gambia in 1965 with a population of about 316,000.

CHAPTER VI

The Replacement of the Creoles and Consolidation of British Rule

'Every office from that of the Governorship downwards
has been held by a black or coloured man. . . . No
amount of disparagement of their descendants will
obliterate the fact.'

THE GOLD COAST INDEPENDENT, 1919

A traveller to the British settlements on the West Coast of
Africa in about 1870 might have transacted his business with
the Government almost entirely with African senior officials.
The Collector of Customs, the Colonial Secretary, the Medical
Officer, the Director of Education and District Commissioner could
all have been black. Thirty years later all would probably have been
white.

Three phases can be distinguished in the development of the
government services in British West Africa. In the first, from about
1830 to 1898, Africans and men of African descent were frequently
employed in responsible positions; in the second, from about 1898
to 1940, they seldom held senior posts; in the third and final phase,
from the 1940s until the various territories became independent, there
was a policy of progressive Africanization.

The Company of Merchants Trading to West Africa, as well as its
predecessors, had held forts on the Gold Coast since the 17th century,
and the Gambia was briefly a British Crown Colony in the 18th
century; but it was only with the settlement of Sierra Leone that the
responsibility for the administration of African Colonies began to
arouse much public interest in Britain. Through the agency of a
Company incorporated by Act of Parliament Sierra Leone was
settled in 1791 as a home for the liberated slaves who were in England

119

and for the American negroes who had sided with the British in the American War of Independence. These were joined by 'recaptives', slaves liberated by the Royal Navy. In 1808 the British Government, which needed a naval base in West Africa, took over Sierra Leone from the Company as a Crown Colony. Under the Company schools had been established in Freetown from the earliest days, and it was from these that the British Government was to find staff not only for the Colony but for the Gold Coast Settlements, for which it acquired direct responsibility in 1843, and later for Lagos.

Whilst the Sierra Leone venture was enthusiastically supported by the evangelicals in England, the expense and the heavy death rate among troops and British officials stationed there made it unpopular in Parliament. In the course of a debate in the House of Commons in 1830 therefore Sir George Murray, the Secretary of State for the Colonies, announced his intention 'as far as possible to fill all the Civil Offices of Sierra Leone with people of colour ... who were not likely to suffer in their health. He hoped finally to make Sierra Leone a free African Colony.'[1]

This policy was at first carried out through the appointment as government officials of West Indians of African or mixed descent. Thus John Carr, a Trinidadian who had been called to the English Bar, was sent out as Queen's Advocate, became Chief Justice in 1841 and acted as Governor. Dr. William Fergusson, an Afro-West Indian with a British medical degree, served as a government doctor in Freetown from 1815 and eventually was appointed as Governor of Sierra Leone in 1844; his son became Colonial Secretary in 1848. Robert Dougan, another Afro-West Indian, acted as Governor in 1854, after spending thirty-three years in Freetown, first in business and then as Queen's Advocate. In 1858 however the Secretary of State received a petition from Africans in Sierra Leone protesting against Afro-West Indians being given senior posts, and he ruled that no more should be sent out.

By this time Creoles, as men born in Sierra Leone came to be called, were beginning to be appointed to senior posts, and such appointments continued until about 1895. George Nicol, of mixed British and African descent and educated in England, became Colonial Secretary in 1859. Thomas Lawson, a Creole of the second generation to be educated in England, became Chief Inspector of Police in 1856; his son was sent on a government scholarship to England to be trained as an engineer, and returned as Assistant

Colonial Surveyor in 1867. Three other scholarships to Britain were provided to train Africans as doctors, who were posted as Staff Assistant Surgeons in the Army on their return in 1859. The posts of Secretary for Native Affairs and Queen's Advocate were normally held by Creoles in the second half of the century. A regular method of entry to government service was established in 1868 when competitive examinations were held for clerkships.[2]

At several periods in the mid-19th century the Governor of Sierra Leone was responsible for the administration of the Gold Coast and for a time for Lagos also. This facilitated the appointment of Sierra Leoneans to the other colonies on the West Coast, particularly when there was a Governor in Freetown like Pope-Hennessy or at Cape Coast such as Sir Benjamin Pine who publicly indicated that it was his intention to replace Europeans with Africans. Such measures indeed seemed almost inevitable in 1865, when Parliament adopted a report by a Select Committee which recommended that

'the object of our policy should be to encourage in the natives the exercise of those qualities which may render it possible for us more and more to transfer to them the administration of all the Governments, with a view of our ultimate withdrawal from all, except, probably Sierra Leone'.[3]

Whilst Sierra Leoneans could be found at this time in the Gold Coast as Chief Medical Officer, Colonial Treasurer and Solicitor General, Africans or men of mixed descent who had been born on the Gold Coast itself now began to study in Sierra Leone and even in England and returned to occupy senior posts. As early as 1850 James Bannerman, a merchant who was the son of a Scottish father and an African mother, became Lieutenant Governor of Cape Coast, and two of his sons acted as Commandants of Winneba and Christiansborg.[4] One of the most remarkable careers in the Gold Coast in the 19th century was that of George Ekem Ferguson, who was a quarter Scottish and threequarters African. Educated in Freetown, he taught at the Wesley School in Cape Coast and was engaged there as shorthand writer to the Governor in 1881 at the age of 17. After serving as Secretary to the Board of Education and clerk to the Queen's Advocate, he was sent to London to study map making. On his return most of his time was spent in mapping the interior, for which he won an award from the Royal Geographical Society of London. But his services were also used in negotiations with frontier tribes, and he was killed on an expedition against the Sofas at the age of 35. Joseph Chamberlain awarded Ferguson's widow a captain's pension and Guggisberg characteristically set up a memorial to him at Achimota thirty years later.[5] In the latter part of the century the most senior African Civil Servant in the Gold Coast was H. Vroom, who was Secretary for Native Affairs and was made a C.M.G. In 1883 seven of the District Commissioners were Africans.[6]

When in 1853 the British Government, appalled by the continuing mortality among European officers, decided to train West Africans as medical doctors at the expense of the British army medical staff, the C.M.S. Mission in Freetown was asked to find candidates. They selected James Africanus Horton, the son of an Ibo recaptive carpenter, and W. B. Davies, the son of a Yoruba recaptive. Horton took his M.D. at Edinburgh in 1858 and Davies at St. Andrews in 1859. Both subsequently served all along the West Coast and retired with the rank of Surgeon-Major in 1880. Horton was a man of considerable versatility. He acted from time to time as an administrator and published several medical studies. He is best remembered for his advocacy of a West African University and for his rebuttal of pseudo-scientific publications about the inferiority of the negro race which emanated from the Anthropological Society in London.[7]

Many of the slaves who were recaptured by the Royal Navy were Yoruba from Western Nigeria who had been taken prisoner in the tribal wars of the 1820s. Though they were resettled in Sierra Leone, a number of recaptives and their children made their way back to Nigeria, where together with the descendants of slaves returning direct from Cuba and Brazil, they formed the nucleus of a middle class. In 1875 in Lagos the heads of the Police, of the Posts and Telegraphs and of the Customs departments were all Africans, as was the Registrar of the High Court.[8] The best known African civil servant in Nigeria joined government service only at the end of the period. Henry Carr was the nephew of a military leader in the Yoruba wars. His father had been enslaved and was released in Sierra Leone, but returned to Nigeria. Carr was a student of such brilliance that the missionary headmaster of the Wesleyan School at Lagos took him to live in his family. He went on to Fourah Bay, where he took the Durham B.A. in mathematics and science at the age of 19. After teaching and writing mathematical textbooks for a few years, he was appointed Chief Clerk in the Lagos Secretariat in 1889 and Inspector of Schools in 1892. Most of the rest of his career was passed in the Education Department. Lugard, despite a frankly admitted difficulty in getting on with the educated Coastal Nigerians, had a particular regard for Carr and made him Resident of the Colony of Lagos in 1918, despite opposition from the Colonial Office.[9]

Between about 1893 and 1905 there was a sharp change of policy on the West Coast, and most senior posts were placed in British hands. In 1898 the Governor of Sierra Leone ruled that not only all heads of department but also their principal assistants must be European. The only two African officers in the West African Frontier Force were pensioned off in 1902. In the same year the Colonial Office decided that African doctors might not be members of the new West African Medical service. Henceforth the most senior African doctor was junior to the most recently arrived European, and the African Dr. Renner, who had often acted as head of the Sierra Leone medical department, never did so again in his remaining 11 years of service. In the Gold Coast, where in 1883 out of 43 higher posts in the Civil Service 9 were held by Africans, by 1908 of 274 listed officers only 5 were Africans and these were very junior.[10] Similarly in Sierra Leone, while in 1892 Africans held 18 out of 40 senior posts, by 1912 out of 92 posts they held only 15 and of these 5 were abolished in the next few years.[11] The position of the Creoles at the end of the century has been poignantly described by their historian –

'Hated and despised as they often were, they were yet indispensable, the unrecognized vehicle by which not only British rule but trade, education, and Christianity were conveyed to West Africa. In the churches and schools which must have closed without their ministrations, in mercantile houses and government offices, dependent on their subordinate toil, these gentle pioneers, bringing a European culture which Europeans resented their possessing, could well look round them to see in whatever good Britain brought West Africa in the 19th century a plant which could never have taken roots without their slighted labour.'[12]

In Nigeria the brilliant Henry Carr, who had been drafted into government service from teaching in 1889, had British officers promoted over him in 1903 and again in 1908. In his bitterness he started to study law, in the hope of finding a career outside government.[13]

The new policy of Europeanization can largely no doubt be attributed to Ross's discovery of the means of transmission of malaria. The insistence of Parliament and of the Colonial Office on Africanization had been mainly due to the very heavy mortality among Europeans on the West Coast; in one year alone, 1859, half the European population of Freetown had died.[14] In 1897 Ross in India proved that malaria was mosquito borne, and in 1900 the American Army Medical Department showed yellow fever also to be transmitted by mosquito. Ross and his collaborators visited Freetown. On their advice not only was spraying carried out but the European population was moved up the hill. More Europeans now came out to the West Coast; they conducted more business, demanded better and more comprehensive government services and lived in segregated areas.

Once it was decided to retain the West African dependencies, there was an insistence in Parliament that they should pay their way. Chamberlain's determination to 'develop our West African estates' required a more intensive administration, in which there was insistence on more formal qualifications. Thus in the Gold Coast District Commissioners were now required to be barristers or solicitors, but Africans with these qualifications preferred the higher earnings of the Bar. Some of the earlier African administrators had also been traders but such a combination of functions became impossible as civil service procedures were tightened up.

The decision on the replacement of the doctors is the most clearly documented. Ripon as Colonial Secretary in 1893 seems to have instructed the Gold Coast Government that one-third of their doctors should be Africans.[15] The Colonial Office in 1901 set up a Committee on the amalgamation of the West African Medical Services, consisting of the Principal Medical Officers of the Gold Coast, Northern Nigeria and Southern Nigeria, all Europeans, together with two Colonial Office officials. Their report concluded—'The Committee are strongly of the opinion that it is in general inadvisable to employ natives of West Africa as medical officers in the government service. . . . They do not believe either that in professional capabilities West African native doctors are at a par, except in very rare instances, with European doctors or that they possess the confidence of European patients on the Coast. Social conditions, particularly in Southern Nigeria, where European officers live together and have their meals under the "mess" system and in Northern Nigeria, where a large proportion of the European staff consists of officers of the regular army, make it extremely undesirable to introduce native medical officers into those Protectorates.'[16] The Committee was not in favour either of a proposal to employ Indian doctors in West Africa but they gave no reasons for this. Chamberlain minuted on the report that it was 'pretty clear to men of ordinary sense that British officers could not have confidence in Indian or native doctors'.[17]

A contributory factor to the new policy was a long series of scandals in which African administrators had been involved. In the Gold Coast one of the Bannerman brothers had been convicted of embezzlement in 1861 and another of extortion in 1863.[18] Rowland Cole, the Postmaster, was reprimanded for lending money at a 'usurious' rate of interest and Vroom, the Colonial Secretary, resigned after allegations that he had an interest in concessions which he had granted officially. In Sierra Leone Sir Frederic Cardew, retired army officer, strict teetotaller and churchman, who was Governor from 1894 to 1900, was not a man to tolerate corruption. In 1895 when J. H. Spaine, a Creole who was Postmaster of the Colony, was twice acquitted by juries of a charge of embezzlement, Cardew changed the law in order to have him retried and committed, without a jury.[19] About the same time the antipathy of the people of the Protectorate in the interior of Sierra Leone for the Creole administrators from Freetown was violently demonstrated in the Hut Tax Revolt of 1898, and this limited the area in which the services of the latter could be used.

But the change of mood in London was also important. Even when the West Coast Colonies were still regarded as an encumbrance, Kimberley as Secretary of State had minuted in 1873, in light of the Gold Coast scandals, 'I fear except in quite subordinate positions we cannot safely employ natives.'[20] Hemming, who was head of the African Department at the Colonial Office, minuted in 1886 that 'the educated native is the curse of the West Coast' and that 'all natives are incorrigible liars'.[21] Men were now occupying high positions in the Colonial Office and Colonial Service who had been brought up on the pseudo-scientific racial theories of the middle of the century and who were convinced of the supreme ability of the British as administrators. Joseph Chamberlain when he became Colonial Secretary in 1895 declared that 'the British race is the greatest of governing races the world has ever seen'.[22] Even someone as devoted to Africa as Mary Kingsley contributed to the idea that Africans were only fit to be permanent wards because of the mental and physical differences between the black and white races. A new and earnest generation of British colonial officials was emerging from the English public schools, with a more rigid attitude towards wickedness and corruption than their predecessors of the fifties and sixties who, often drunken and sometimes corrupt themselves, were seldom shocked by African behaviour. The replacement of the Africans in the government service was paralleled in the missions. Bishop Crowther, whose appointment had been a striking symbol of African achievement, was succeeded by an Englishman in 1891, when the C.M.S. Committee decided that it would be undesirable to place an African Bishop over European clergymen. While the earlier missionaries like Venn, the Secretary of the C.M.S., had struggled against the detractors of the Negro race, the tactlessness of those who came out in the nineties caused a number of the African ministers in Western Nigeria to secede and set up separate churches.[23]

Yet even some who were predisposed to sympathize with the Creoles felt that they had contributed considerably to the misfortunes which had befallen them. Dr. Blyden, the West Indian Negro who after spending part of his remarkable career as Secretary of State in Liberia, served as an adviser to the Sierra Leone Government, criticized the original settlers in Sierra Leone who 'formed no connection with the indigenous inhabitants, placed themselves in a hostile attitude, constituting themselves as it were a social and political island', and forced the recaptives who arrived later to adopt their manners, their religion, and their social arrangements.[24] Fox-Bourne, the Secretary of the Aborigines Protection Society, deplored the replacement of the Creoles by young Englishmen who took posts in Africa merely as a step to advancement elsewhere; and he had a series of questions asked in Parliament about their exclusion from the medical service. But he could not help admitting that they had 'formed too high an opinion of their own attainments'.[25]

Chamberlain was the first businessman to arrive at the Colonial Office. Like his contemporary Curzon in India, he was keenly interested in efficiency in government and he instructed Lord Selborne, his Parliamentary Under Secretary, to find out how many Colonial officials there were and how they had been appointed. In the course of this survey the possibility was examined of creating a unified service, whose officers could be transferred between territories. The proposal was dropped because service in West Africa was so unpopular that it was felt that the possibility of being transferred there would adversely affect recruitment for other territories. As Chamberlain noted, 'We take inferior men for West Africa and they are not good enough for other Colonies'.[26]

The indifferent quality of the European civil servants in the African Colonies, who were appointed by the patronage of the Secretary of State, emerged from Selborne's inquiry; this led to suggestions that civil servants for the African territories should be recruited by competitive written examination, as was done for Malaya, Hongkong and Ceylon, whose candidates took the I.C.S. examination. But it was concluded that the unpopularity of the West African service would make it impossible to find sufficient candidates for the examination. Moreover it was believed that a man's health would stand up better to the climate of the tropics if he did not go out until he was 25; but only men who had failed in other professions were likely to be candidates for an examination held between the ages of 25 and 30.[27] So until the end entry to the administrative service of the African Colonies was obtained by appointment on interview. 'Patronage ruled the day in Downing Street' wrote Casely Hayford in 1903,[28] contrasting the quality of the British officers in West Africa unfavourably with those who entered the I.C.S. by competition. As Sir Ralph Furse of the Colonial Office later developed and described it, the 'patronage' became systematically organized, with 'a secret list of Oxford and Cambridge tutors in order of reliability of their reports on undergraduates, and a close connexion with headmasters of schools. . . . We learnt to eschew publicity and to rely on personal contacts in the most fruitful quarters. . . . Our methods were mole-like: quiet, persistent and indirect.'[29] Furse believed selection by interview to be a better method than competitive written examinations and he succeeded ultimately in obtaining control of selection of the candidates for Ceylon, Hongkong and Malaya, who had previously taken the I.C.S. examination.

This was not a method of recruitment which tended to produce a type of British civil servant as intellectual as did the Indian Civil Service Examination: it was widely believed that a man with a first class degree would have been regarded by Furse and his interviewers as dangerous. It is interesting to speculate how far the difference between the I.C.S. and Colonial Service types influenced the Indian and African administrators who succeeded them. The Nigerian and Ghanaian Governments when they became independent announced that they would recruit their administrative services by written competitive examination as soon as there were sufficient candidates, and Western Nigeria started to do so in 1964.

Despite Chamberlain's investigation each colony continued to employ its own officials on different salary and pension scales: an American writer observed that officers in the Gold Coast considered themselves superior to those in Sierra Leone, while those in Nigeria considered themselves superior to those in the Gold Coast, and that the Northern Nigerian service was rated highest of all because the officers were required to keep horses and play polo.[30] In the 1920s another vigorous Colonial Secretary, L. S. Amery, again took up the question of a unified service. As a result not only a Colonial Administrative Service but also Colonial Medical, Forestry, Agriculture and other professional services were established. Little consideration was given to the effect which this step would have on the recruitment of local people to the government services, and it tended to block their promotion to higher appointments and to discourage them from joining government service. Although local candidates might be eligible to occupy posts normally held by members of the unified services, they found themselves in competition with British officers who might be transferred from other territories. This competition caused considerable bitterness in the period of retrenchment and of unemployment in the early thirties.

Amery's reforms opened recruitment in the services to Canadians and Australians. But this did not extend to the non-white Commonwealth. Until 1942 candidates for the Colonial Administrative Service were required to be of 'pure European descent'.[31] In the 20th century, unlike the 19th, Africans from one territory did not serve in another. This was in marked contrast to French practice by which Senegalese and Dahomeyans were employed throughout West and Equatorial Africa and West Indians were also used extensively in these areas.*

The period between about 1898 and 1940 was one of administrative consolidation in British West Africa. In 1900 the Colonial Office took over the responsibilities of the Royal Niger Company as

* A curious exception to the British policy was the presence of a few Ceylonese in the I.C.S. and conversely of some Indians in the Ceylon Civil Service.

well as that of the Niger Coast Protectorate from the Foreign Office, and was thenceforward responsible for the administration of all British territories in West Africa. This was the period when Indirect Rule was developed. It would probably be generally agreed that in Northern Nigeria Lugard with his scanty resources had no alternative to introducing Indirect Rule, and that the Fulani Chiefs possessed an apparatus for administration of justice, maintenance of order and collection of taxes which could work under the supervision of British Residents: but in Southern Nigeria and the Gold Coast, where tribal rule had widely broken down and there was an educated middle class, it has been questioned whether Indirect Rule was either effective or appropriate, and whether the hunt to 'find the Chief' was not sometimes a wild goose chase.

For Lugard it was a cardinal principle of British policy that the interests of a large native population should not be subject to the will of a small minority of educated and Europeanized natives.[32] Though the services of clerks from the coast were essential in the North, they were segregated in their own townships and their own schools. In the South it was a cause of great bitterness to the intellectuals who returned from studying overseas to find no adequate opportunities of employment with the native authorities.

In the 1930s the British still believed that independence for the West African countries was not a question which would arise in the foreseeable future. Within this context enthusiasm for Indirect Rule had one curious and unfortunate result. It became established policy that Africans should not be recruited into the Administrative Service. The latter was regarded as a temporary scaffolding round the growing structure of the native administrations. To build Africans into the 'scaffolding', it was argued, would be to create a vested interest which would make its demolition very difficult.[33]

In fact the great expansion of the role of the central government in economic and social development was to mean that more administrative officers, with wider duties, would be required after independence, for which the West African governments would have been much better prepared had they recruited African administrative officers before 1942. But in the late thirties, as Dr. Perham has observed, 'There was an atmosphere of almost unlimited time to complete the task, regarded then as hardly begun, of building a new Nigeria from bottom up'.[34]

In the Gold Coast and Sierra Leone it was never forgotten, as

The Gold Coast Independent said in 1919, that 'every office from that of the Governorship downwards has been held by a black or coloured man. . . . No amount of disparaging their descendants will obliterate the fact'.[35] The system of government was not only more complex than that of the 19th century, but the hierarchies were now more rigid. They had come to be modelled on the sharp differentiation between the administrative and clerical services which existed in the British civil service of the time. But what in England reflected a class structure in Africa reflected a race structure.[36] The African, however bright, was now confined to a 'Native Subordinate Service', with no chance for occasional distinction such as had existed in the looser arrangements of the 19th century.

All services of the governments were not equally rigid: Sir Hugh Clifford, for example, who was Governor of the Gold Coast from 1913 to 1919, was surprised by the small attempt made to use local people in senior posts throughout the service by comparison with Ceylon where he had previously served, and he appointed some Africans as legal officers. But the first overall plan for Africanization of the services in any British territory was formulated by his successor, Sir Gordon Guggisberg, in 1925.

Guggisberg in much of his thinking was some twenty years ahead of his time. His memory still commands great respect in Ghana, like that of Ripon in India. He was neither British nor a professional administrator. Canadian by birth and of Swiss descent, he had gone to Europe as a child, passed through Woolwich, and joined the Royal Engineers. Between 1900 and 1914 he was mainly employed in survey work on the West Coast of Africa and formed a high regard for the potential abilities of Africans with whom he was working. He commanded an infantry brigade in France in the First World War and, profoundly affected by the meaningless slaughter, resolved to devote the rest of his life to the service of his fellow men.

Guggisberg saw, and stated publicly, that it was a misguided policy to expect a colony to finance its development from its own revenues. This, he said, was to put the cart before the horse, for the amount of a colony's revenue depends entirely on the development of its natural resources.[37] He drew up a 10 year development plan but realized that the government could not afford to expand its expatriate stuff sufficiently to implement it. He therefore produced a scheme in 1925 for progressive Africanization of the services under which in twenty years time 231 out of 550 senior posts were to be filled by Africans, who in 1925 held only 27 such posts.[38] At the same time he founded Achimota College, one of whose principal objects was to educate Africans for government service.

The plan was not carried out. Guggisberg's successors were unenthusiastic. Whilst he had been prepared to employ Africans even with the risk of a slight loss of efficiency, they insisted that 'standards' could not be reduced and did not insist on departmental training schemes. The output of Achimota students dropped when its budget was reduced during the depression of 1929–32, and some of those Africans who had been appointed to government posts were retrenched together with the expatriates during that period of stringency. In 1946 there were only 89 Africans in senior posts instead of the 231 anticipated.[39]

The Guggisberg plan thus proved to be a false start. Effective overall Africanization programmes only commenced in West Africa after the Second World War. Before considering the way in which these were carried out, however, it is necessary to examine the educational policies adopted in West Africa, which were greatly to influence the course of Africanization.

REFERENCES

[1] Hansard, House of Commons Debates, 15 June, 1830, Col. 404.
[2] The examples in these two paragraphs are from C. Fyfe's *Sierra Leone*, London, 1962.
[3] P.P. 1865 V, p. 412.
[4] D. Kimble, *Political History of Ghana*, Oxford, 1963, Chapter II.
[5] M. J. Sampson, *Gold Coast Men of Affairs*, London, 1937, p. 129.
[6] Kimble, op. cit., Chapter II.
[7] L. C. Gwam in *Ibadan*, June, 1964.
[8] J. F. A. Ajayi, *Milestones in Nigerian History*, Ibadan, 1962, p. 20.
[9] L. C. Gwam, 'Dr. Henry Carr', in *Ibadan*, November, 1963, and M. Perham, *Lugard*, Vol. II, London, 1960, p. 605.
[10] Kimble, op. cit., p. 100.
[11] Fyfe, op. cit., p. 615.
[12] Fyfe, op. cit., p. 619.
[13] L. C. Gwam, 'Dr. Henry Carr' in *Ibadan*, November, 1963.
[14] Fyfe, op. cit., p. 296.
[15] *Anti-Slavery Reporter and Aborigines Friend*, April, 1911.
[16] C.O. 96. 390, December, 1901, *Report of the Committee on amalgamation of the medical services in the W. African colonies.*
[17] C.O. 96. 403, 29 April, 1902.
[18] Kimble, op. cit., p. 67.

[19] Fyfe, op. cit., p. 532.

[20] Kimble, op. cit., p. 94.

[21] ibid., p. 91.

[22] Speech at the Imperial Institute, printed in G. Bennett, *Concept of Empire*, London, 1962, p. 315.

[23] J. B. Webster, *African Churches among the Yoruba*, Oxford, 1964.

[24] Quoted by H. R. Fox-Bourne in *Black and White in West Africa*, Transactions of Aborigines Protection Society, 1901–1903, p. 85.

[25] ibid., p. 49.

[26] C.O. 885/7, Misc. 123, 28 August, 1899.

[27] C.O. 885/7, Misc. 123, *Minutes on Proposed Re-organization*, March, 1900.

[28] Casely Hayford, *Gold Coast Native Institutions*, London, 1903, p. 218.

[29] Sir R. Furse, *Aucuparius*, London, 1962, p. 223.

[30] Robert Heussler, *Yesterday's Rulers*, London, 1963, p. 39.

[31] Kenneth Robinson, *Dilemmas of Trusteeship*, London, 1965, p. 43.

[32] Sir F. D. Lugard, *Report on the Amalgamations of Northern and Southern Nigeria and Administration 1912–19*, Cmd 468, 1920, p. 19.

[33] See M. Perham, *Native Administration in Nigeria*, London, 1962 edition p. 361, and O. Awolowo, *Path to African Freedom*, London, 1947, p. 110.

[34] M. Perham, op. cit., p. xi.

[35] Kimble, op. cit., p. 106.

[36] J. S. Coleman in *Nigeria, Background to Nationalism*, Berkeley, 1958, p. 155, and a number of American writers have been struck by this point.

[37] *The Gold Coast: a Review of the Events of 1920–26*, Accra, 1927, p. 197.

[38] ibid., p. 254.

[39] *Statement on Africanization of the Public Service Gold Coast Government*, Accra, 1954, p. 1.

CHAPTER VII

West Africa — Educational Policies

'The idea that elementary education does not fit a child for anything is of European origin.'

PROF. B. FAFUNYA, UNIVERSITY OF
NIGERIA, 1964

In 1960, the year of independence, the Nigerian Government invited a Commission under Sir Eric Ashby to advise on its overall educational needs. This Commission was perhaps the first in any of the developing countries to base an educational plan on a manpower forecast; it consisted of an equal number of Nigerian, British and American educationists, and its report was regarded as unusually authoritative.

'Although the quantity of higher education at present available in Nigeria is insufficient,' the report stated, 'the quality is beyond reproach. Unfortunately other forms of education beyond secondary school have developed less favourably. There is a profound reason for this. . . . The first western schooling brought to Nigeria was a literary education, and once civil rule was established the expatriate administrators were graduates, most of them graduates in arts. And so the literary tradition and the university degree have become indelible symbols of prestige in Nigeria; by contrast technology, agriculture and other practical subjects . . . have not won esteem'.[1]

The extent to which Africans were available to staff the government services at independence reflected the results of the educational policies of the colonial period which, both in West and East Africa, can be broadly divided into three periods.

In the first, up to about 1924, education was left to the missionaries with little government intervention; in the second, from about 1925–1935, the governments recognized their overall responsibility, and stress was laid on primary and vocational education related to the

133

agricultural environment; in the third, from about 1945 until self-government, the emphasis was on the creation of institutions of higher education modelled on those of England. As the territories became self-governing they usually entered a fourth stage in which primary and secondary education were greatly expanded and an attempt was made to relate higher education to manpower needs.

Before the coming of the Europeans there had been no schools on the Coast, though Koranic schools had existed on a considerable scale in Northern Nigeria. A few early attempts were made by traders and missionaries to educate Africans in England, but London proved to be the 'Black Man's Grave'. Of three boys sent to London by the Society for the Propagation of the Gospel in 1754, one died of consumption and one in a mental home. The survivor, Philip Quaque, was ordained, married an English wife, and from 1766 for some forty years ran a school in Cape Coast Castle which produced clerks for the Company.[2] Zachary Macaulay, Governor of Sierra Leone, when he returned to London in 1794 took 21 boys and 4 girls with him to be educated, but the climate proved fatal to most of them.[3]

In the early days of the Sierra Leone settlement all children of the settlers were educated at the expense of the Company, and the British Government made a grant to the schools when it took over the Colony. Generally, however, education was left to the missionaries in West Africa throughout the 19th century, the most active societies being the C.M.S. on the Coast and the Basel Mission inland. Primary education concentrated on literacy, for ability to read the Bible was for some missions a required test before baptism. The earliest secondary schools were established in Sierra Leone in 1827, in Lagos in 1859, and in Cape Coast in 1875. These were founded to produce teachers and catechists for the missions and clerks for the governments and merchants; the education was only secondary in name. In the 1840s the C.M.S., faced with a staff crisis owing to the heavy death rate among Europeans, founded the Fourah Bay College in Sierra Leone to train African missionaries: Fourah Bay became affiliated as a University College to Durham University in 1876, and its students took the Durham degree locally. It always remained primarily a theological college with very small numbers, and Greek and Latin were required for entry. Even in 1942 there were only 25 students and the rate of failures was high. But Fourah Bay provided a higher education for a few men who were to do much to shape African nationalism in British West Africa in the late 19th century and it served as a visible proof that university education was feasible in the region. The majority of its students came from the Gold Coast and Nigeria.

After the early days in Sierra Leone little was done by the British Government for education in Africa before the First World War. It is estimated that at the end of the 19th century the Government was spending not more than £10,000 a year on education in all the West African territories together.[4] The Government's aid to education was given in grants-in-aid to mission schools, based on numbers and examination results, and it only occasionally established its own schools in areas where there were no missions. The missionaries were not interested in professional training or in higher education except for the ministry. When a missionary on leave from Sierra Leone who was giving evidence to the Select Committee of the British Parliament in 1865 was asked whether any of the schools gave a training in agriculture, he replied that none did so because 'we consider it our duty to preach the gospel'.[5]

It will be recollected that this same Select Committee of Parliament proposed a gradual withdrawal of British administrators in West Africa. Dr. James Africanus Horton, who was one of the first Sierra Leoneans to take a medical degree in England, wrote a book in 1868 with the title *West African Countries and Peoples, British and Native, with the requirements necessary for establishing that self-government recommended by the House of Commons 1865, and Vindication of the African Race*. In this he proposed that Fourah Bay should become the 'University of Western Africa' which would produce administrators and professional officers who could replace the British: it should offer degree courses in classics, English language and literature, French, German, Hebrew and theology, but should give special importance to mathematics and natural science.[6] Dr. Edward Blyden, the West Indian Negro, while in Freetown in 1872, proposed a different sort of university, which would release the educational system from the 'despotic Europeanizing influences which had warped and crushed the Negro mind'.[7] Pope-Hennessy, who was Governor-in-Chief of West Africa at the time, was impressed by Blyden's arguments and envisaged an institution which would not only educate the sons of rich Africans but where, 'like in the Irish universities and some of the Continental universities of our time, even the poorest youths who had talents and a real taste for knowledge might by scholarships or fellowships have an opportunity of cultivating learning'.[8] This warm response, however, was by no means typical of the Colonial Office attitude.

The nationalist Casely Hayford in the Gold Coast in the early 20th century continued the argument for a university, suggesting that teaching must be in the vernacular but 'in working correspondence with one of the best teaching institutions in Japan, England, Germany and America',[9] and the Conference of Africans of British West Africa in 1920 which he organized called for the founding of a 'British West African University on such lines as would preserve in the students a sense of African nationality'.[10] About the same time Lugard was very tentatively suggesting that the teachers college and technical institute in Northern Nigeria might one day develop into the University of West Africa.[11]

The London *Times* greeted the news of Fourah Bay's affiliation by inquiring whether Durham University next intended to affiliate itself to the Zoo.[12] Not only was the British Government unresponsive to the demand for higher education, but in the second half of the 19th century British administrators became increasingly critical of the mission education and its products. Some of their suspicions may have been caused by the assistance which Sierra Leoneans had given to chiefs in the Gold Coast and to the Yoruba in finding a legal argument for asserting their independence. By the end of the century statements were common such as that of the Governor of Southern Nigeria, who said in 1896 that 'the young African educated in Europe imbibes ideas which instead of assisting him in after life, tend rather to make him dissatisfied with his surroundings when he returns to his country, and really unfit him for the post he is destined to take in his national sphere'.[13] The attitude became deeply embedded; as late as 1937 Lord Hailey, coming to Africa after India, referred to the 'preference for the uneducated over the educated native which is so much more conspicuous in British than in French territories', and attributed this partly to the difficult position of an educated class of Africans within the system of indirect rule.[14]

When Lugard took over Northern Nigeria on behalf of the British Government from the Royal Niger Company in 1900 and subdued the emirates, there was an opportunity to introduce a quite different system of education. Christian missions were excluded until 1927 from the Muslim areas. Instead it was the enthusiastic Director of Education of the Government, Hanns Vischer, who established schools for the sons of chiefs, for teachers and for apprentices. Vischer was determined 'to avoid the creation of a Babu class'.[15] Teaching was in the vernacular language, Hausa; there was great emphasis on character-building, games and manual labour.

Such a system, though its quality might be good, was much more expensive to operate, with British graduate government teachers, than that of the missionaries, in which those who knew a little could be used to teach those who knew less. The missionaries, relegated to the pagan regions, had by 1913 three times as many pupils as there were in the government schools of Northern Nigeria.

Lugard himself, when he returned to Nigeria as Governor General of the whole country in 1913, would have liked to amalgamate the education systems of North and South. He wished to bring the missions into the emirates and to set up English language schools there to produce clerks, as well as a technical school to teach the use of steam and power machinery. He was over-ruled by the Colonial Office which by now was more enthusiastic than its founder about the pure doctrine of 'Indirect Rule'.[16] As the Colonial Under-Secretary proudly, though somewhat incoherently, told Parliament in 1917 'If honourable members look into a system of education like that of Northern Nigeria they will find it one of the most remarkable developments that has ever taken place under British rule. An attempt has been made there where you have a black population, to get inside the native mind and to develop their own system of local education, thus making sure that at the end you do not drag it across, so to speak, into the European rut.'[17]

Yet by 1920 not a single Northerner was employed as a clerk by the government. Clifford, who was Governor General at that time, informed the legislature that education in the North, practically confined to the vernacular and Arabic, was the exclusive perquisite of the ruling classes whose children were given just sufficient knowledge to enable them to fill posts in the Native Authority: though it may be added that he was even more critical of the hedge school education which was developing in the South. In 1934 the North, with a population of eleven millions still had a school enrolment of only 10,000 compared with 178,000 in a population of nine millions in the South. The three great crises of the 1914 War, the economic depression of 1929, and the 1939 War had a much greater effect in curtailing the staff of the government schools of the North than in the areas where the schools were staffed by missionaries.

137

Lugard's views on education, as expressed both in his Memoranda as Governor General and in the *Dual Mandate*, written after his retirement, had a considerable effect on British colonial policy. He had been born in India and had served there as a young officer. In the *Dual Mandate*, he drew attention to the disastrous results of the Indian educational policy which had produced great numbers of unemployed graduates with a purely literary education. As Governor General of Nigeria he laid down the principle, subsequently approved by the Colonial Office, 'that the primary object of all schools should be the formation of character and habits of discipline, rather than the mere acquisition of a certain amount of book-learning and technical skill'.[18] Secondary education, he insisted, should be in boarding schools with a high proportion of British staff, a prefect system, organized games and religious and moral instruction. This of course was a type of school which territories living off their own revenues could not afford to set up on any large scale.

While the theories of Lugard and of Hanns Vischer, who became an educational adviser to the Colonial Office in 1922, were one important influence on educational policy between the Wars, another was that of the Phelps-Stokes Missions. The Phelps-Stokes Foundation of the U.S.A. sent missions first to West Africa in 1921 and then to East Africa in 1924 which between them produced the earliest overall survey of African education. The missions were mainly composed of American and British missionaries and of experts in industrial and agricultural education; and their leader, Jesse Jones, was Principal of the Hampton Institute, where the American Negro educationist, Booker T. Washington, had started his career. Hanns Vischer was a member of the second mission. The reports urged that the British Government should accept a responsibility for education instead of leaving it almost entirely to the missionaries. Their main theme was that too much time was being given to a purely literary education and not enough to agricultural and vocational education. Recollecting the unrest which had been caused in India by an overproduction of clerks, they eulogized the methods of practical rural education which Booker T. Washington had introduced for the American Negroes. In general they urged that mass education and training of teachers should be given priority over higher education for the few, though they looked forward ultimately to a time when Africa would have its own colleges.[19]

Under the influence of these reports and of the missionary

organizations, the Secretary of State for the Colonies in 1925 set up an Advisory Committee on African Education. The Indian experience on this committee was considerable. Lugard, who was a member, was at this time much impressed by Valentine Chirol's book on *Indian Unrest*. Another member, Sir Michael Sadler, had been Chairman of the Calcutta University Commission, whose melancholy report has already been noticed. J. H. Oldham had served as a missionary in India. Arthur Mayhew, who was Joint Secretary with Vischer, had been a member of the Indian Educational Service and wrote a book on education in India which was often quoted in the annual Education Reports of the African governments. He argued that in India the government had failed in its responsibility to guide educational policy and had allowed private proprietors of colleges to set deplorably low standards, which were confirmed by the examination system of the Indian universities. He therefore proposed that Africa should rely on external examining bodies in order to establish and maintain its standards. Mayhew admitted by 1938, however, that 'there is a tendency [in Africa], which though natural is capable of perversion, to guard against a surplus production of graduates which may stimulate unrest and discontent'.[20]

The Advisory Committee in 1925 for the first time published a definitive statement on British educational policy in tropical Africa. 'Education,' they said, 'should be adapted to the mentality, aptitudes, occupations and traditions of the various peoples: care must be taken to avoid a hiatus between the educated class and the rest of the community'. The first task of African education, they maintained, was 'to raise the standard alike of character and efficiency of the bulk of the people', though they added that 'as resources permit the door of advancement through higher education in Africa must be increasingly opened for those who by character, ability and temperament show themselves fitted to profit by such education'. The greatest importance must be attached to religious teaching and moral instruction. 'Field games and social relations and intercourse are influences at least as important as class room instruction'.[21]

There can be little doubt that English standards and English literary curricula had generally been too closely followed in West Africa. As early as the 1840s successive governors of Sierra Leone had criticized the missionaries for giving a purely literary education to students who might find themselves unemployed.[22] Some of the missions subsequently tried to set up vocational training schools but

139

with little success. Traditions were too deeply established in West Africa by the 1920s, however, for the new policies of the Advisory Committee to have anything like the effect which they had in East Africa. There was strong African opposition to developing a curriculum more suited to African needs. When in 1922 the Sierra Leone Government proposed to substitute a West African examination for the Cambridge local examination, parents, students and the press successfully agitated to preserve this direct link with the British educational system, even though it meant studying Latin, Greek and English geography.[23] In Nigeria, Chief Awolowo has recounted how the English principal of the Wesley College, which he attended in the 1920s, became unpopular for his encouragement of West African languages and for insisting on the dignity of manual labour.[24] In Fourah Bay about the same time there was a storm of protest when carpentry and masonry were made compulsory. To most students of this generation the examination which opened the way to British educational qualifications was all important, and activities which were not related to this were unnecessary burdens in a heavy curriculum.

It is this which explains the unpopularity of the Yaba College which was opened in Nigeria in 1932. Although the Governor announced that ultimately it was hoped that it would be possible for students at Yaba to take external degrees, in fact the College never did more than award a diploma which had no validity outside Nigeria because, unlike Fourah Bay, it had no British affiliation. Africans were trained as medical, agricultural and veterinary assistants, and the output was limited to the number of posts available in government service. The Nigerian with a Yaba diploma earned a salary far lower than that of his colleagues who had managed to go to England and take a degree, which in some cases took no longer than the Yaba course.

Only at Achimota College in the Gold Coast perhaps were the new policies developed with real success. Guggisberg recruited a remarkable team in A. G. Fraser, who had been Principal of Trinity College, Kandy, in Ceylon, and J. E. K. Aggrey, an African born in the Gold Coast who had taught for twenty years in America and had been a member of both the Phelps-Stokes Missions. Aggrey used to say that no one should be allowed to graduate in theology without passing an examination in agriculture. When he and Fraser insisted that their staff and students get out into the villages to study African languages and customs, Achimota became involved in the controversy of the American negroes on education, between those who followed Booker T. Washington in emphasizing the need for mass education and those who supported Dubois in scorning this policy as one which condemned the negroes to be hewers of wood and drawers of water and who emphasized the need to form a negro elite. Achimota survived the criticism because Fraser and Aggrey so evidently believed in advancing the African as rapidly as possible and in advancing Achimota itself to be a university. When Fraser was asked to visit Northern Nigeria to report on education, though he started out by believing in the legend that the Northern Nigerian approach was the best in Africa, he ended by accusing the government of being afraid of education, of having no outlook beyond the present and little beyond the past.[25]

By the Second World War, despite the 19th century dreams, there was still no University of West Africa. Achimota had reached the intermediate level; Yaba awarded its own diplomas: and there were a handful of graduates from Fourah Bay with external degrees, mostly in theology, from Durham. Most West Africans with degrees had obtained them abroad. During the Second War, however, there was a notable change of policy in London. The Labour Party from within the British coalition government was obliged to bear in mind the criticisms which it had made while in opposition that the development of the colonies was neglected. In 1945 the Asquith Commission on Higher Education in the Colonies and the Elliott Commission on Higher Education in West Africa clearly stated the principle that the immediate development of university education was an unescapable corollary of a policy which aimed at colonial self-government. The old dogma that every colony should pay for its own social services was now virtually abandoned and substantial support became available for the new universities from the Colonial Development and Welfare Fund.

The majority of the Elliott Commission proposed that there should be three University Colleges, one in Nigeria, one in the Gold Coast and one in Sierra Leone. The Secretary of State, however, approved the minority report which proposed that there should be a single University College of West Africa, situated at Ibadan in Nigeria. Eventually the Gold Coast was allowed to develop its University College on condition that the funds were raised locally. Fourah Bay too managed to survive to attain the same status. Ibadan opened in

1948 with students from Yaba, and the University College of the Gold Coast in the same year with students from Achimota.

The spirit in which postwar higher education was developed may be summed up in the Elliott Commission's words: 'All agree that African academic standards in no way inferior to those of British Universities are essential . . . quality before quantity must be the motto'.[26] The new University Colleges entered into a special relationship with London University: their students took London external degrees; their staff were approved by London; and external examiners were provided by London. The colleges were entirely residential.

The rapid erection and staffing of the new universities and the aid given to them by the British universities through the Inter-University Council has been described with natural satisfaction by some of those who played a leading part in the developments immediately after the Second War. As the West African countries moved towards independence, however, there was criticism both in Britain and in Africa of the strict adherence of the new universities to the standards of London and the conventions of Cambridge. The entry requirements were raised when those of the British universities changed from 'O level' to 'A level' and remained much higher than those demanded by American, Canadian or Australian universities.

The Asquith Commission had expected that higher education in the Colonies would be cheaper than in the United Kingdom. In fact the cost per student in the early years in Africa turned out to be about double that in the United Kingdom. At Ibadan in the medical faculty, it was three times as much.[27] Staff-pupil ratios were low and staff salaries high. Ibadan in 1950 found it necessary to raise the salaries of the Nigerian staff to the same level as that of the British, including the expatriate allowance.

Sir Eric Ashby has suggested that at this period the national need in Nigeria and Ghana was for a sprinkling of highly specialized experts and scholars and a broad stream of less differentiated graduates with general degrees to man the Civil Service and to teach in schools. But the desire to emulate even the fashions of British academic life was irresistible'.[28] Awolowo's party, the Action Group, in Nigeria asked why after eight years of activity Ibadan was not teaching engineering, law, economics and public administration but Latin, Greek and Ancient History.[29] The Nigerian Parliamentary Commission on Africanization in 1959 asserted that Ibadan had contributed very little to the solution of the manpower problem and the

Nigerianization of the public services. The university authorities replied that the government had never consulted with them on these questions.[30]

Dr. Dike, the first Nigerian to become Vice Chancellor of Ibadan, summed up the results of the London relationship in a lecture in 1964. On the positive side, he concluded, standards had been established which made Ibadan's degrees universally acceptable. On the other hand, maintenance of these standards had meant that the number of graduates produced was small. There had been too much emphasis, he felt, on literary subjects, too little on natural sciences and agriculture.[31]

It may seem strange that an elitist policy should have been introduced in the new African universities just at the time when it was being abandoned in England. The Asquith and Elliott Commissions and those who implemented their reports were concerned, however, that the graduates of the new universities should be unquestionably as well qualified as the British officers whom they were to succeed. In order to convince the colonial governments, with their entrenched prejudices about 'standards', of the capability of the Africans, they considered that the latter must be given the opportunity to attain exactly the same qualifications as the Europeans. African nationalist opinion at first supported them on this, insisting that 'we will have no more Yabas'. The spectre of the Calcutta University, with its huge numbers and low standards also haunted the British educational planners. Yet the question still may be asked as to whether academic standards might not have been maintained in a simpler setting, following perhaps the Scottish rather than the English pattern, and with an emphasis on studies which were more nearly related to the urgent national needs for higher manpower.

As popularly elected governments came into power, schoolteachers, who unlike civil servants were allowed to participate in politics, occupied up to 50% of the seats in the legislatures. The new governments responded to the fervent desire of the electorate and of the legislators for more education. Primary enrolment rose by 142% in the Western Region of Nigeria between 1955 and 1960 and by 200% in Ghana between 1951 and 1955. There was a considerable expansion of secondary schools also. With pressure from below for higher education, and as the manpower needs of development plans were realized, universities which produced only small numbers of graduates, studying classics and English literature rather than agriculture and economics, came increasingly under attack. So were the

143

policies by which the study of applied science and technology was relegated to Colleges of Arts, Science and Technology which did not have university status.

In Ghana President Nkrumah insisted, when the University College became a University, independent of London, that the standard of its degrees must remain as high as ever. But he himself had studied in America as well as Britain, and after independence the College of Arts, Science and Technology was upgraded to become the Kwame Nkrumah University of Science and Technology. 'The ivory tower concept of the University is dead,' he said, '. . . everything will be done to place a premium on the study of science and technology'.[32]

President Azikiwe of Nigeria had also studied in America where he had been particularly impressed by the Land Grant Colleges with their willingness to include vocational subjects, their rejection of elitism and their concentration on farming and rural life. Azikiwe was openly critical of the Ibadan model. 'We cannot afford,' he said, 'to continue to produce an upper class of parasites who shall prey upon a stagnant and sterile class of workers and peasants'.[33] In 1955 he founded the University of Nigeria at Nsukka. Here students ate in cafeterias instead of being waited upon, and might even work their way through college. The American system of 'credits' was introduced, so that there was less emphasis on final examinations. Despite the sneers of Ibadan, the earliest batch of Nsukka graduates obtained the top places in the Civil Service Examination in 1964 when for the first time this became competitive in the Western Region.

In Nigeria, as well as Ghana, other new universities were also set up after independence. In addition to Ibadan and Nsukka, the Western Region started its own University of Ife and the Northern Region fulfilled Lugard's dream by establishing the Ahmadu Bello University at Zaria on the foundations of the old College of Arts, Science and Technology. In Lagos a university was founded which was to be primarily non-residential.

But by independence only Ibadan was producing graduates and those at a rate of barely 100 per year. Nor had they yet much experience. In the medical, engineering and educational services the immediate successors to the British were the graduates of Yaba and Achimota, many of whom had supplemented their pre-war diplomas with British degrees, acquired by visits or by correspondence courses and external examination.

Though the Northern Region also expanded its educational services in the fifties, it lagged far behind the rest of West Africa. The Katsina Teachers Training College, founded in 1921 and run on the lines of an English Public School, had until 1952 provided the only opportunity in the region for a full secondary education. At independence the Prime Minister of Nigeria, the Premier of the Northern Region and most of the ministers and higher civil servants had been educated at Katsina and had subsequently served as teachers. At the secondary level in 1962 only 418 Northerners passed School Certificate, and the Northern Region was no farther advanced educationally than the East African countries at this stage. Within the Region itself, statistics showed the great discrepancies which had arisen from the earlier educational policies. In Ilorin and Kabba Provinces, which had been pagan and where the missionaries had established schools, 40% of the children aged six to thirteen were enrolled in 1962. In the Muslim Provinces of Kano and Katsina, from which the missionaries had long been excluded, the proportion was only 5%.[34]

Although the importance of professional education had been stressed by the Elliott Commission in 1945, its subsequent progress was generally disappointing. At Ibadan engineering was abandoned in 1951; economics was not taught until 1956; forestry, though planned, was not started before independence. Medicine had been one of the earliest professions to be studied by West Africans. Sierra Leoneans had qualified in England from the 1860s and in Nigeria and Ghana from the 1890s. Successive commissions had however commented on the lack of a medical school in West Africa and a faculty was eventually established at Ibadan. Medicine and veterinary science however were described by the Ashby Commission in 1960 as both suffering 'through a mistaken but understandable belief that standards of attainment for Nigerians practising in Nigeria must be acceptable to the bodies which legislate for Englishmen practising in England . . .'.[35] Some factors which hampered the development of professional education in Africa as a whole will be considered in Chapter XII. A principal reason in West Africa had been that secondary education was mainly in the hands of the missions, whose schools were neither staffed nor equipped to teach the science which was needed as a basis for professional studies. But, as the Ashby Commission had noted, there was also a question of prestige. A number of the professional officers who were trained preferred, when a chance arose, to transfer to administrative posts.

How little effect the policies of Phelps-Stokes and the Advisory Committee had generally in West Africa could be seen from the report of a Nuffield Foundation Mission in 1953 which found that the Cambridge School Certificate Examination dominated the curriculum of the secondary schools on the West Coast far more completely than the various School Certificates had ever dominated the grammar schools in England. 'Many of the examinations which clutter the educational system of the West Coast,' they added, 'have lost any educational justification they once may have had, and are retained in spite of their pernicious effects because they are convenient pegs on which the government–and consequently other employers–can hang their jobs'.[36]

The coastal area of former British West Africa provides almost a classic example of a cycle which has been observed by sociologists in many colonies. In the first stage the people are suspicious of the new foreign schools, to which the chiefs send their slaves instead of their sons. In the second stage the economic advantages of western education are appreciated. At this point it is almost impossible for the foreigner to try to adapt the curriculum or examinations to local needs, for the local people insist on an opportunity to obtain exactly the same western certificates and diplomas as are held by expatriates, in order to qualify for senior positions in government service. Only in the final stage, after independence, is it usually possible for a national government to inaugurate a locally oriented system of education because it now also controls the means of entry to the government service.[37]

Only after independence could a Nigerian Professor of Education refreshingly maintain that 'the curriculum in Africa south of the Sahara before the advent of the European consisted of the following essentials: moral instruction and civics, on-the-job training, trading, hunting, farming, fishing, etc. for boys and domestic science for girls and sanitation. . . . The idea that elementary education does not fit a child for anything is of European origin and there is no conceivable reason why Nigeria or any other under-developed country should accept it as gospel truth'.[38]

Much can be criticized in the educational system which developed in West Africa. With the honourable exception of Achimota and the pitifully small effort in Northern Nigeria, it was seldom related to the environment. It made little attempt to mobilize the one great unused asset of Africa, under-employed adult labour. In the secondary schools, the many had to study a curriculum which was of value only to the few who would go on to universities. Yet in one way and another the system succeeded, except in Northern Nigeria, in producing a substantial number of West Africans who were able to continue and obtain university degrees, mostly abroad, by the time of independence, and to take over the senior posts in the Services from the British. It will be seen later how in East Africa, by contrast, the one-sided emphasis of the recommendations of the Phelps-Stokes Mission and of the Advisory Committee's statement of 1925 resulted in an almost disastrous lack of higher manpower, when independence came years before it was anticipated by those who had been responsible for the educational policies of the governments. It will also be seen in the next chapter how inadequate the much praised educational system proved in Northern Nigeria whose lack of indigenous administrators delayed the independence of the whole Federation.

REFERENCES

[1] *Investment in Education* (Ashby Report), Lagos, 1960, p. 5.

[2] F. L. Bartels, 'Philip Quaque' in *Transactions of Gold Coast Historical Society*, Vol. I, Part V.

[3] D. L. Sumner, *Education in Sierra Leone*, London, 1963, p. 11.

[4] Colin Newbury, *West African Commonwealth*, Cambridge, 1964, p. 35.

[5] F. H. Hilliard, *Short History of Education in British West Africa*, London, 1957, p. 30.

[6] J. A. B. Horton, *West African Countries and Peoples*, London, 1868, p. 202.

[7] Quoted by E. Ashby, *African Universities and Western Tradition*, London, 1964, p. 12.

[8] J. Pope-Hennessy, *Verandah*, London, 1964, p. 118.

[9] Quoted in E. Ashby, *African Universities and Western Tradition*, London, 1964, p. 13.

[10] ibid., p. 14.

[11] Lord Lugard, *Instructions to Political Officers*, London, 1919, p. 138.

[12] Hilliard, op. cit., p. 30.

[13] J. S. Coleman, *Nigeria, Background to Nationalism*, London, 1958, p. 122.

[14] Lord Hailey, *An African Survey*, London, 1945 edition, p. 258.

[15] Vischer's Memorandum of 1908, quoted in S. F. Graham, *History of Education in Northern Nigeria* (unpublished London Ph.D. thesis), 1955, p. 191.

[16] M. Perham, *Lugard, the Years of Authority*, Vol. II, London, 1960, Chapter XXV.

[17] Sir A. Steel Maitland, Hansard House of Commons Debates, 14 August, 1917, Col. 1055.

[18] Lord Lugard, *The Dual Mandate*, London, 1922, p. 431.

[19] Phelps-Stokes Fund, *Education in Africa*, New York, 1922, and *Education in East Africa*, 1925. Godfrey N. Brown, in an article on 'British Educational Policy in West and Central Africa', *Journal of Modern African Studies*, 2, 3, 1964, analyzes the composition and influence of these missions.

[20] A. Mayhew, *Education in the Colonial Empire*, London, 1938, p. 179.

[21] Advisory Committee on Native Education in the British Tropical African Colonies, *Education Policy in British Tropical Africa*, Cmd 2374, 1925, p. 4.

[22] D. L. Sumner, op. cit., pp. 69–70.

[23] R. W. Cole, *Kossoh Town Boy*, London, 1960, p. 186.

[24] O. Awolowo, *Awo*, Cambridge, 1960, p. 115.

[25] W. E. F. Ward, *Fraser of Trinity and Achimota*, London, 1965, pp. 222–224.

[26] *Report of the Commission on Higher Education in West Africa* (Elliott Commission), Cmd 6655, 1945, p. 122.

[27] K. Mellanby, *The Birth of Nigeria's University*, London, 1958, p. 118 and p. 189.

[28] Ashby, op. cit., p. 32.

[29] Ashby, op. cit., p. 57

[30] *Report of Nigerian Parliamentary Commission on Africanization*, S.P. 6, 1959, p. VI and p. 51.

[31] K. O. Dike, Paper at Nigerian Seminar on Manpower Problems, Lagos, 1964.

[32] Ashby, op. cit., p. 64.

[33] *University of Nigeria Calendar*, 1963–64, p. 5.

[34] *School Statistics of N. Nigeria* 1962, Kaduna, 1963, p. 15.

[35] Ashby Report, p. 23.

[36] Nuffield Foundation, *Report on African Education*, Oxford, 1953, p. 9.

[37] An article by Sir Christopher Cox on 'The Impact of British Education on the Indigenous Peoples of Overseas Territories', *Colonial Review*, December, 1956, p. 230, develops this point as does Margaret Read in *Education and Social Change in Tropical Areas*, London, 1955, p. 105.

[38] Dr. Babs Fafunya. Unpublished Paper at Nigerian Seminar on Manpower Problems, 1964.

CHAPTER VIII

Africanization

GHANA – NIGERIA – WESTERN NIGERIA –
EASTERN NIGERIA – NORTHERN NIGERIA
– SIERRA LEONE – THE ARMED FORCES
– OTHER SERVICES – COMPENSATION

'The strains and stresses for an independent country to
be administered preponderantly by overseas civil servants would be intolerable. They would be more so than
the harm that could be done to the country by any
lowering of standards.'
FINAL REPORT OF PARLIAMENTARY COMMITTEE
ON NIGERIANIZATION, 1959

After the First World War the official files are still closed: an
account of the attitudes of the British and West African
Governments and of local leaders to Africanization of the
services must now depend mainly on reports on Africanization, Legislative Assembly debates, references in memoirs, and on the remini-
scences, which often cannot be attributed, of those who participated
in the process of the transfer of power either on the British or on the
African side.

The administrative machine, with which discussion on Africanization was mainly concerned, changed considerably over the period.
Initially it was the District Officer, or under indirect rule the Resident,
who was the obvious symbol of power. Like the District Magistrate
or Deputy Commissioner in India, the Resident in Nigeria and in the
Gold Coast was responsible for maintaining law and order and was
the general representative of the government, with at least a co-
ordinating function in relation to the representatives of technical
departments in his Province or District. He either had judicial
powers or the duty of inspecting native courts: and if he was not

149

directly responsible, as in India, for collecting revenue, he was concerned that the native authorities made equitable assessments and efficient collections. At a time when considerably more attention was being given to the place of Africans in local than in central government, the question which absorbed the British during the inter-war and immediately post-war years was not so much whether the Resident and District Officer would be Africanized as whether their offices would be maintained at all. Consequently the first West Africans were only appointed experimentally as administrative officers in the forties, though African doctors and judges had been appointed some years earlier.

While the pattern in the Provinces and Districts changed little through the period of British rule, the central secretariat expanded greatly in the last fifteen to twenty years. In earlier years the Governor, who was usually but not always a colonial civil servant, was able to despatch the business of government through the Colonial Secretary, with whom the Residents or District Officers and heads of department corresponded. As the colony's budget increased, a Financial Secretary was added. At this stage the Colonial Secretary and Financial Secretary and one or two other departmental heads, such as the Director of Health and head of the Police, would sit on the Governor's Executive Council, as well as in the Legislative Council. As the economic and social activities of the government increased, the Colonial and Financial Secretary could no longer deal with the files of all the professional departments. In some territories civil servants were appointed as 'Members' or 'Ministers' who became responsible not only for the supervision of a group of Departments but for answering questions about their activities in the Legislative Assembly. In the last stage before independence African non-officials or members of the predominant party were appointed as Ministers, and senior civil servants responsible to them became Permanent Secretaries, the Ministry being usually responsible for several Departments.

To the Africans therefore it was apparent that the senior British officials at headquarters had not only an administrative but a political role. One effect was to make Africanization of the posts of Permanent Secretary as important a symbol as that of the senior officers in Provinces and Districts: another was to add greatly to the desirability of posts in the administrative service, in which, with the rapid promotion which was possible at the time of independence, Africans sometimes became Permanent Secretaries in their mid-thirties, often supervising the work of professional heads of departments who had much longer experience.

Once malaria and yellow fever came under control, it does not seem that there was much pressure from the Colonial Office on the territorial governments to Africanize the services, at least until the Labour Government came into office in 1945. Individual governors seem to have been wholly responsible for whatever initiatives were taken on this question and, apart from the Guggisberg period in Ghana, the West African governments did not show much interest in Africanization until the Second War. At the West African National Conference which Casely Hayford organized in 1920, however, delegates from the Gold Coast, Nigeria, Gambia and Sierra Leone demanded Africanization of judicial posts and of the West African medical staffs; press and politicians never allowed the governments entirely to forget the issues.

The Second World War brought about a considerable change. The difficulty of recruiting expatriates was in itself an incentive to Africanization of posts: immediately after the War, Colonial Development and Welfare funds remained unspent because staff were not available. But there was also a new spirit in London. Sir Ralph Furse at the Colonial Office in a remarkable memorandum drew attention to the fact that after the fall of Singapore public opinion in England demanded a different sort of colonial service. 'The educated African is moving towards the front of the stage,' he pointed out, and must be recruited and trained to share responsibilities with the British in the services.[1] Lord Hailey, whose range of knowledge of Indian and African administration was almost unique, reminded the government of some lessons of Indian history. 'There is no doubt,' he told the House of Lords in 1942, 'that where we promise self-government to the colonial peoples the first criterion that many of them will apply in judging our intentions is the extent to which we admit them to our administrative services. Here in their view is the substance of power, and it appeals to them – and in particular to the educated classes – as of more importance than the slow evolution of popular institutions'. He pointed out that in 1938 there had been thirty-eight fully qualified African doctors in government service and two African judges of the Supreme Court, so that the ability of Africans could hardly be called in question. In the press of the Gold Coast and to a certain extent in Nigeria, he asserted, the one absorbing topic was the appointment of Africans to the Administrative Service.[2] The Labour Government after winning the election of 1945 announced that 'if progressive advancement along the road to self-government within the framework of the British Commonwealth of Nations is to be a reality, the public services of the Colonies must be adapted to local conditions and must to the greatest extent be staffed by local people. . . . The first objective of post-war organization will be to provide necessary conditions to enable colonial people to staff their own services'.[3] A million pound scholarship scheme was set up to accelerate the process. 'Shared training with British officers in this country' was seen as providing 'the best remedy for one of the defects in the British colonial practice of the past–i.e., that we were less successful in our dealings with the colonial intelligentsia than with the primitive population'. But it was insisted that colonial entrants to administrative courses must be graduates and no less well equipped than the home entrants.

While the Gold Coast (which became Ghana in 1957), Nigeria and Sierra Leone each advanced by orderly stages to independence over a period of about eight years, there were some differences in the way in which their governments handled the question of Africanization.

GHANA

The Gold Coast Government started an inquiry in 1941 into the scope for appointment of Africans in each department of government and into the qualifications required for such posts. The report, which did not appear until 1944, laid considerable stress on maintenance of standards. While it recognized that 'given the necessary facilities for training, Africans possessed the ability to qualify themselves academically and technically for the highest posts', a warning was sounded on the dangers of corruption owing to pressure on government officers by their relatives. 'Officers not up to the standards in every respect will have to be eliminated from the service at the earliest stage if government is to ensure the maintenance of the quality of its public service.' There were at this time eleven African medical officers and three agricultural officers in government service, and scholarships were being provided to the United Kingdom for university studies. But even a university degree was not to be regarded as more than 'a ticket permitting a candidate to enter the competition which has as its prize appointment to a senior post'. Progress in departmental training could be seen. The Police and

Public Works Department were selecting candidates for training in the U.K. and a special appointments board was set up to select scholars and to nominate Africans for promotion.[4]

In 1942 the first two Ghanaians were appointed to the Administrative Service: K. A. Busia, who had an Oxford degree, left the service after a few years for academic work and politics; A. L. Adu, who was a Cambridge graduate, in due course became head of the civil service and then was seconded to posts with international organizations in East Africa.* In 1943 the Governor, Sir Alan Burns, declared that it was the Government's policy 'to appoint Africans to superior appointments in preference to Europeans wherever suitable Africans could be found, and further to take all practicable measures by way of scholarships, training schemes and the like to augment the numbers of Africans suitable for such appointments'[5]. Only one more African was appointed to the Administrative Service however before 1950.

The rapid constitutional developments in the Gold Coast after the War were accompanied by an almost continuous flow of reports on Africanization. There was a Select Committee of the Legislature on Africanization in 1950.[6] In 1951 the Lidbury Commission on the Civil Service in the Gold Coast[7] gave special attention to Africanization in its report: a Select Committee of the Legislature under K. A. Gbedemah[8] reviewed the Lidbury Report in 1952. In 1953 a working party of civil servants under A. L. Adu reviewed the Africanization programme,[9] and in 1954 the Government issued a statement on the programme of Africanization of the Public Service.[10]

A rapid evolution of policy can be seen in these reports. The report of 1950 established as general principles:

1. That while there should be no lowering of standards, vacancies should be filled by Africans wherever possible;

* This name occurs so frequently in this study that a biographical note may be useful. — A. L. Adu, C.M.G., O.B.E., born 1914, educated Achimota and Cambridge, M.A., Natural Science Tripos. Taught Achimota 1939; entered Gold Coast Civil Service 1942. Commissioner for Africanization 1950, Director of Recruitment and Training 1952, Secretary to Cabinet and Head of Civil Service 1959. Chairman of Nyasaland Localization Committee 1960 and of Tanganyika Local Salaries Commission, 1961, Secretary-General, East African Common Services Organization (1962), Regional Representative in East Africa, U.N. Technical Assistance Board 1964, Deputy Secretary General, Commonwealth Secretariat, 1965, Author of *The Civil Service in New African States*, 1965.

2. That promotions should be by merit, irrespective of race;

3. That future recruitment of expatriates, except in the administrative service and police, should be on contract;

4. That retrenchment of expatriates should not be contemplated.

The Lidbury Commission of 1951 found the principal weakness of the Gold Coast civil service to be the lack of opportunity for Africans to develop by experience the qualities necessary for promotion. This owed its origin to the old distinction between 'European' and 'African' posts, though they were now called 'senior' and 'junior' posts: transfer from one to the other was much more difficult than it would have been in the British civil service. The Commission recommended, and the Government approved, new classifications of administrative, executive, clerical and subclerical services, with regular promotion possibilities between them. There was still great emphasis that 'standards' must not be lowered.[11] The Select Committee of 1952 made the customary genuflection in the direction of 'standards', but suggested that a university degree should be an adequate qualification for an African to be admitted to the administrative service, without further written examination, as it was indeed for the expatriates.[12]

It was left to the Adu Committee of 1953 to raise many of the fundamental issues which had to be faced if there were to be rapid Africanization. At this stage, they argued, a policy must be established which would place Africans in the key posts of the administration and would eventually produce a sufficient number of Africans to fill all the posts in the civil service. There were many Africans whose practical experience could offset lack of academic qualifications. The transformation of the service from one which was predominantly expatriate to one which was indigenous was bound to be accompanied by some disruption of the services. During the takeover there would inevitably be a reduction in the standard and extent of services provided to the public: but this issue had never been frankly put to the public. British 'standards' should not be regarded as sacrosanct. American degrees should be recognized as a qualification; men who had failed School Certificate should be considered for technical posts. Above all there must be a much greater emphasis on in-service training. An officer had the same right, they suggested, to receive training in the civil service as he had to receive a salary. The Committee believed that the great majority of overseas civil servants were in sympathy with an Africanization policy, which they hoped would 'be completed in the atmosphere of a coming-of-age party rather than of a divorce court'.[13]

The philosophy of the Adu Committee proved somewhat too advanced for the government. Ghana's approach to Africanization was more gradual than that of most other countries. By 1954 there were four African heads of departments and ten assistant secretaries. By 1958 Africans occupied 69% of the posts in superscale and the next two grades, but even in 1959, two years after independence, half the Permanent Secretaries were still expatriates.

Dr. Nkrumah became Leader of Government Business in 1951; the Gold Coast did not become independent, as 'Ghana', until 1957. In the interim the services were considerably expanded in order to staff new development schemes. The increase in the number of Africans in senior posts was not therefore matched by a corresponding decrease in the number of British officials. While the number of Africans rose from 544 in 1952 to 1,984 in 1958, the number of overseas officers fell from 1,332 to 880.[14] Nor was there less need for expatriates after independence, though these were professionals and technicians instead of administrators. For although Ghana was better off than most other states in tropical Africa, the manpower shortage in engineering, medicine and veterinary science was serious for a government whose electorate clamoured for better services. As one indication of this, shortly after independence the Legislative Assembly demanded that pharmacists should be permitted to undertake medical practice. The Government did not accept the proposal, but instead engaged an additional hundred expatriate doctors. Even in 1964 it was estimated that specialist doctors would not be entirely replaced by Ghanaians for twenty years, nor engineers for ten years, though forty or fifty of the latter were now graduating each year. It was also considered that it would take twenty years to staff the University fully with Ghanaians.

Ghana set a precedent for several other former British states in Africa by replacing the provincial and district officers by political appointees. Administrative officers were however maintained in the districts as secretaries to the new government agents. More administrative officers were now required in the Secretariat to deal with development programmes. The average age of the men at the top of the civil services at independence, as Permanent Secretaries and in equivalent posts, was thirty-eight. About half had entered the administrative service direct and had around ten years' experience in government. The others had entered government through the clerical service and had fifteen to twenty years' service. About 70% of the top civil servants had studied at Ghana's three great secondary schools, Achimota, Mfantsipim and Adisadel. The salary of a Permanent Secretary was £2,300 in 1964, while that of a Minister was £2,700, both lower than in Nigeria. The Ghana civil service which was Africanized gradually over several years, could be favourably compared in 1964 with that of any other African state. But many of its earliest Permanent Secretaries, of the first generation of graduates, were serving abroad with International Organizations: the former prefects of Achimota had not found it easy to adjust to the policy and practice of Nkrumahism.

NIGERIA

The history of Africanization in Nigeria is more complex than that in Ghana as from 1954 not only was there a Federal Civil Service, but each of the Regions, Western, Eastern and Northern,[15] independently recruited its own civil service through a separate Public Service Commission.

Because British rule was consolidated later in Nigeria than in Sierra Leone and the Gold Coast, the earliest Africans to hold senior posts in the government services were at first mostly persons referred to as 'native foreigners'. Some were from Sierra Leone and the Gold Coast, a few were West Indians and 'Brazilians' descended from West Africans who had been slaves in Brazil. By the Second World War the number of native foreigners was beginning to decline and Dr. Azikiwe started to press for Nigerianization of the services. This was one of the points made in a memorandum submitted to the Secretary of State by a delegation of journalists of which he was a member in 1943; in the same year Azikiwe suggested publicly that if 200 fellowships a year were awarded for five years the government services could be wholly staffed by Nigerians in seven years' time.[16]

After the War, the government began to show more interest. While in 1939 there had been only twenty-three Africans in senior posts, forty-two were appointed in 1947. The Acting Governor informed the Legislative Council in 1948 that a speedier advance was limited by the shortage of candidates, especially in the professional and technical fields. He had been shocked to find that there were only two Nigerians taking the veterinary diploma course.[17] Azikiwe, now a member of the Legislative Council, continued to demand that the fellowships programme be greatly increased, that Africans be commissioned in the Royal West African Frontier Force, and that Nigerian doctors with medical degrees from the U.S.A. and Asia should be allowed to practise.[18]

In 1948 Sir John MacPherson and Hugh Foot (later to become Lord Caradon) arrived as Governor and Chief Secretary respectively. Determined to retain the political initiative at this stage, they set up a Commission in 1948 to make recommendations about the recruitment and training of Nigerians for senior posts in the government service. Foot was Chairman; Azikiwe was a member and signed the report.

The Report noted that of 172 Nigerians in the senior service, 48 were in the medical and 23 in the judicial service. Nigerians represented less than 10% of the total strength of the service and their average age was forty-three.

The Foot Commission established the lines upon which Nigerianization was to proceed. No non-Nigerian was in future to be appointed if a suitable Nigerian were available and a Public Service Commission was to make selections for appointments and promotions. A detailed scheme was prepared for each department for scholarships abroad; scholarships were also to be awarded to the University College of Ibadan and to secondary schools: in all schemes special consideration was to be given to the needs of the backward Northern Province. Every year there was to be a review of the junior service for promotions, and departments were urged to give high priority to in-service training.[19]

A pious reference was made to the traditional belief that the 'scaffolding' of the administrative service was destined to disappear, but meanwhile it was decided to continue Nigerian recruitment to the service, which had started experimentally in 1943. It was also accepted that if Nigerian scholars could not be placed in the U.K., whose universities at this time reserved 90% of their places for British ex-servicemen, study in the Dominions and U.S.A. should be considered.

By the time that the Nigerian Civil Service was divided between the Federal Government and the Regions, some results of the Foot Commission's work could be seen. In 1952, the proportion of Nigerians in the senior service had risen to 19%, most having been promoted from the junior service. While the scholarship scheme had been carried out, far more Nigerians, 1,288 out of 1,588, were studying privately. The report of Sir Sidney Phillipson and S. O. Adebo on Nigerianization in 1954 frankly raised some basic issues. They concluded that it was possible, though unprecedented, for a self-governing country to have a civil service which in its senior ranks was predominantly expatriate, provided that the number gradually decreased. They firmly insisted that there must be no lowering of administrative and professional standards; and they opposed both the appointment of Nigerian understudies to expatriates in super-scale posts and the principle of compensatory retirement terms for expatriates. There must be, they said, no departure from the principle of equal treatment between British and Nigerians in the service.[20]

The details of the several reports and statements on Africanization which appeared between 1954 and independence need not detain us. They show how problems and policies changed as independence drew nearer. In 1956 the greatly expanded Federal scholarship programme was limited only by lack of qualified candidates. Of 1,300 applicants for scholarships, only 130 had the appropriate qualifications.[21] In the same year a programme was started for training Nigerian diplomats by attaching them as supernumeraries in Nigerian offices and British embassies overseas.[22]

The main difficulty was not to find Nigerian administrators but professional officers. The bottleneck was in the secondary schools, poorly provided with laboratories, and in 1957 the government set up an emergency science training scheme in Lagos at which 200 students were taught mathematics and science to G.C.E. (A) level.[23] The administrators in the Federal Government were almost entirely drawn from the Western and Eastern Regions. In 1957 the North, which contained 55% of the country's population, provided only 1% of the Federal civil service.

Now the earlier principles on 'standards' began to be abandoned. In 1957 compensation schemes for expatriates were introduced and in 1958 a Committee of the Federal Parliament put forward the view, subsequently accepted by the Government, that 'Nigeria is not yet at a stage when rigid standards of quality and performance can reasonably be demanded of the Public Service. In a period of transition a temporary deterioration must be expected and must be tolerated if the new status of the service is to be successfully achieved'.[24] The Parliamentary Committee also challenged the

Phillipson-Adebo thesis that it was acceptable for expatriates to serve in senior positions in an independent government. Being ultimately responsible to the Secretary of State for the Colonies, the British could not, it was now suggested, give an undivided loyalty to Nigeria; and the Committee therefore pressed for immediate and complete Nigerianization of the senior administrative posts.[25] This proposal the Government rejected; but a number of supernumeraries were appointed as deputy secretaries. In June 1960, just before independence, about 60% of the Federal senior service posts were held by Nigerians.

One of the greatest fears of the Northern Region was that in an independent Nigeria their services would be flooded by the more highly educated Yoruba from the West and Ibo from the East. The backwardness of their own people not only caused the Northern Leaders to ask for internal self-government later than in the Western and Eastern Regions: it also made them insist that the public services of each Region should be independently recruited. Under the constitution the Federal Government was responsible for little beyond foreign affairs, defence, currency, communications and the oversight of certain public corporations. The residual functions were with the regional governments, which became responsible for their own public services from 1954. The Western and Eastern Regions became internally self-governing in 1957 and the Northern Region in 1959.

THE WESTERN REGION OF NIGERIA

Nigerianization advanced much more rapidly in the Western and Eastern Regions than in the North, particularly in the West, where the missionary schools had been first established and which sent 1,000 scholars abroad between 1952 and 1960. In 1952, the Western Region Government adopted its 'frigidaire' policy by which votes for expatriation pay were frozen and could not be released without approval by the Regional Executive Council. In 1955 the Government however reaffirmed that promotion within the service should not take account of race and that there would be no lowering of standards for entry into the civil service.

At the stage of Regional internal self-government in 1957, compensation schemes came into effect for expatriates. Certain posts such as Secretary to the Cabinet were now reserved for Nigerians. Chief S. O. Adebo, who had been closely associated with the Federal

Government's Nigerianization programme, became head of the service, and the Government also appointed six supernumerary Senior Assistant Secretaries to work with the expatriate Permanent Secretaries. Just before independence in 1960, three of the fourteen Permanent Secretaries were Nigerians, and six other Nigerians had acted as Permanent Secretary on occasion. At independence, when the Government decided to reserve all posts of Permanent Secretary and head of department for Africans, there were thus experienced men available to take up the posts.

Of the six supernumeraries who understudied and succeeded the British Permanent Secretaries, three were university graduates. One had been a principal agricultural officer who had taken the Trinidad diploma in tropical agriculture. One was an education officer, posted as students' officer in London. One came from the Federal Ministry of Finance. One was an administrative officer, who had been acting director of recruitment in the Public Service Commission, and one was a lawyer with first class honours who had lectured at the London School of Economics. These and other senior Nigerian officers formed during the transitional period the 'Adebo Club', presided over informally by the Chief Secretary, who did much to set and stabilize the traditions of the new service.

In the Provinces the Residents were abolished and the District Officers became local government advisers, whose duties were to advise the newly formed local councils, though occasionally when local government broke down, the 'local government adviser' was appointed as 'sole administrator'. In normal circumstances, however, the local government adviser could look after a larger area than the old District Officer. Fewer administrative officers now therefore worked in the field than in the Secretariat, where increasing numbers were required to plan and staff development schemes. It was even argued that two different types of administrative officer should now be recruited and that while in the field the old qualification of a general arts degree might still be appropriate, for secretariat work, which was mainly concerned with development, a more thorough grounding in economics and perhaps sociology would be preferable. A greater degree of specialization, by which officials normally remained in the same departments, as in the United Kingdom, also now seemed necessary.[26] In the interim period a number of senior administrative posts were held by doctors, engineers, agricultural officers and teachers. Power and prestige seemed to have attracted them to these positions rather than better salaries than they would have earned in their professions. This seemed likely to prove a temporary phase. By 1964 the supply of graduate candidates had so increased that a competitive written examination was held for entry into the administrative class.

THE EASTERN REGION OF NIGERIA

Nigerianization in the Eastern Region developed along similar though more gradual lines to those in the West. At independence about half the senior posts were still in expatriate hands and some expatriates still served as Permanent Secretaries until 1962. All but two of the Nigerians who succeeded them were graduates of British universities, several having started in the education service and taken external degrees from London University.

As in the Western Region, the Resident was abolished and the District Officer's functions changed. He no longer had the responsibility for reviewing decisions of native authority courts which had previously taken up much of his time.

Donald Kingsley, an American from the Ford Foundation, who reported on the Eastern Nigerian public service in 1961, immediately after independence, found that the average age of the administrative service was thirty-three and the average length of service only three and a half years. Nigerians straight from university had replaced experienced expatriates. He concluded that the first stage of Nigerianization had been carried out with notable success in the Region but made some basic criticisms which were repeated in his reports on the other regions. There had been virtually no training of administrative officers for work in the central ministries; they had been trained for the work of the old time District Officer rather than for the requirements of the kind of administration now emerging. Within the secretariat there was too much association of training with formal schooling, and a tendency to think that the former ended rather than began with a school certificate or a degree. Kingsley considered that the requirement of a school certificate for entry into the clerical service was too high and indeed irrelevant: an examination in use of English and typing would have been more appropriate. Many clerks were spending working hours preparing for the examination which might enable them to escape from the clerical service.[27]

THE NORTHERN REGION OF NIGERIA

The British had assumed during the period of indirect rule in Northern Nigeria that the emirates or 'native authorities' would very gradually develop into democratically elected local authorities. Little attention was given to the ultimate position at the centre. Meanwhile the native authorities were mainly staffed by relations of the Emirs, whose incompetence often exasperated the British technical officers. Even the British Resident was however only an adviser who could neither hear complaints nor give orders direct. He might be able to protect senior staff against arbitrary dismissal but he had little success in obtaining the dismissal of incompetents.[28] Crocker, an Australian who served as an administrative officer in Nigeria in the thirties, wrote bitterly 'when cadets and quite junior A.D.O.'s asked "how are you going to develop these emirates which you have turned into medieval monarchies into modern states or communities" . . . such men are marked down as temperamentally unsuited for life in Nigeria'.[29] Since Lugard's time, Crocker considered, the autocracies had been strengthened and the villages neglected.

As for the point of view of the native authorities, Ahmadu Bello's reaction as a District Head was probably typical when, during the shortage of British administrative officers which arose in the Second World War, he recorded thankfully that 'we no longer had to listen to a stream of advice and exhortation from the variety of administrative officers who had moved across our vision before the War. Some of these people could never realize that we had been administering our units long before they were thought of in this country'. He went on to assert that 'when the British came to this country they found that we had our Chiefs, Schools, Judges and all that was necessary for civilization'.[30] The Emir of Abuja was even more scathing. 'The administrative officer seems to many people,' he told the Legislative Council in 1949, 'just someone living in an office amongst letters and files, making some more letters and files for another officer in another office to deal with and so on. It is rather like a snake swallowing its own tail–very much hard work, but no good can come of it'.[31]

It is surprising that at least from the publication of the Foot Report in 1948 there was not more active interest in Africanization in the Northern Region Government. Some of the Residents, who were all of course British, are said to have dismissed the new ideas as

'Footrot', and to have told the Emirs whom they advised that there would be no changes in their lifetime. Little was done to expand secondary education or training programmes in the Region until the first African ministers were appointed in 1952. There was no Northern Nigerian in the Administrative Service until 1955.

Sir Ahmadu Bello, Sardauna of Sokoto, the first Premier of the Region, like most of his ministers had passed through the Katsina Teachers Training School and had been an administrator under the native authority of Sokoto, serving first as a District Head and then at headquarters.[32] Native authority officials, unlike officials of the regional government, were allowed to participate in politics. From his first involvement in politics, Ahmadu Bello was clear as to priorities. In 1953, he told the Regional House of Assembly 'There are two points we have got to tackle rigidly, and as soon as we have a firm grip on them then self-government is at hand. . . . They are the Northernization of the Civil Service and of Local Government services'.[33] He saw that in order to Northernize he temporarily needed more expatriates as teachers, and brought in British officers who were being 'Africanized' in the Sudan. The Zaria Institute of Administration was the apple of his eye: eight expatriate administrative officers were placed on its staff.

In the North more than anywhere the theory had prevailed that the administrative officers would one day become redundant. Ahmadu Bello and his ministers however found it essential to retain them. After independence, the Resident was replaced by a Provincial Commissioner with ministerial status, but beside him was a Provincial Secretary through whom all orders were transmitted, and the District Officer continued to function at the lower level. More administrative officers were also needed for the expanding secretariat. There were two possible sources, the small trickle of university graduates and the officials of the native authorities. The Institute of Administration at Zaria from 1953 ran courses at all levels, for district heads, accountants and local government administrators: but its greatest achievement was the success of its one-year courses to train administrative officers for the regional government. About one hundred men were trained as Assistant District Officers between 1957 and 1961. Most of them came from the junior or clerical service of the native authorities and had School Certificate and some seven years' experience in government service.

A few months after Nigerian independence in 1961 a somewhat

sombre view of the Northern Government's administrative policy was taken by Kingsley and Rucker of the Ford Foundation.[34] At that time Northerners held only 28% of the administrative, 25% of the executive and 5% of professional posts. Northernization had been accompanied by a lowering of standards and efficiency which would be felt for some years to come.

Kingsley and Rucker suggested that 'there had been no systematic review of entrance qualifications in the light of Northernization policy either in terms of relevance to Nigerian conditions or needs or of their practicability. In a number of technical and professional areas the continuance of entrance requirements related to conditions in the U.K. is unrealistic and almost certainly unnecessary.' As in Kingsley's reports on the other Regions, the training of administrative officers was stated to be too much related to the needs of district work and too little to that of the Secretariat. Training for supervisory and technical posts was unnecessarily long–far longer than in the United States.

The North was in no hurry to get rid of its expatriates: indeed its leaders blamed the Western and Eastern politicians for making it difficult for the North to retain them. By the end of 1961, however, half the administrative officers were Northerners, and by 1964 all the Permanent Secretaries. These were mostly men who had come up from the ranks. In 1964 they were generally older than their counterparts in the West and East, though a notable exception was the head of the service, a London graduate of thirty-six. By that time 180 out of 211 British administrative officers had departed, as had 86% of the doctors and 81% of the agricultural officers. In public works and education the percentage was lower, 68% and 63%.

SIERRA LEONE

Sierra Leone had its first Commission on Africanization in 1949 and several reports on the question appeared before independence in 1961. The pattern was similar to that in Ghana and Southern Nigeria. Between 1953 and 1959 the number of Africans in the senior service increased from 166 to 381, but the number of expatriates did not decrease correspondingly. On the contrary, there was an increase, if officers on contract as well as those who were pensionable are included.

The bottleneck in the secondary schools became very marked when the British universities raised their entry qualifications in 1948. Of the 21 secondary schools in Sierra Leone only 11 taught even up to School Certificate in 1956. In that year 109 boys and girls passed School Certificate and only 6 Higher Certificate. Of the 108 School Certificate holders 72 obtained scholarships for further study. In these circumstances it was useless for the government to expect to obtain clerks with School Certificate, and they were recruited below this level by examination.

Fourah Bay produced only 8 graduates in 1956. These, who held external pass degrees from Durham University were less favourably placed in government service than were the graduates who had studied overseas.[35] The attitude of the Sinker Commission of 1953 on this grievance was adamant. 'We have been told at present,' they wrote, 'that there are few if any suitable openings for graduates from Fourah Bay in government service. Direct entry to the administrative service is normally dependent on the possession of an honours degree, and amongst expatriate candidates only those with exceptional qualities of adaptability and personality are selected. We think that the same standards should be preserved for African candidates'.[36] This was a bold assertion in view of the difficulty which had always been experienced in finding British officers who were prepared to serve in Sierra Leone. A few years later, however, the Gorsuch Commission pointed out that the government was debasing Fourah Bay's degrees by this discrimination against its graduates. and they were admitted to the administrative service.[37] British cultural prestige always remained high in Sierra Leone: as late as 1957 a regulation was passed authorizing Sierra Leone officers who earned over £720 a year to take their leave in Britain in every alternate year.[38]

THE ARMED FORCES[39]

Africanization of army officers started rather later than that of the higher civil service in West Africa. Azikiwe pressed for Africanization of the officer corps in the 1940s but other Nigerian political leaders such as Awolowo and H. O. Davies appeared apprehensive lest an African officer corps might be created which would constitute an alternative elite to the politicians. Both in Ghana and Nigeria the British recruited the other ranks of the R.W.A.F.F. from the Muslim North, and the axiom came to be accepted that it was easier to educate a fighting man than to militarize a softer schoolboy. When it came to finding African officers, who were required to hold a School Certificate, however, it was necessary to draw on the educated classes of the South. The Nigerian Parliamentary Committee in 1959 considered that too much emphasis was being placed on educational qualifications for officers and that more N.C.O.'s should be commissioned.[40] In 1961, out of 300 officers in the Nigerian Army, there were 81 Africans, but of these 60% were Ibos. Subsequently Nigeria tried to reach a percentage both of officers and men of 50% from the North and 25% each from the West and South.

It is interesting, in light of the strong opposition of Congress to a policy of 'segregation' in the Indian Army, to note that the Parliamentary Committee on Nigerianization urged that whole units should be completely Africanized before independence.[41]

Africanization of the Nigerian Army was complicated by regional factors. The Northern leaders wished to retain the services of expatriate officers so long as there were no Northerners qualified and available to replace them. Western and Eastern Region leaders on the other hand pressed for immediate Africanization. There was still a British Commander-in-Chief four years after independence.

In Ghana there was difficulty in finding graduates who wished to train as officers and the main source of officer recruitment was from Warrant Officers and N.C.O.'s in the Army Education Service. The first Ghanaians were sent to officer cadet schools in the U.K. in 1953, and at independence there were 60 Ghanaians out of 283 officers. British officers, including the Commander-in-Chief, were however maintained in executive positions until Ghana became involved in the Congo three years after independence. Ghana sent officers for training not only to Sandhurst but to India, Pakistan and the Soviet Union, and set up its own military academy in 1960. A typical Ghana army officer, just after independence, would have a School Certificate and between six months to three years military education. He would more likely be the son of a peasant cocoa farmer than of a professional man, for the latter was inclined to regard the civil service or the Bar as having greateresti prge than the army.

While the army was not under the control of the individual West African governments before independence, the police force was, and here Africanization was more advanced. Sierra Leone had Africanized half its gazetted posts in 1960 before independence, the most senior Africans being Assistant Commissioners. Ghana completed Africanization of the police in 1960. The position in Nigeria was

166

more complicated. Although the police force was controlled by the Federal Government and recruited by a Federal police commission, Native Authorities and local councils also sometimes maintained police forces. The Nigerian contingent which policed Leopoldville under Nigerian officers in 1960 was described by several observers as the most efficient police force under the U.N. command.

OTHER SERVICES

There was considerable variation in the degree of Africanization in the different professions and technical services. A Sierra Leone Government Report of 1959 describes a situation which was typical on the West Coast. 'Figures show how uneven Africanization has been. The law, medicine and accounting have made rapid strides, whereas administration, agriculture, geology and veterinary science have lagged behind and recruitment to them needs to be stimulated. It is not every boy with a sound secondary education who is willing to train for an outdoor job if he can obtain an indoor one.'[42] In the same year the Nigerian Parliament's Africanization Committee described the situation in the Agricultural Research Department as 'pathetic' and blamed the secondary schools for not providing sound teaching in science.[43] While agriculture was the principal economic activity of West Africa, in 1959 in Nigeria only 7% of university students were studying in this field, in Ghana 6% and in Sierra Leone none. Of one thousand Nigerians known to be studying in the U.K. in 1958, only 3% were studying agriculture.

Africans had made most progress in medicine and law, even though law could only be studied abroad, because these professions had been open to them in private practice since the 19th century. In January 1963 there were 391 Nigerian and 218 expatriate medical officers in the service of the four Nigerian Governments. Except in the North, where most of the doctors were British and Pakistani, the expatriate doctors were mainly specialists, recruited from many countries. At this time Nigeria was still heavily dependent on expatriate engineers. The four Governments had 125 Nigerian civil engineers and 183 expatriates, while there were 183 vacancies. Each Government had, however, sufficient Nigerian engineers to man key positions. As the British engineers departed they were partly replaced by Tamils from Ceylon. It was also found, at least in the Western Region, that a Divisional Engineer could cover several divisions if he were given adequate administrative support. The position in agriculture was not quite as bad as had been anticipated. There were 329 Nigerian agricultural officers, 91 expatriates and 147 vacancies. The majority of the veterinarians were, however, still expatriates.

The position in the government posts which required a degree or professional qualification in 1963 was as follows:[44]

	Nigerians	Expatriates	Vacancies
Western Region	1,990	169	622
Eastern Region	974	195	191
Northern Region	579	627	396
Federal Government	2,072	658	934

The North thus still had more expatriates than local officers at this level while the proportions in the West and East were relatively small. In the Federal Government about half the expatriates were classified as 'senior managerial and administrative staff'. It appeared that many of them were being retained deliberately until they could be replaced by Northerners.

COMPENSATION

When India and the Sudan had become independent, the new governments had not wished to retain the services of expatriate officers. With these precedents, the compensation arrangements which were at first evolved in West Africa were more designed to safeguard the financial position of the expatriates than to persuade them to continue to serve as long as required. Both in Ghana and Nigeria, however, the expatriates left more rapidly than they could be replaced. In Ghana, where ambitious development schemes could have been slowed down without the expatriates, this caused the government after independence to introduce more generous terms.

The history in Nigeria was complicated and need only be briefly summarized.[45] In 1957 the British Government offered to place its officers on a Special List, which would entitle them to be considered for employment in other territories should their services no longer be required in Nigeria. Few officers chose this alternative: most preferred to accept immediate compensation. Subsequently an immediate advance payment of compensation was offered to those who agreed to stay. The Nigerian Governments, however, were left with the feeling that the arrangements made for compensation, for which

ultimately or immediately they had to pay, had tended to cause their
expatriate officers to leave their service at a critical time. They consequently refused to re-employ on contract any officer who had
received compensation. The subject is a complex one which will be
considered in other regions also in this study. In general it may
be stated that a far better climate would have been created if the
British Government had voluntarily accepted to pay a larger share
of the compensation. At the same time it must be recognized, as
Kenneth Younger has pointed out, that there has almost always been
a danger period immediately before and after independence when
relations between the new governments and the expatriates become
delicate.[46] It has never been easy for the new governments to strike
a balance between those actions which are intended to hasten
Africanization and satisfy the electorate and those which on the
other hand may allay the anxieties of the essential expatriates and
induce them to stay.

Localization in West Africa would have proceeded more smoothly
but for the long exclusion of Africans from the administrative
service and from posts which were occupied by members of other
unified services. Except in the Northern Region of Nigeria the process took place gradually, however, over a period of about ten to
twelve years and Africans with adequate qualifications, usually
acquired abroad, were generally available and able to prevent serious
loss of efficiency. Three distinct stages can be seen. In the first,
Africans were trained largely through scholarships to fill vacant
posts but 'standards' were said to be unchangeable. In the second
stage Africans were given priority over the expatriates in employment but not in promotion. In the third phase, which usually came
only when elected governments took office, key posts were usually
placed in African hands even if this meant that they were promoted
over expatriates with longer experience.

The new heads of departments, owing to their extensive scholarship experience, were sometimes better qualified academically than
the British whom they succeeded. There was a considerable shortage
of professional and administrative staff at the middle levels, but it
was sometimes less alarming than statistics would appear to indicate,
since many departments had carried forward their vacancies year
after year. Several departments, faced with the necessity of dilution
and of using men with diplomas to do work previously done by men

with degrees, found that this did not result in much loss of efficiency. The position in Northern Nigeria was quite different, determined as the government was not to allow Southerners to replace the expatriates. Breakdown was, however, avoided by retaining the British officials and by devoting considerable energy and resources to crash training courses.

One of the most striking differences in the administrative services of the West African governments before and after independence was in the relative position of the officers serving in the Secretariat and those in the field. In the British days the majority preferred to be Residents or District Officers, to have their own commands, rather than to work in the Secretariat. Ahmadu Bello, when first Premier of the Northern Region, complained that his British officers were always intriguing to get back to the Provinces.[47] After independence, it was the politician who had the supreme authority in Province and District, and flew the national flag on his house and car, while the civil servant dealt with the papers. Partly for reasons of prestige, therefore, African civil servants preferred to work in the capital, but partly too for social reasons. The educational facilities of the capital meant more to them than they did to the expatriate, who sent his children to England to be educated.

Perhaps the main unanswered question in West Africa was whether the governments and institutions financed by the governments, such as public corporations and universities, could continue to maintain the same structure of salary and perquisites for the senior staff as the colonial government had established for a much smaller number of expatriates. It was probably inevitable that Africans should demand and obtain the same terms as their expatriate colleagues, but the result was that the differential between the top and bottom salaries in the government service was far higher than in the western world. The political importance of the problem was much greater than in more industrialized countries: in Nigeria at independence 60% of those employed outside agriculture were listed as public employees.[48]

REFERENCES

[1] Printed in *Post War Training for the Colonial Service*, Col 198, 1946, Appendix, p. 20.
[2] Hansard, House of Lords Debates, 6 May, 1942, Col. 912 ff.
[3] *Organization of the Colonial Service*, Col 197, 1946, p. 3.
[4] Gold Coast S.P.1, Accra, 1944.

[5] *Report of the Select Committee of the Legislative Council on Africanization*, S.P. 1, Accra, 1950, p. 8.

[6] ibid.

[7] *Report of Commission on the Civil Service of the Gold Coast* (Lidbury Report), S.P. IV, Accra, 1951.

[8] *Report of Select Committee on the Lidbury Report* (Gbedemah Report), S.P. III, Accra, 1952.

[9] Final Report of Working Party to Review the Africanization Programme ('Adu Report' -Unpublished). Accra, 1953.

[10] *Statement on Programme of the Africanization of the Public Service*, Accra, 1954.

[11] *Lidbury Report*, op. cit., pp. 18–25.

[12] *Gbedemah Report*, op. cit., p. 3.

[13] Though this report is unpublished, its conclusions are summarized in A. L. Adu, *The Civil Service in New African States*, London, 1965, p. 88.

[14] K. Younger, *The Public Service in New States*, London, 1960, p. 33.

[15] Another Regional Government, for the Midwest, was established in 1964.

[16] Nigeria Legislative Council Debates, 9 March, 1948, p. 412.

[17] ibid., 2 March, 1948, p. 7.

[18] ibid., 10 March, 1948, p. 428.

[19] *Report of the Commission on Recruitment and Training of Nigerians for Senior Posts in Government* (Foot Report), Lagos, 1948.

[20] Sir S. Phillipson and S. O. Adebo, *Nigerianization of the Civil Service*, Lagos, 1954, pp. 48–55.

[21] *Statement of Federal Government on Higher Training of Nigerians*, Lagos, S.P. 4 of 1956.

[22] *Training of Nigerians for Representation Overseas*, Lagos, S.P. 11 of 1956.

[23] *Annual Report of Nigerianization Officer for* 1957, Lagos, 1958, p. 4.

[24] *Matters Arising from the Final Report of the Parliamentary Committee on the Nigerianization of the Federal Public Service*, Lagos, S.P. 2 of 1960.

[25] *Views of the Government of the Federation on the Interim Report of the Committee on Nigerianization*, Lagos, 1958, p. 15.

[26] A. Adedeji, 'The Public Service in a Developing Country', Seminar on Public Administration in a Developing Economy, University of Ife, 1964.

[27] J. Donald Kingsley, *Staff Development, Eastern Nigeria Public Service*, Enugu, 1961.

[28] M. G. Smith, *Government in Zazzau*, London, 1960, p. 272 ff.

[29] W. R. Crocker, *Nigeria*, London, 1936, p. 216.

[30] Ahmadu Bello, *My Life*, London, 1962, p. 63 and p. 75.

[31] Nigeria Legislative Council Debates, 15 March, 1949, p. 442.

[32] Ahmadu Bello, op. cit.

[33] ibid., p. 140.

[34] In an unpublished report.

[35] *Report of the Commission on the Civil Service of Sierra Leone* (Gorsuch Report), Freetown, 1957, pp. 5–6.

171

[36] *Report of the Commission on the Civil Service of Sierra Leone* 1953 (Sinker Report), Freetown, 1953, p. 7.

[37] *Gorsuch Report*, op. cit., pp. 6–7.

[38] ibid., p. 53.

[39] W. F. Gutteridge, *Military Institutions and Power in the New States*, London, 1965, is the main source for this section.

[40] *Final Report of Parliamentary Committee on Nigerianization*, Nigeria Government S.P. 6 of 1959, op. cit., p. 35.

[41] ibid., p. 35.

[42] *Government Statement on Africanization*, S.P. 4 of 1959, Freetown, 1959, p. 3.

[43] Nigerian Federal Government S.P. 6 of 1959, op. cit., p. 23.

[44] Statistics from papers on Seminar on Manpower Problems, Lagos, 1964.

[45] A detailed account is given by K. Younger, op. cit., p. 13.

[46] ibid., p. 75. See also A. L. Adu, op. cit., pp. 82–86.

[47] Ahmadu Bello, op. cit., p. 88.

[48] Taylor Cole, Bureaucracy in Transition: Independent Nigeria in *Public Administration*, Winter, 1960. Thomas Balogh has also written on this problem in 'Economics of Education and Planning', *Comparative Education*, October, 1964, and elsewhere.

PART THREE

East Africa

Tanganyika became independent in 1961 with a population of about 9,400,000; Uganda in 1962 with a population of about 6,500,000; Kenya in 1963 with a population of about 7,300,000. Zanzibar became independent in 1964 with a population of about 300,000 but in the same year joined with Tanganyika in the United Republic of Tanzania.

CHAPTER IX

Common Problems

THE ASIANS IN THE SERVICES – THE CIVIL SERVICE
STRUCTURE – THE COMMON SERVICES – THE
UNIVERSITY – DEFENCE

'The Government recognizes that many Asiatics are
permanently settled in the country but considers that
the natives are still more permanent' -
CHIEF SECRETARY OF UGANDA IN THE
LEGISLATIVE COUNCIL, 1928

The European influence was much more recent in East Africa than in West Africa. Not only had the West Coast been in contact with Europeans for centuries but both among the Yoruba and the Fulani there were large towns and relatively advanced forms of government. In East Africa distances were enormous and the population scattered, except among the lakes of the interior. Even at independence the few towns appeared more Asian than African. Education developed late. Whilst in the Gold Coast even at the end of the 19th century there were about 200 Africans with higher education, in Tanganyika the first African graduate was only 38 at independence, and he was Prime Minister.

The late development of western education and the suddenness with which independence came caused the government services of all the East African territories to be less well prepared than those in West Africa. In the next chapter the differences between the territories will be seen; in this chapter some of their common problems and common institutions will be considered.

THE ASIANS IN THE SERVICES

One of the most striking characteristics of the government services

175

in East Africa was the predominant position of the Asian community in the middle levels between the Europeans at the top and the Africans at the bottom.

The Asians did not first come to East Africa in order, as is sometimes believed, to build the Uganda railway. They were there before the British and before the Germans, managing the Customs office for the Sultan of Zanzibar, trading and financing the Arab slave-traders. The British brought in Punjabis to build the railways, but they also recruited clerks and artisans in Bombay. By the 1920s the territorial governments had three separate salary scales for Europeans, Asians and Africans. Right up to independence, although the Asians were little more than 2% of the population of Kenya and about 1% in Tanganyika and Uganda, the number of posts which they held in the middle levels far exceeded this proportion, as can be seen from the following table compiled in 1961.

Numbers of government officers in positions normally demanding higher education, excluding teachers[1]

	Europeans	Asians	Africans
Uganda	650	150	250
Tanganyika	727	83	200
Kenya	1,250	450	180

Numbers of government officers in positions normally demanding secondary education, excluding teachers

	Europeans	Asians	Africans
Uganda	700	350	600
Tanganyika	898	996	879
Kenya	1,900	2,600	900

Asians also provided 50% of the graduate teachers and had almost a monopoly of the engineering and legal professions: Asian doctors outnumbered Africans by 8 to 1.

Even in 1961 in Kenya and Tanganyika, though not in Uganda, more Asians than Africans passed School Certificate. Mainly concentrated in the cities, they had organized their own secondary schools long before the Africans had any secondary education, and until Tom Mboya's airlift started in 1959, many more Asians than Africans went abroad for higher education, mostly to India.

176

The presence of the Asian community meant that there was less economic pressure on the territorial governments than there was in West Africa to educate and train Africans in order to provide cheap subordinate personnel for the government. Under the policies of 'multiracialism' which were current in the fifties it was also assumed that the best man ought to be allowed to come to the top irrespective of race. Only in Uganda was a policy of 'Africanization' followed, but Uganda had no European settlers, and a higher level of African education than the other territories. Tanganyika, Kenya and the East African Common Services Organization maintained a policy of 'localization' until 1961.

The position of the Asians was complicated by their varying status. Some, whether born in India or in East Africa, had the right of paid passages to India every fifth year. In Uganda this privilege was cancelled at independence, and several hundred Asians in the East African Common Services Organization then put in their resignations in 1963, apparently in the expectation that they might persuade the administration not to take similar steps. Instead the resignations were accepted and the posts Africanized. The varying treatment of the Asians in the territorial governments after independence will be seen in the next chapter. In all of them, and in the E.A.C.S.O., there was some ambiguity as to whether, and to what extent, 'localization' meant 'Africanization'.

THE CIVIL SERVICE STRUCTURE

Until the 1950s the services of the three territories were organized on similar lines, with a differentiation between European posts at the top, Asian posts at the middle level and African posts at the bottom. The Holmes Commission, which in 1947–48 reported on Civil Service Structure and Salaries in East Africa, found that 'salaries rest in effect on a racial basis'. They maintained however that this was justifiable: 'Generally speaking,' they said, 'the European surpasses the Asian in such matters as sense of public service, judgement and readiness to take responsibility' and 'Subject to individual exceptions the African is at the present time markedly inferior to the Asian of the same educational qualifications in such matters as sense of responsibility, judgement, application to duty and output of work'. They stated that these conclusions were proved 'beyond argument' by the similar difference in salaries paid to these three races in business and industry. Pointing out that the indigenous peoples of East Africa were removed by little more than fifty years from a state of society far more primitive than that of Britain at the beginning of the Christian era, the Commission sensed a danger that 'in a laudable desire to enable Africans to participate to a greater extent than at present in the public services, governments may be tempted to seek to replace Europeans by Africans with inferior professional or technical qualifications'. Nothing, they felt, could be more inimical to the future interests of the territories or of the Africans themselves. They proposed that in the higher posts Asians and Africans should be paid three-fifths of the salary of an officer recruited from Britain. In locally recruited posts separate European, Asian and African salary scales were proposed, which were justified by comparison with the rates paid in business and elsewhere.[2]

It was only in 1953 that the Secretary of State, by authorizing individual governors to make appointments in the salary range of £1,000 a year or above, made it possible for the territorial governments to appoint Africans to the most senior posts. In the following year the Lidbury Commission on the Civil Services of East Africa made recommendations which, when accepted by the governments, considerably advanced the framework of Africanization. The same basic salary scales were established for all races: the principle was established that the territories should now aim as far as possible to staff their services with local people; and in 1955 each of the territories set up a Public Service Commission, one of whose duties was to ensure that no one was recruited from outside the territory if a local person were available.[3] Finally in 1960 the Flemming Report[4] recommended that in future expatriates should only be recruited on contract and no longer on pensionable terms.

In these developments a similar pattern to that of West Africa can be seen. Indeed several of those who served in these Commissions had been concerned with Africanization in West Africa. In the earlier stages the precedents were somewhat misleading. The East African Governments and their advisers did not realize that they would have a far shorter time than had Ghana and Nigeria in which to prepare for independence. But in the years immediately preceding and following independence West African experience may have tipped the balance between breakdown and the effective maintenance of the services. Adu of Ghana and Udoji of Nigeria brought an air of reality to the East African Common Service Organization. David

Anderson, who had served in Ghana, was successively staff development adviser in Tanganyika and Kenya. Luke of Sierra Leone was
one of the Africanization Commissioners in Uganda.

The British East African territories, unlike those in West Africa, were
contiguous, and in the 1920s the Kenya settlers, led by Lord Delamere, agitated for the three territories to be formed into a federation.
Though L. S. Amery, then Secretary of State for the Colonies, was
interested in a 'closer union', Sir Donald Cameron as Governor of
Tanganyika successfully maintained that Tanganyika was a mandate
held by Britain from the League of Nations to be administered in
the interests of its inhabitants, which could not be subordinated to
those of a settler government. Important interests in Uganda were
also nervous of commercial and industrial exploitation from Nairobi.

The arrangements for co-operation which emerged were however
much closer than those in West Africa. A Conference of the three
Governors first met in 1925 and acquired a permanent secretariat.
In 1948 this was replaced by an East African High Commission whose
Administrator, together with the Postmaster General and the General
Manager of the East African Railways, were not only responsible to
the three Governors but to a Central Legislative Assembly, consisting
of members elected by the Legislative Assemblies of the three territories. The East African Railways and Harbours, Posts and Tele-
communications, Income Tax and Customs administrations were
maintained as common services, as well as a number of research
institutions. The East Africa High Commission, inclusive of the
Railways and Harbours and Posts and Telegraphs administrations,
had more employees than any of the individual governments: it
recruited its own staff and had an imposing headquarters building in
Nairobi. Many people saw it as the framework of an East African
Federation which would be formed by the three governments after
they became independent.

It might have been expected that the question of localization of
these important services would have received considerable attention.
There were two main obstacles, which were related. In the first place,
nobody knew whether the High Commission would continue after
the individual territories became independent. Secondly, the High
Commission, which was not responsible for education and had no

scholarship schemes, was in a weak position to attract educated Africans, who preferred what seemed to be more secure careers in the services of their own territories. Before independence the recommendations of the Holmes and Lidbury reports were accepted in principle by the E.A.H.C. as well as by the territories but Lidbury's proposal that a training grade should be set up for Africans was not implemented because of the expense involved. In 1961 Sir Richard Ramage wrote a report on 'localization' of the E.A.H.C. services, recommending that preference should be given to Africans in recruitment, that special training should be organized for them and that they should be promoted to supernumerary posts for three year periods. Ramage appeared to be assuming, unrealistically as it proved, that none of the territories would be independent for another three years. He did not therefore propose that Africans should immediately be appointed substantially to senior posts nor did he make any recommendations which would have affected the career and promotion prospects of expatriates.[5] His report was thus better received by non-Africans than by Africans.

When Tanganyika became independent at the end of 1961 the High Commission was reconstituted as the East African Common Services Organization, whose chief executive became 'Secretary General' instead of Administrator, and whose officials became responsible to committees of Ministers from the three territories instead of to the Governors. The Central Legislative Assembly remained in being. A. L. Adu, the former Commissioner of Africanization in Ghana, was appointed as the first Secretary General. A policy of 'Africanization' instead of 'localization' was now adopted and the Public Service Commissions were instructed to give preference to Africans both in recruitment and in promotion. In 1962 an Africanization Commission was set up under the Chairmanship of J. O. Udoji, the Chief Secretary of Eastern Nigeria, to advise the Organization on further measures. Its report[6] is of great interest, particularly in showing how the problems of East Africa looked to those with experience of Africanization in Ghana and Nigeria. The subsequent debate on it in the Central Legislative Assembly is illustrative of similar discussions on the subject which were going on in the legislatures of the territories.

The Commission found that of the 567 posts in the top Administrative and Professional class 88% were held by Europeans, 4% by Asians, and only 8% by Africans. At the next level, of 3,624 Executive and Technical posts only 12% were held by Africans, while 46% were held by Asians and 42% by Europeans. 'In an African Colonial Service with a normal racial structure,' they wrote, 'it is usual to find Africans at all levels of the Service, but with the nationals of the imperial power dominating only the top posts. In such a case Africanization is a simple process of advancing Africans already at the administrative and professional level one or two steps before they reach the top policy advising posts.' But in E.A.C.S.O., the Africans were found only at the executive and technical level. 'To advance the material at this level at the top will either break the person or break the service.'[7]

Nevertheless the Udoji Commission considered that Africanization was a matter of great urgency for the same political and financial reasons as had applied in West Africa and because over 1,000 expatriate officers had retired or given notice. They recommended a policy by which 'all key and policy advisory posts in the short run be held by Africans, and in the long run reduction and ultimate elimination of the predominance of non-Africans at all levels', though they added that there was no intention of wholesale displacement of non-Africans.

This brought them to the question of standards.[8] 'Every other head of department we interviewed reminded us of his responsibility to maintain standards and of the impossibility of accelerating the rate of Africanization without lowering standards.' . . . 'It appeared that everybody was making a fetish of standards.' But to apply the standards of Whitehall or Washington to East Africa, they maintained, was irrelevant: standards need only be absolute in two circumstances, either where safety of life or where honesty and integrity were concerned. They suggested that present educational requirements could be lowered: specifically that clerical and technical grades did not need School Certificate; that supervisory and executive grades did not need Higher Certificate; and that university degrees should not be required for entry to administrative and professional grades.

Yet even with these lowered qualifications, where were the Africans to be found, when the territorial governments themselves were thousands short of high level manpower? The Commission was strongly critical of an educational policy under which half the places in the University of East Africa were left vacant because there were insufficient candidates with Higher Certificate to fill them. They suggested that the University should accept entrants with School

Certificate. Meanwhile they proposed a massive scholarship programme abroad, by which 360 Africans should be sent to institutions of higher education in Europe, U.S.A. and elsewhere which
would accept entrants with School Certificate and train them for
work with E.A.C.S.O.

The administration of E.A.C.S.O. accepted most of these recommendations, though with the qualification that standards could not
be lowered to the point where the railways and posts and telegraphs
ceased to pay their way.[9] Subsequently the Udoji Report was debated
in the Central Legislative Assembly, which consisted of members of
the parliaments of the three territories. Their speeches showed how
charged with emotion the issue of Africanization had become. 'It is
very difficult,' said one member, 'to convince our people to stand up
in a public place and say "now we have become independent, we are
governing this country", when they see a white stationmaster at the
railway station and a white nurse in the clinic'. Much suspicion of
the Europeans was voiced. 'Expatriates do not want to leave and they
try to have an excuse in saying we are not up to standard' said one
member, or as another put it 'How can you expect an expatriate to
pull you up the ladder when he himself is at the top?' Even more
revealing, another asserted that 'statements that the African is unreliable, irresponsible and has no integrity have made our minds so
dumb, and we believe we cannot do the thing even when we are
given the opportunity. If you go into the room where an expatriate
shuts himself up all day you may well find that a schoolboy could do
what he is doing'. And yet, as another member admitted, no African
with a degree wanted to go into the railways or posts and telegraphs.
If he could not be a politician his next preference would be to become
a permanent secretary or diplomat.[10]

Dawson Mwanyumba, one of the Kenya Ministers, pointed out
in reply to the debate that in fact the current problem was to persuade
the British officials to stay. The Authority was trying to avoid a
situation in which Africanization was pushed too fast and in which,
as in the Congo, the expatriates had to be invited to come back.
There was no point, he suggested, in replacing the British with
Russians or Americans who did not know local conditions. Adu
reminded the House that Ghana, which had started its Africanization schemes in 1950, had not dispensed with its expatriate administrative officers until 1960, and added that it was inconsistent for
members to press for Africanization of the posts and telegraphs but

to complain when telephone calls took longer to put through.[11] Adu resigned shortly afterwards and was replaced by a Tanganyikan. In 1964 East Africans were also appointed as General Manager of the East African Railways and Postmaster General.

THE UNIVERSITY

In addition to the Common Services, the territories at independence shared the University of East Africa. Of its three component University Colleges, Makerere in Uganda was the oldest. This had started as a technical school in 1922 and its history will be seen in the next chapter. Makerere entered into a relationship with London University in 1949, its first graduates taking degrees in 1953. The University College of Nairobi was founded in 1954 as the Royal Technical College; it subsequently, however, considerably changed its character and ran arts as well as professional courses. The University College of Dar-es-Salaam was opened in 1961, with the first Law Faculty in East Africa. Thus, while each of the Colleges continued to run general courses, each also had departments which were not duplicated elsewhere and in which students from the other territories could be enrolled. From 1963 the London relationship ended and the University of East Africa awarded its own degrees which were recognized in the United Kingdom.

While the co-operation of the three governments in maintaining a single university and avoiding duplication of effort has been generally commended, we have seen how the Udoji Commission criticized the 'standards' which were maintained: at a time when the governments and the Common Services were anxiously waiting for every African graduate who was turned out, the Colleges appeared to be restricting their output.

The difficulty arose from the relationship with London University. When the British universities in 1949 raised their entry qualification to the possession of the Higher Certificate, for a time several of the African University Colleges were allowed to continue to receive students with School Certificate and to run 4 year instead of 3 year courses. In 1960, however, Makerere and the Royal College ceased to do this. Thus exactly at the most critical moment before independence they had empty places. To some extent this embarrassing situation could be explained as being due to the transfer of first year university work to the new VI forms of the secondary schools. Some defended the colleges also by maintaining that at a time of expansion it was right for the number of places to exceed the demand. But hundreds of East Africans who might have filled these places were studying in the U.S.A. and in Eastern Europe and elsewhere, wherever a Higher Certificate was not required as a condition of admission. To future British historians, the educational policy of the colonial power in the last days of empire is likely to seem extraordinary. To the French, who have made cultural ties the most lasting bond with their former colonies, the indifference of the British to the consequences of their policy may well be quite incomprehensible.

Its results may be symbolized in the story of a secondary school boy in Nyasaland in 1958 who told his mother that he wanted to go to America, where he had heard that Africans could find places in the colleges. She gave him her blessing and a bag of flour, and he set off to walk to America. After fifteen months and many adventures he arrived in Kampala in Uganda to learn that if he could reach America his fees would be paid, but that he must get there on his own. So he walked on to Khartoum, where he was picked up by a student airlift, two years and 2,500 miles after leaving home. He returned from America to occupy a distinguished seat at his country's independence celebrations. This was the type of enthusiast who was lost by the institutions of higher education in British Africa and in Britain itself.[12]

The question of university standards was complicated by the fact that the university staff were mostly British, who were inclined to insist that they would not teach at what they considered to be a pre-university VI form level, though at an earlier period in England itself the majority of students had taken pass degrees; and as we have seen in relation to West Africa, the specialized honours courses which were organized in the African universities were possibly less useful at this stage to African governments than would be courses which led to a larger output of potential administrators with broad pass degrees.[13] The exodus to universities in America and other countries outside the British system was to cause considerable problems as to recognition of their degrees in the government services when they returned.

DEFENCE

East Africa's defence force was the King's African Rifles for which, until Tanganyika became independent, the East African Defence Committee in Nairobi had overall responsibility. Its battalions were recruited on a territorial basis. As in India and in West Africa they tended to be selected from 'martial tribes'. Thus in Uganda the Acholi and in Kenya the Kamba were strongly represented, while more educated and politically influential tribes, such as the Baganda in Uganda and the Kikuyu in Kenya, were seldom recruited. When the military authorities began to be concerned with localization, officer candidates were pre-selected by the territories but were finally selected by the command headquarters. The results have been described as 'bizarre, and significant of the lack of realism which periodically invaded the politics of the East African countries during the last five years'.[14] In Kenya and Tanganyika the policy of multi-racialism and of high educational standards prevailed. The result was that at the end of 1961 at independence Tanganyika had accepted only two Africans and one Asian for training as officers. In Kenya by this time only local Europeans and Asians had been commissioned as no suitable African applicant from secondary school could be found. In Uganda only three African officers had been selected.

It was Kenya which first saw the danger of such a situation in light of the lessons of the Congo. From December 1961 the School Certificate qualification was no longer demanded and commissions were given to the effendis, locally commissioned officers whose status corresponded to that of Viceroy's Commissioned Officers in India. At the same time N.C.O.s were sent to England to be trained as officers. Thus by April 1963, six months before independence, Kenya had 84 African officers, about half the total number.

A long term Africanization measure, modelled on British experience in India, failed dismally. A 'junior leaders company' was formed of 150 boys from the three territories who were given pre-military training as potential officer cadets. They mutinied in March 1963, complaining that they had been called 'baboons and monkeys' by the staff and that they had been relegated for not passing examinations. Eighty-three of them were dismissed.

Early in 1964 there were much more serious mutinies, first in the Tanganyikan Army and then in those of Kenya and Uganda. The Tanganyika mutiny seems to have been partly due to discontent among African N.C.O.s because the pace of Africanization had not kept up with that of Kenya, though it appears that, unknown to the mutineers, the Government already had plans by which all officers would be Africans by the end of 1965. In none of the territories had Africanization in the army kept pace with that in the Civil Service. N.C.O.s and troops considered that they had a right to higher pay when they saw the rapid promotion of their civilian friends and relations. All three mutinies were put down by the intervention of British troops called in by the independent Governments, but not before the Tanganyikan mutineers had deported their British officers. Though the leaders were given severe sentences, the position was never restored. For better or worse, executive posts were now rapidly Africanized, and responsibility for military training was shared by foreign missions as diverse in Tanganyika as those from the U.K., West Germany, and China.

REFERENCES

[1] Table compiled from Guy Hunter's report to East African University on *High Level Manpower in East Africa*, 1962, unpublished.

[2] *Report of the Commission on the Civil Services of Kenya, Tanganyika, Uganda and Zanzibar*, 1947–48 (Holmes Report) HMSO Col/223, 1948, pp. 23–28.

[3] *Report of the Commission on the East African Territories and East African High Commission* 1953–54 (Lidbury Report), London, Crown Agents, 1954.

[4] *Report of the Commission on the Public Services of the East African Territories of the East African High Commission* (Flemming Report), Entebbe, 1960.

[5] *Report on the Localization of the Civil Service of the East Africa High Commission* (Ramage Report), Nairobi, 1961, p. 17 and passim.

[6] *Report of the Africanization Commission* (Udoji Report), E.A.C.S.O., Nairobi, 1963.

[7] ibid., p. 5.

[8] ibid., p. 17.

[9] E.A.C.S.O., Nairobi, S.P. No. 1 of 1963, p. 2.

[10] *Proceedings of the Central Legislative Assembly Debates*, Vol. II— 2 Nov., E.A.C.S.O., Nairobi, 1963, pp. 622–646 and 665–673.

[11] ibid., pp. 673–681 and pp. 726–738.

[12] *Reporter*, Nairobi, 19 June, 1964, p. 32.

[13] See Sir Eric Ashby, *African Universities and Western Tradition*, p. 32. Also Sir A. Carr Saunders, *New Universities Overseas*, p. 133.

[14] W. Gutteridge, op. cit., *Military Institutions in New States*, p. 109, which is the main source for this section.

CHAPTER X

The Territories

TANGANYIKA – UGANDA – KENYA

'If the mission's timetable were accepted it would not mean self-government but either administrative and economic collapse or the vesting of excessive power in a largely non-African civil service.'

–U.K. GOVERNMENT'S OBSERVATIONS IN 1955 ON A UNITED NATIONS MISSION'S PROPOSAL THAT TANGANYIKA BECOME SELF-GOVERNING IN 1974

Whilst, as has been seen in the previous chapter, the East African territories had both common problems and joint institutions, the differences in their political history considerably affected the way in which their public services developed. The most important factors were in Uganda the missionary influence and the treaties with the Kingdoms; in Kenya the European settlers and in Tanganyika the Mandate and Trusteeship relationship. These resulted in Tanganyika being both the most backward of the three territories educationally and yet the first to become independent.

TANGANYIKA

The British conquered Tanganyika from the Germans in the First World War and retained it under a Mandate from the League of Nations. The Germans had administered Tanganyika through a system of direct rule in which African subordinate officials were responsible to German district officers for the administration of sub-districts. They relied mainly on Swahili speaking Africans, many of whom had previously been employed by the Sultan of Zanzibar.

The British, once the emergency problems of the postwar period were over, introduced a system of indirect rule. Sir Donald Cameron, who was Governor from 1925 to 1931, had served in the West Indies and Nigeria. He was determined to avoid creating a system of education and administration such as, he considered, had turned out Africans who were 'incomplete and bad imitations of white men' in the West Indies and Sierra Leone.[1] Under his system of native administration, which was a modified form of that established in Northern Nigeria, he intended that 'the position of the chiefs will be guarded against assaults which may be made against it by Europeanized natives seeking to obtain political control of the country',[2] though he believed that after a few generations indirect rule would provide 'stepping stones' to a wider form of political organization. A corollary to his policy was an educational system which did not over-emphasize the literary side, and he adopted the memorandum of 1925 of the Advisory Committee as his 'Charter of education'.[3]

Cameron's policies were enthusiastically supported by his Director of Education, Rivers-Smith, whose annual reports throw considerable light on the reasons for Tanganyika's subsequent educational backwardness. Under German rule an extensive network of mission schools had been supplemented by government schools at regional headquarters, to which the brighter boys proceeded in order to learn the German language and enter the administration. This educational system was almost entirely disrupted during the war of 1914–18. Under the British the missionaries continued to carry the main load, though from 1925 they received grants-in-aid. The government, however, between 1926 and 1931 set up 'central' or 'middle' schools, which were senior primary boarding schools, in each Province; in several of these priority was given to educating the sons of chiefs.

'Agriculture,' wrote Rivers-Smith in his first annual report in 1923, 'shall be the keynote of our educational programme'. It was his intention 'to reduce to the minimum the class who, as a result of being able to read and write, despise the calling of their parents though unfitted for anything better'.[4] The door was not to be closed to the boy of proven ability but educational activities should be rigidly limited to the country's employment needs: a sufficient number of boys would be trained for clerical and technical work, and there would be schools for the sons of chiefs. Beyond this, education should be concentrated on community life and agricultural activities.

The number to whom English was taught was deliberately restricted. Thus there would be little fear for many years that Tanganyika would be subjected to political agitation from within, provided that 'the brake on education' was 'firmly though wisely applied'.[5]

By inculcating the spirit of the English Public School Rivers-Smith believed that he was making an important contribution to the system of indirect rule, for 'the Prefect System made possible the full realization of the British ideal to delegate authority to those who by heredity ought to possess and exercise it.'[6] One of his officers, A. T. Lacey, who ran the school for the sons of Chiefs at Tabora, also believed that 'the underlying principle of the English Public School holds good all over the earth'; Lacey opposed the introduction of the teaching of English, and his prefects were chosen for their smartness at drill.[7] Rivers-Smith had a particular horror of urbanism, which he considered would reduce the country's population to an uneconomic level by spreading venereal disease.[8] The fundamental necessity, he wrote in 1926, was to foster the African's aptitude for agriculture 'in order that Africa may fulfil her obligations to meet continually growing demands for her products'.[9] In 1929 he suggested that 'until the African has developed a right sense of values, a matter of generations, it may be that his interests will be best served by avoiding the confusion which arises through a misunderstanding of such terms as secondary school, high school, or college'.[10] In 1930 he reported that 'no secondary education in the sense generally accepted in European countries is yet given or required'.[11] All post-primary education was still vocational, and in the following year the Acting Director stated that 'There will be no need to provide University education for the children of this territory for many years'.[12] Rivers-Smith was seldom optimistic about African intellectual capacity, and quoted with approval in one of his later reports a missionary's statement that 'the material is bad. It is the iron hand of heredity. Generations of intemperance and incredible sexual excess do not produce brain power.'[13]

After the departure of Rivers-Smith in 1930, his successor had little chance to develop a different policy, for in the economic crisis the budget of the education department was progressively reduced from £122,000 in 1931 to £72,000 in 1935. The money was saved by reductions in European staff. These were made mainly at the expense of the higher classes in the central schools, thus curtailing the prospects of Tanganyikan students who wanted to go to Makerere College in Uganda for a full secondary education. Most of the central schools indeed were now closed. In 1936 the budgetary position began to improve, but again from 1939 to 1945 European staff were greatly reduced in order to serve in the armed forces or in other departments of government. Both the economic crisis and the War in the long run however may have helped to accelerate Africanization of the services, for departments which could not obtain Europeans now became interested in training local people to replace them.

The Permanent Commission on Mandates of the League of Nations did not do much to press the mandatory power to train and recruit local inhabitants for the government services. They obtained an assurance in 1933 that preference would be given to local inhabitants in the subordinate services, but this appears to have been an economy measure. A statement in 1938 that it was the firmly established policy to employ Africans 'in any posts for which their capacities fitted them' was not very meaningful either in theory or in practice.[14]

Under the Trusteeship Agreement which was made with the United Nations in 1946, however, the British Government as administering authority was bound 'to assure to the inhabitants of Tanganyika a progressively increasing share in the administrative and other services of the territory'. The U.N. Trusteeship Council, through its annual questionnaires and its triennial visiting missions, showed a continuous interest in the point. In 1947 a ten year plan for development of education was initiated: but though the primary enrolment target figure was exceeded, only half the projected enrolment in secondary schools was obtained, as an inadequate number of suitable candidates came up from the primary schools. By 1956 Tanganyika had 156 students on post-secondary courses at Makerere but it was never able to take up its full quota of places there. Unlucky right until the end, the Education Department was obliged by financial stringency to curtail a 5 year plan for expansion of secondary schools which was launched in 1957. At the time of independence the level of African secondary school enrolment in Tanganyika in relation to the population was only half that of Uganda or Kenya.

The British Government was able to report to the United Nations in 1954 that in accordance with the Lidbury Report's recommendations it had, like the other East African governments, decided gradually to replace expatriate officers in Tanganyika by local people, and had established its civil service on non-racial lines. But it described as 'ill-informed' the comments of the U.N. Visiting Mission in that year that the pace of educational expansion had been too slow;[15] and the Governor two years later, though stating that it was necessary to train Africans for the civil service, insisted that 'standards must not be lowered at any cost' and that those Africans who could not absorb either the training or traditions of the service must be relentlessly weeded out.[16]

No one, of course, foresaw the final acceleration towards independence. In 1954 the U.N. Visiting Mission proposed that a time-table should be set up to achieve self-government in twenty years. The United Kingdom Government replied that such a time-table 'would not mean self-government but either administrative and economic collapse or the vesting of excessive power in a largely non-African civil service.' They added that they did not consider it justifiable in any circumstances to adopt policies which might tend to lower the standards of Administrative Officers.[17] In 1956 the nationalist leader Julius Nyerere was proposing independence by 1968: in 1959 he asked for it in 1964: but he got it in 1961. Not much perhaps could be done at the last moment to expand the educational system. The University College in Dar-es-Salaam was opened in 1961. In the same year Nyerere started Kivukoni College, modelled on Ruskin College, Oxford, to provide a year's course in government for party workers and trade union officials. British officials appeared unenthusiastic about this venture, which did not fit into normal educational or administrative procedures. Nyerere himself was aware of the importance of localization. In December 1959 he stated that 'before independence we must have a minimum of local men in the Civil Service'.[18] Though attacked by the Tanganyika Federation of Labour for not accelerating Africanization, he maintained that local people of any race should be equally eligible for the civil service. With very limited resources, he gave priority to replacing Europeans by Africans in the districts, 'where contact with the people is closest',[19] and a number of African officers were trained and appointed as District Officers. But in the Secretariat in the months before independence there were few signs of Africanization at senior levels. Even in such sensitive posts as Permanent Secretary of Foreign Affairs or Permanent Secretary to the Prime Minister it was openly assumed that the expatriates would continue for years after independence. And, as a Ford Foundation report pointed out, at a time when the main problem was to adjust the job content to the reduced qualifications

191

of available candidates, almost every ministry was announcing its intention to raise its entry standards.[20] Despite mounting criticism from T.A.N.U. back-benchers, the question of Africanization was not thrashed out in public reports or parliamentary commissions as it had been in Ghana and Nigeria and was being in Uganda. A remark of a member of the Legislature Council in June 1961 reflected the widespread disquiet. 'Africanization,' he said, 'is a word widely talked of in the bars and outside this Assembly. The policy of the Prime Minister needs full explanation to the people'.[21]

When party workers and Members of Parliament visited the Secretariat after independence and found the principal offices still full of white faces, there was an explosion of pent up feeling which contributed to the temporary retirement of Nyerere as Prime Minister. Most of the expatriate Permanent Secretaries were replaced almost overnight by Africans who had no opportunity to understudy them and several of whom had only a primary education. The new Prime Minister, Rashidi Kawawa, yielded to the storm, and abandoned Nyerere's multiracial approach. He announced to the National Assembly in February 1962 that he was setting up an Africanization Commission which would 'ensure that every single post in the civil service either has an African already in it, or an African starting to take it over, or a plan for training an African to fill it'.[22]

The Commission, which was headed by S. A. Maswanya, Minister without Portfolio, reported in June 1963, and its recommendations were accepted. Now for the first time, eighteen months after independence, a plan for the future of the services was published. Immediately, priority was given to placing Africans in sensitive and key posts; throughout the services when an African was qualified and suitable he was to be offered an appointment, if necessary by replacement of a non-Tanganyikan. Eventually the racial inbalance of the services would thus be corrected and at that stage the civil service would be open to Tanganyikans of all races without discrimination.

Administrative posts were Africanized very rapidly after independence. Provincial and Deputy Commissioners were replaced by political Regional and Area Commissioners and the expatriates who did not leave mostly either became Secretaries at the Area or Regional level or were transferred to the judiciary. In the Secretariat the first African Permanent Secretaries were replaced by others with better qualifications. By 1964 several of these posts were held by young Makerere graduates. Others were former teachers; the remainder had long years in government service, having started in the clerical service and been transferred to the administrative service as district officers.

The position in the professional departments at independence was even more difficult. In 1962 in the Forestry Department all 44 professional posts were held by expatriates and the first 4 Africans were only expected to graduate in 1965. There were no African engineers or geologists, and none were expected to qualify in the foreseeable future. Progress in the Health Department, owing to the early development of the Makerere medical school, was more encouraging, and there were 17 African medical officers. 60% of the gazetted officers in the police were Africans.[23]

Although in September 1963 expatriates still filled 45% of the senior posts on the professional side, they left more rapidly than they could be replaced by qualified Africans. Whilst the Ministry of Agriculture still retained about half of its British officers in September 1964, in order to replace the others and to staff development schemes it had obtained the services of Israelis, Indians, Danes, Italians, and Norwegians as well as of Russian veterinarians who did not speak English but were accompanied by interpreters.

The Education Department was also severely affected. 105 British education officers, mostly secondary school teachers, left in 1962. There were only 20 Tanganyikan graduate teachers in 1963, and many of the best qualified Africans had been promoted to senior posts in other departments. The departing British were to some extent replaced by young American volunteers, but newspapers published complaints that these strayed from the School Certificate curriculum.

The departure of the expatriates immediately after independence was accelerated by the lack of a clear statement by the government of its Africanization policy.[24] The army mutiny of 1964 which led to a feeling of insecurity, and in some cases high tempers over the way in which the Dar-es-Salaam Club was taken over by the government also precipitated decisions to leave.

The speed of Africanization at the higher levels increased the difficulty of staffing at the middle level. The government was so concerned at the competition between departments for the services of School Certificate holders that it made an advance allocation of those who were expected to pass the examination in December 1962. Of 955 African boys and girls available, 420 were to move up to the Higher School Certificate class. Teacher training obtained 300. The specialized services, such as health, agriculture, and community development, received only about a third of their requirement for immediate employment or departmental training. The common cadres, which provided the secretarial, accounting and clerical grades, obtained no allocation at all.[25]

Not only were the common cadres weakened at independence by promotions from their ranks, but they also lost the services of the wives of expatriate officials who had filled most of the posts of private secretaries and now departed with their husbands. At the same time, as the Maswanya Commission noted, 'The popular pressure for Africanization both from inside and outside the Civil Service tends to concentrate on the common cadres. This is partly because of the comparatively large number of posts, mostly concentrated in the ministry headquarters, and also because the generalized nature of most of the posts precludes a precise definition of the "qualities" and "qualifications" required in terms of educational achievement or of certificates and diplomas'.[26] By 1963, in fact, the main pressure was on Africanization of the Asian posts at the middle level, since the Europeans at the top level had already been replaced insofar as there were qualified Africans available. The Asians were given two years after independence in which to decide whether to take Tanganyikan citizenship. It is estimated that about 25% of those in government service did so. In January 1964 President Nyerere announced that the period in which preference was to be given to Africans was over, and that from this time there would be no discrimination between Tanganyikan citizens in government appointments.[27]

Much could be added on the melancholy results of the failure of the Tanganyikan Government to prepare the Services for independence. Though the Mzumbe school trained district officers before independence, an Institute of Administration which trained Secretariat officers was only set up after independence. One reason why it was so difficult to find Africans for the government service at independence was that the secondary school leaving age was raised in 1961. The educational weakness could not be rapidly overcome at independence. In 1962 there were 205 Tanganyikans in the University of East Africa and another 349 overseas. Until they returned and gained experience makeshift arrangements had to continue. Administrative standards inevitably dropped and imperilled development plans, for which in 1964 the government sought to recruit an additional 440 foreign experts.[28]

The relationship between the civil service and the party after independence appeared somewhat uneasy. African civil servants, who under British rule had not been allowed to join the party, were now inclined to allege that the latter was staffed by men who had not been bright enough to enter government service. On the other hand politicians were unlikely to give the customary respect to the advice of civil servants when the latter were less well acquainted with their functions and held lower educational qualifications than the ministers themselves. In an attempt to improve the relationship in 1964 civil servants were urged by the government to join the party, and in some cases the heads of government offices led their staff in procession to enrol.

UGANDA

Of the three East African territories Uganda was the most far-sighted in its approach to localization. Unlike Kenya, which was dominated by white settlers, or Tanganyika, which was conquered from the Germans, Uganda was a territory where the missionaries for long held the initiative. Summoned by an appeal from the explorer, H. M. Stanley, and initially encouraged by a ruler who saw them as a counterpoise to Egyptian influence from the north, British C.M.S. missionaries arrived in Uganda in 1877, followed by French White Fathers in 1879. It was only in 1888 that the British government gave responsibility for the administration in the country to the Imperial British East Africa Company: when the Company decided to withdraw, the C.M.S. led the campaign for the retention of Uganda which persuaded a divided Liberal Government to establish a Protectorate.

Though described as a Protectorate, Uganda included four kingdoms with a 'treaty' relationship with Britain, of which Buganda was the most important. In light of the treaty relationships very little land was alienated to British settlers. In Buganda an upper class existed, some of whose sons were educated first at missionary schools for the sons of chiefs and later in England. The government of the Kabaka of Uganda employed a number of these on their return. There were other factors in Uganda's educational advance. English was the lingua franca, instead of Swahili which was used in Kenya and Tanganyika. Cotton and coffee, produced by peasant farmers, provided the revenue from which the government was able to finance secondary education.

As early as 1900 Sir Harry Johnston was urging the missionaries to produce African clerks for the government. His European staff was very small, and agents from Buganda were used in extending British rule outside that kingdom. They were not always recruited with care. Postlethwaite found in Busoga in 1918 that most of them were 'ex-interpreters, office boys and even an old Provincial Commissioner's cook'.[29] He sent them home and used local Busoga interpreters instead.

Sir Hesketh Bell stated a policy as Governor in 1906, which on the whole was consistently applied. 'Our policy should be the creation of an essentially African state, which should prove by its stability and honest government that pure-bred Africans are really capable of governing themselves without suppressing the traditions of their race or abandoning manners and customs which are not consistent with humanity'; though he added that there must be 'a complete disregard of the vociferations of any semi-educated group, which may, long before the country is fit for such a thing, clamour for complete self-government'.[30]

Elementary and secondary education in Uganda were left entirely in the hands of the missions until 1924, when in light of the Phelps-Stokes Report the government set up an Education Department and a system of grants and supervision. The missions appeared more interested than the government in the formation of an elite: the C.M.S. on the inspiration of A. G. Fraser established King's School, Budo, on Public School lines. The government, in a country which was mainly administered by an unusual system of indirect rule, was anxious to do nothing which might upset the existing social order. In 1933 the Department of Education considered that an annual output of 69 graduates from junior secondary schools was adequate. Even when full School Certificate courses began at Makerere all students were required to promise to enter one of the professional courses subsequently. Between 1925 and 1935 the government in fact wanted post primary education to be vocational.[31]

What distinguishes Uganda from Tanganyika and Kenya is the early vision. Hussey, a great Director of Education, who came from the Sudan to Uganda and eventually went on to Nigeria to found Yaba College, took it for granted in 1925 that Makerere was 'destined to become the University College for the Protectorate'.[32] Hussey was an enthusiast for Africanization of the services, pointing out that the savings in salaries which would result from this would exceed the government's entire education budget. He was however considerably influenced by Mayhew's book on Indian education. He wished 'to avoid at all costs ruthless westernization accomplished through the medium of education'. The object rather should be 'to allow African education to develop on its own soil, while making use of teachers and literature from Europe', to foster an African culture 'different but in no way inferior to the cultures of Europe and America'.[33] He was always on his guard, in light of India's experience, of turning out 'a class of senior educated misfits who are likely to feel a grievance against the system that produced them and become eventually dangerous',[34] and he started at Budo a 'yeomen farmers course' for boys who did not show sufficient promise on the literary side.

When Hussey left in 1929, the courses at Makerere were still all professional. His successor, E. G. Morris, felt that there was bound to be prejudice against the educated African in government and that it was better not to pay him a salary commensurate to his educational qualifications until he had proved his worth.[35] In 1933, however, he suggested, without effect, that it might be time for an administrative cadet service for Africans to be formed from the boys who were now taking School Certificate.[36] In the following year some of the junior secondary classes were closed because the number of pupils being sent up to Makerere exceeded the requirements of the country.

There was an early emphasis on technical education. Makerere College was first set up in 1921 for training of artisans; it later became a secondary school which by 1935 was producing students who passed School Certificate. This caused the Governor, Sir Bernard Bourdillon, to reflect on the dangers of too much secondary education;[37] his successor, Sir Philip Mitchell, had a much more positive attitude to the development of an educated African class and caused the Secretary of State to send out a Commission on Higher Education in East Africa in 1937 under the chairmanship of Lord de la Warr.

Its report has considerable interest, for the commission asked the three governments to forecast their needs for Africans with higher and secondary education over the next ten years. The replies were 910 for Uganda, 346 for Kenya and 415 for Tanganyika, which reflected how considerably in advance of the other territories was Uganda's policy on the question at this time. The Commission still saw the role of Africans as assistants to European administrators and specialists, but it recommended that a Higher College be established at Makerere which as soon as possible should become the University College of East Africa. It also stated firmly that the danger of creating a class of educated unemployed was negligible.[38]

Although places at Makerere were open to students from Kenya and Tanganyika, whose governments contributed to its budget, there is no doubt that its establishment in Uganda, close to the capital, provided a constant stimulus to local educational progress. Much earlier than in Tanganyika and Kenya there was a policy that Africans should be advanced in the government services. In 1929 government departments were instructed that all clerical staff should be African if possible and that Asians should only be engaged on a temporary basis. 'The Government recognizes,' the Chief Secretary told the Legislative Council in 1928, 'that many Asiatics are permanently settled in the country, but considers that the natives are still more permanent'.[39]

In the final stages also Uganda was more conscious than Kenya or Tanganyika of the need for Africanization of the services. Sir Andrew Cohen, who was Governor from 1952 to 1957, probably considered that independence would not come until about 1970; but even to work within this concept proved considerably more realistic than the policies of his neighbours. In 1952 he appointed two committees. The first under Bernard de Bunsen, Principal of Makerere College, reviewed the educational system and made proposals which brought about a rapid expansion of secondary education. The second under J. V. Wild, was a Standing Committee on Recruitment, Training and Promotion of Africans to Higher Posts. This committee over the next three years maintained pressure on the departments of government to think in terms of Africanization, and it produced a plan by which 25% of administrative and professional posts were to be Africanized by 1962. Its final report in 1955 seems somewhat unimaginative in light of subsequent developments. It stated that it would be 'disastrous for the Service and hence for the country' if the standards of the Civil Service were lowered. There was no intention to suggest appointment of Africans to higher posts merely because they were Africans: places could easily be found for qualified Africans through the normal process of wastage. The report recommended successfully, however, that supernumerary vacancies should be created for qualified Africans where no immediate vacancies were available. It also reorganized the scholarship programme, and could claim when it handed over its work to a permanent Public Service

Commission in 1955 that it had 'started the first trickle of Africans into higher posts'.[40] Cohen's announcement when he appointed the Committee was notably far-sighted in stating that in future, when government servants were considered for promotion, experience in government service might be regarded as a substitute for academic qualifications.[41]

Like the other East African countries, Uganda in 1954 created a unified civil service of all races and in the following year set up a Public Services Commission, one of whose duties was to ensure that no recruitment should be made outside East Africa if a qualified local person were available. Between 1952 and 1958 secondary school enrolment was almost doubled, and scholarship schemes were greatly expanded.

In 1961, eighteen months before independence, whilst the Government still insisted that administrative standards must not be lowered, it modified a policy established in 1958 by which qualifications acquired by Ugandans in India and the U.S.A. could only fit them for appointments if they were recognized in the United Kingdom. It was more frank at this stage than Tanganyika or Kenya in openly referring to its objective as 'Africanization' rather than 'localization'. Whilst showing that the numbers of Africans in senior posts had risen from 5 in 1952 to 130 in 1961, the government admitted that Africans were not obtaining sufficient experience in the very top or Superscale posts. To this end it introduced a scheme before independence by which Africans might be promoted over the heads of expatriates and the latter compensated. A training centre for administrative officers was also set up, modelled on that of Northern Nigeria.[42]

Early in 1962, six months before independence, D. J. K. Nabete, one of the cabinet ministers, and T. L. Luke, a civil servant from Sierra Leone, were appointed as Africanization Commissioners. Their recommendations showed a thorough study of the history of Africanization elsewhere and of the lessons of the Congo, in light of which they indicated guiding principles. Certain politically sensitive posts should be listed immediately as 'Reserved' and filled by Africans by independence. These should include all posts in the Ministry of Foreign Affairs. Four African Permanent Secretaries should be appointed before independence, and understudies chosen immediately for these posts in the remaining ministries. Standards must be flexible. Most of the progress achieved in Africanization, they believed, had been due to a temporary and reasonable reduction of standards. Pass degrees had been accepted in place of honours degrees and experience in place of university studies. This temporary relaxation was better than leaving the posts vacant.

At this stage about one-third of administrative posts and one-fifth of professional posts were filled by Ugandans. The Commissioners concluded that 'the measures taken between 1952 and 1959 though producing no spectacular result, prepared the ground for the bumper crop now being harvested'. They estimated that it should be possible to Africanize all but a few scientific technical and teaching posts in five years and the rest in ten years, though they appreciated the difficulty of retaining a sufficient number of expatriates meanwhile. They suggested that the first priority should be to use the limited output from secondary schools and universities in the administration, while expatriates were retained in the teaching profession.[43]

The Ministers in their statement in the Nabete-Luke report were less satisfied than the Commissioners with progress in Africanization, which they described as having been 'intolerably slow' before independence. 'The Government believes,' they said, 'that the previous colonial administration has laid too much stress on maintenance of standards in a territory which has comparatively slender resources of finance and manpower. Staffing at senior levels has been too lavish, and Government is determined to reduce the Civil Service establishment to a level which the country is capable of achieving'.[44] Somewhat surprisingly they objected at this point, on the verge of independence, to the use of the term 'Africanization' and declared that in future 'Ugandanization' would be used. Considerable efforts were made to induce expatriates to remain by giving them extra increments and allowing them to continue indefinitely, with the right to retire at any time. Only 7 expatriate officers were asked to retire before independence, but 484 out of 1,150 of those with pension rights had given notice of retirement.

The Africans who took over from the British in Uganda were rather better educated and more experienced than those who did so in Kenya and considerably more so than those in Tanganyika. At the beginning of 1965 all the Permanent Secretaries and ten out of twelve district commissioners were graduates. While the Provincial Commissioners were abolished, civil servants were retained as deputy commissioners. Though Uganda was more advanced than the other two territories it retained its expatriate administrators longer; there were still four British Permanent Secretaries two years after independence.

KENYA

Though the dominant position of the European settlers for long delayed Africanization in Kenya, in the last stages it helped indirectly to accelerate it. What is now Kenya was administered by the Imperial British East Africa Company from 1888 and became a British Protectorate in 1895. European settlement in the Highlands started about 1902. Neither the settlers nor the British administrators had much interest in the education of Africans. Dundas, who was a District Officer from 1908–1914 found that most Europeans considered African education 'unwise if not pernicious',[45] and until 1924 it was left to the missionaries, except insofar as the government from 1911 made grants for industrial training or in respect of Africans who passed departmental examinations. When the Government began to recognize a responsibility for African education the Education Department's native policy was described by the Director in 1924 as based on Booker T. Washington's manual 'Working with hands'.[46] 'Just as hard work has been found useful in the training of mentally defective children,' he wrote in his annual report for 1926, 'so the most useful training which the African can receive in his present condition is continual contact with material processes.'[47] Three-fifths of the time at government central schools was devoted to gardening and handicrafts.

Such an approach was not generally accepted by the missionaries. Dr. Norman Leys protested that 'what the African in Kenya needs is knowledge, enlightenment, the acquisition of the appetite that makes men seek the truth. He needs them exactly as the whole human race needs them. . . . No people in the world has a keener appetite for education or a greater aptitude for learning'.[48] The Government's policy, he suggested, was a disastrous amalgam of the views of the settlers, who wanted the Africans only to be trained as efficient labourers, and of the ill-founded theories of the anthropologists who had invented an 'African mentality'.[49]

The government's favourite educational institution was the Jeanes School, founded on the advice of the Phelps-Stokes mission in 1925. Here 'Africans of high character and tactful disposition but not of high intellectual attainment' were trained as supervisors, whose duties would be to ensure that the village schools gave children an education which would not divide them from village life and cause them to seek employment in the towns. The Protestant Missionaries founded in the same year the Alliance High School, which was the first institution to provide secondary education for Africans. In 1933 the Director of Education considered that the missionaries were spending a disproportionate amount of money on the central boarding schools as opposed to the elementary schools. He had a battle on two fronts; for at the same time the Local Native Councils were pressing to be allowed to use their funds for extending secondary instead of elementary education, in spite of the Director's assurance that the present facilities provided in central schools, secondary schools and at Makerere were disproportionate to the needs of the African Community.[50] The enthusiasm for 'literary' education was also shown when the Kikuyu Independent Schools, which were started by the Kikuyu after their rift with the Scottish missionaries, taught in English instead of the vernacular even in the first grade.

The economic crisis of 1929 and the Second World War had a similar effect in Kenya as in Tanganyika. The budget for African education was cut in the thirties and development of secondary education curtailed in the forties. From about 1934 Africans began to be employed in office jobs; but the Pim Report of 1936 on Kenya's financial position pointed out that the Kenya Government was not using Africans as extensively as were the other East African governments, and that European administrative officers were doing work which was carried out elsewhere by clerks.[51] We have already seen that the Kenya Government showed less interest than Uganda and Tanganyika in using Africans in the services, when the de la Warr Commission in 1937 asked the three governments to forecast their needs for Africans with higher education.[52] Meanwhile those Kenyans who were taking professional courses at Makerere would sometimes try to move to South African universities in order to take arts degrees, because they were dissatisfied with the status which their Makerere qualifications would bring them.[53]

Even after the Second War the Kenya Government's reluctance to use Africans continued to be noted. The Lidbury Commission in 1954 were struck by the number of European clerks who were drawing relatively high salaries but performing minor duties.[54] In 1955 Europeans represented 28% of the total number of officers in the administrative and professional grades of government service, compared with 18% in Tanganyika and 16% in Uganda. The Royal

Commission on East Africa in that year found that there was far less chance for the African in the public service to rise to the higher appointments in Kenya than in the other territories.[55]

Throughout the Colonial period Kenya was 'more intensively' administered than its neighbours. Initially this was because the European settlers demanded a high standard of services, and because there was no Indirect Rule; the trend was accentuated during the Mau Mau emergency. The Economy Commission of 1962 considered that 'the point of economical administration had been reached and passed'. They questioned whether for example 18 government architects were needed, or 78 expatriate personal secretaries, or a police force as large as that of Tanganyika and Uganda combined, and they generally criticized the overgrading of work.[56]

The fact that Kenya had twice as many expatriate officers as Tanganyika or Uganda, however, meant that in the closing stages before independence a proportionately greater staff effort could be devoted to Africanization and training schemes. In 1960 there were only five Africans in senior posts; in 1961 several African Assistant Secretaries were appointed. When at independence in December 1963 the British Permanent Secretaries were replaced by Africans, all of these were graduates and half had worked in the ministries over which they now presided. Though their average age was only 33, the results of expanded higher education were apparent in Nairobi at independence, as they had not been in Dar-es-Salaam. Below the Permanent Secretaries most of the Assistant Secretaries and District Offices had been through six month courses at the Kenya Institute of Administration which had been running for over two years before independence, mainly with American money and British staff. Elspeth Huxley was charmed and Tom Mboya contemptuous at the 'messnights where they punctiliously passed the port to the left' and other activities 'designed to turn out replicas of the British Officer and gentleman',[57] but the common training was an important factor in an administrative transition which was much smoother in Kenya than in Tanganyika.

The government had been stimulated by private initiative. Tom Mboya, the political and trade union leader, in 1959 persuaded American private organizations and colleges to give scholarships to several hundred Africans, mostly from Kenya, whose educational attainments did not allow them to enter the University of East Africa. How casually the scheme operated has been recounted by several of the scholars.[58] The first airlifts were of clerks and primary school teachers, secretaries, draughtsmen and laboratory assistants, surveyors and postal clerks, salesmen and health inspectors. Many of these failed to complete their courses: later the scheme was tightened up and a School Certificate and aptitude test were required. The American scheme was paralleled by the airlift organized by Oginga Odinga, subsequently Vice-President of Kenya, to Communist countries. In the last year before independence only 220 Kenya Africans studied in the United Kingdom compared with 1,356 elsewhere abroad.[59]

Kenya had not only more European officials but more Asian officials than Uganda or Tanganyika. There were also more Asians than Africans in secondary schools and in the University College, Nairobi. In 1961 the Chief Secretary announced that it was the government's policy to move towards a position where the proportions of the population were more accurately reflected in the services; Mr. Kenyatta as Prime Minister in 1963 subsequently endorsed this policy. There was not in Kenya, as in Tanganyika or in E.A.C.S.O., even after independence, however, an official policy of 'Africanization': it remained 'localization'.

Both the British and the Africans in Kenya on the whole made good use of the extra two years and of the lessons learnt from Tanganyika's experience. Mboya's memoirs show how this breathing space enabled K.A.N.U. leaders to develop a policy of localization instead of floating with the tide of popular feeling. Mboya's first priority was Africanization of the top administrative officers and in the army and police; the next was in agriculture, education and forestry, which, though less sensitive, could have political content. Other professional departments such as medical, legal, and health, he suggested, need not be unduly disturbed before independence.[60] Whether through government policy or individual preference, half the Africans who were pursuing higher studies in 1962 were taking general courses.

Kenya, like Tanganyika, placed political commissioners in the districts after independence. The Constitution was the result of a compromise between the K.A.N.U. party, which was centralist, and K.A.D.U. whose strength was based on the support of the smaller tribes. In the first year of independence there were regional assemblies, regional executives and even regional public service commissions. Whilst this ponderous structure increased pressure on the civil service, its existence perhaps restrained the K.A.N.U. government from attempting to merge the civil service with the party: indeed the neutrality of the civil service appeared advantageous to the government in the coastal areas where its strength was weak.

It will have been seen that the administrative and professional services in East Africa were in a far less satisfactory condition at independence than they were in West Africa. The main reason was that the acceleration to independence came with unexpected suddenness. Even in the late fifties, there was no anticipation that within a few years these territories would be independent African states whose governments would be determined to staff key positions with Africans, whether they were qualified or not. In January 1959 the British government was still planning for the three territories to become independent between 1970 and 1975.[61]

Behind the lack of preparedness was the sad story of African education, which never had time to establish roots between the successive blows of the 1914 War, the 1929 economic crisis and the War of 1939. African education was affected not only by these fortuitous disasters, but by the local interpretation of the Phelps-Stokes Report and of the Colonial Office Advisory Committee's policies of the 1920s. Obsessed with the dangers of creating a class of educated unemployed, the East African Governments failed to educate the minimum numbers required to staff the higher ranks of their services. Even in 1939 Sir Donald Cameron noted that 90% of the clerks in the Secretariat and Customs in Tanganyika were still foreigners and that the government had failed to provide secondary education to produce Africans who could go on to qualify as medical assistants, engineers and teachers. 'We ought to have been able to do better than this,' he concluded.[62] The quality of secondary education at independence in East Africa, where it was mainly in the hands of trained British teachers, was probably higher than in West Africa, where the expansion in the fifties had led to a dilution of teaching staff. There was not, however, except on a small scale in Buganda, a middle class who could afford to send their sons to schools abroad. Indeed the towns were more Indian than African, and it was the Asians who fulfilled the middle class role which in West Africa was occupied by people from the coastal tribes. The British could not have developed East Africa without the Asians, but eventually the Asians blocked the progress of the Africans.

Above the Asians were the Europeans. It was important that even in Kenya, unlike Southern Rhodesia, the white settlers were never a major element in the services, and most senior posts were filled from England. The independent governments had little desire to replace the European expatriates by local Asians. The shrewder African politicians recognized that the main problem indeed was not how to get rid of the expatriates but how to persuade them to stay until Africans were trained to replace them.

In East Africa, owing to the educational backwardness, the governments were far more dependent on expatriates at independence than those of West Africa. It was estimated in 1961 that for another five years there would not even be enough new higher manpower to replace wastage.

The effect of the compensation arrangements on the departure of expatriates has been seen in West Africa. The Udoji Report contained an interesting analysis of the reasons for the departure of expatriate officials in East Africa. The retirement rate was lowest among those who were under 35 on the one hand and over 45 on the other: it was highest between the ages of 40 and 45, and next highest in 40–45 age-group. The Commission concluded that most officers between 35 and 40 retired because they anticipated a drop in educational standards in East Africa and desired to educate their children in England. Those in the 40–45 age-group were influenced by the fact that their compensation sum could not be increased after the age of 41 and by the difficulty of starting on a new career in England after this age.[63]

Africanization, as in West Africa, had advanced further in the medical services than elsewhere, but the legal profession, which was the other outlet for the West African middle class, was monopolized by the Asians, and there was no Law Faculty in East Africa until 1961.[64] The obstacles to Africanization in the other professional services will be considered more generally in Chapter XII. The retrenchment in secondary education in the 1930s considerably retarded the progress of Africans in all of them.

One feature which has been noted in West Africa was repeated in East Africa. In each region the countries which were relatively most advanced, Ghana and Uganda, retained the services of British Permanent Secretaries for a longer period after independence than did their neighbours. In East Africa this was perhaps due to the fact that only in Uganda had there been a long term policy on Africanization which had been explained to the public over a period of years. Pressure for immediate Africanization was therefore less than it was in Tanganyika and Kenya, where no reports on Africanization were published before independence and the realities of the situation were less well understood by members of Parliament and party organizers.

REFERENCES

[1] Sir Donald Cameron, Address to Empire Parliamentary Association, London, 1927, p. 5.

[2] ibid., p. 6.

[3] Sir Donald Cameron, *My Tanganyika Service and Some Nigeria*, London, 1939, p. 127.

[4] Tanganyika Government *Education Report for* 1923, p. 5.

[5] Tanganyika Government *Education Report for* 1926, p. 10 and p. 12.

[6] Tanganyika Government *Education Report for* 1925, p. 8.

[7] Tanganyika Government *Education Report for* 1925, p. 50 and 1926, p. 41.

[8] Tanganyika Government *Education Report for* 1926, p. 21.

[9] Tanganyika Government *Education Report for* 1926, p. 21.

[10] Tanganyika Government *Education Report for* 1929, p. 7.

[11] Tanganyika Government *Education Report for* 1930, p. 3.

[12] Tanganyika Government *Education Report for* 1931, p. 7.

[13] Tanganyika Government *Education Report for* 1929, p. 27.

[14] B. Chidzero, *Tanganyika and International Trusteeship*, London, 1961, p. 128.

[15] *Observations of Administering Authority on the Report of U.N. Visiting Mission*, U.N. document T/1162, 1955, p. 48.

[16] Tanganyika Legislative Council Reports, Vol. 31, p. 11.

[17] op. cit., U.N. document T/1162, 1955, p. 24 and p. 32.

[18] J. Clagett Taylor, *Political Development of Tanganyika*, London, 1963, p. 275.

[19] J. Nyerere, Tanganyika National Assembly Debates, 31 May, 1961, Col. 817.

[20] J. L. Thurston, *Human Resources and Training*. Ford Foundation 1960 (Unpublished).

[21] Tanganyika National Assembly Debates, 1 June, 1961. Col. 886.

[22] ibid., 17 February, 1962. Col. 281.

[23] *Report of the Africanization Commission* (Maswanya Report), 1962, Dar-es-Salaam, 1963.

[24] G. Tobias, *Survey of High Level Manpower Requirements in Tanganyika*, Ford Foundation, 1962, p. 9.

[25] *Report of the Africanization Commission* 1962, Dar-es-Salaam, 1963, p. 37.

[26] ibid., p. 34.

[27] *Africanization of the Civil Service, Annual Report for 1963*, Dar-es-Salaam, 1964.

[28] *Tanganyika Five Year Plan*, Dar-es-Salaam, 1964, p. 86.

[29] J. R. P. Postlethwaite, *I Look Back*, London, 1947, p. 75.

30 Sir Hesketh Bell, *Glimpses of a Governor's Life*, London, 1946, p. 122.
31 C. Pratt in *History of East Africa*, Vol. II, pp. 525–534.
32 *Uganda Education Department Report for 1925*, Entebbe, 1926, p. 6.
33 *Uganda Education Department Report for 1926*, p. 5.
34 *Uganda Education Department Report for 1928*, p. 7.
35 *Uganda Education Department Report for 1930*, p. 13.
36 *Uganda Education Department Report for 1933*, p. 15.
37 *Report of the Commissioners for Africanization*, Part I, Entebbe, 1962, p. 18.
38 *Higher Education in Africa* (de la Warr Report), HMSO, 1937, Col. No. 142.
39 C. Pratt in *History of East Africa* (ed. V. T. Harlow et al.), Vol. II, Oxford, 1965. p. 515,
40 *Final Report of Standing Committee on Recruitment, Training and Promotion of Africans*, Entebbe, 1955.
41 ibid., p. 9.
42 *Future Developments in the Public Services in Uganda*, S.P. 2 of 1961, Entebbe.
43 *Report of the Commissioners for Africanization*, Entebbe, 1962, Part I, p. 17 ff.
44 *Statement on Reports of Commissioners for Africanization*, S.P. 7 of 1962, Entebbe, pp. 2–3.
45 Sir Chas. Dundas, *African Crossroads*, London, 1925, p. 138.
46 Kenya Government *Education Department Annual Report*, 1924, p. 19.
47 Kenya Government *Education Department Annual Report*, 1926, p. 15.
48 Norman Leys, *Kenya*, London, 1926, pp. 4–8.
49 Norman Leys, *Last Chance in Kenya*, London, 1931, pp. 106–113.
50 Kenya Government *Education Department Annual Report*, 1933, pp. 25–26.
51 *Report of Commission on Financial Position of Kenya*, HMSO, Col. 116, 1936, pp. 55–62.
52 See p. 197 above.
53 Kenya Government *Education Department Annual Report*, 1936, p. 63.
54 *Lidbury Report*, p. 65.
55 *East Africa Royal Commission Report*–Cmd 9475, 1955, p. 180.
56 Kenya Government *Report of the Economy Commission*, Nairobi, 1962, p. 42.
57 Tom Mboya, *Freedom and After*, London, 1963, p. 154. Elspeth Huxley, *Forks and Hopes*, London, 1964, p. 125.
58 e.g. R. M. Gatheru, *Child of Two Worlds*, London, 1964, p. 114.
59 Kenya Ministry of Education, *Annual Summary Report*, 1962, p. 19.
60 Tom Mboya, *Freedom and After*, London, 1963, pp. 153–157.
61 See Sir Michael Blundell's account of the Conference of Governors at Chequers in 1959 in *So Rough a Wind*, London, 1964, p. 262.
62 Sir Donald Cameron, *My Tanganyika Service*, op. cit., p. 128.
63 *Udoji Report*, op. cit., p. 24.
64 See Guy Hunter, *Education for a Developing Region*, pp. 64–69, for an analysis of the higher manpower situation.

PART FOUR

Comparisons and Reflections

CHAPTER XI

The French and other Empires

THE FRENCH IN TROPICAL AFRICA – THE BELGIANS IN
TROPICAL AFRICA – THE AMERICANS IN THE
PHILIPPINES – THE DUTCH IN INDONESIA

'To the man whom we prevent from being the first in his
country because his country is a colony there must be
the possibility of being the first among us.'
ARTHUR GIRAULT, 1903

An appreciation of the British approach to the development of
the government services and of its results may become more
realistic if some consideration is given to what happened
under other contemporary colonial empires. The French colonies of
West and Equatorial Africa have comparative interest because they
were adjacent to British territories with populations of similar culture
and levels of development. Events in the Belgian Congo had a considerable impact on the progress of localization in the neighbouring
British territories of East Africa. In Asia the experience of the
Philippines under American rule and of Indonesia under the Dutch
merit a reference since their administrations were often compared by
travellers with that of British India.

THE FRENCH IN TROPICAL AFRICA

In tracing the development of the government services in British
Africa, the most informative documents have generally been reports
on Africanization policy by commissions which were set up by the
local legislature or executive. Little similar documentation exists in
the former French colonies of tropical Africa. Here the initiative on

Africanization did not rest with a local governor or legislature but with the French cabinet or in the French Parliament in Paris.

Before the latter part of the 19th century, French colonial policy, inspired by the Revolutionary ideals of universal equality and fraternity, was assimilationist. The inhabitants of the West Indian colonies, as well as those of the four communes of Senegal which were acquired before that time, had full rights as citizens, including that to participate in election of representatives to the French legislature and to compete for the highest administrative positions on the same terms as the metropolitan French. In the remainder of the West and Equatorial African territories, however, which were acquired in the second half of the 19th century, there was no citizenship by birth: the Africans remained French 'subjects' and seldom acquired citizenship.

French rule in tropical Africa was direct rather than indirect. The Governors General of West and Equatorial Africa were responsible to the Minister for the Colonies in Paris. Under them was a hierarchy of Governors of Territories, provincial and district commissioners, and at the bottom the African chiefs of groups of villages (chefs de canton) who were appointed by the government.

There were three categories of civil servant. Those in the general cadre required a university degree and could be posted in any French territory throughout the world or in the Colonial Ministry. Those in the upper cadre had a secondary education and could be posted throughout a group of territories, such as French West Africa or French Equatorial Africa. Those in the local cadre had primary education and were employed within one territory only.

The French administrators of the top, or general, cadre were more intensively trained than their British counterparts. Usually they attended one of half a dozen lycées (or secondary schools) in France, the work of whose higher classes had a specialized bearing on colonial affairs. They then took a three-year university course at the École Nationale de la France d'Outre-Mer, which later became the École des Hautes Études d'Outre-Mer.

Until 1946 it was only possible for French citizens to enter the Ecole Nationale, and it was virtually barred to Africans, though L. S. Senghor from one of the privileged communes of Senegal was on its staff and a number of West Indians passed through, such as Eboué who became Governor General of Equatorial Africa in the Second War. In 1946 all inhabitants of the colonies became citizens, but by

1954 there were only two African students at the E. N. F. O. M. and in 1955 three. Even at the middle level, the upper cadre, which required secondary education, in 1954 in French Equatorial Africa only 88 out of 1,327[1] officers were Africans, and an American observer who made a study of Africanization of the services of West Africa in 1955 found the situation in the French territories considerably less advanced than in the British.[2]

The main reason lay in the limited local facilities for education. Before 1945 there were no institutions in French West Africa at which university degrees could be obtained, and in French Equatorial Africa it was not even possible to take a full secondary course. A few clerks and accountants had been trained in Senegal from 1816. Faidherbe, who was Governor in 1854, set up a school for the sons of chiefs at Dakar which eventually became in 1912 the William Ponty School. Here teachers and medical and agricultural auxiliaries were trained, but their diplomas had no validity in France, and admissions were restricted in accordance witn the number of posts available in the administration. Georges Hardy, who was Director of Education in French West Africa in the 1920s, proclaimed that 'the danger is never to teach too little; it is to teach too much'.[3]

For the rest, the children who only studied in primary schools, education before 1945 had a strong practical bias. In the rural areas in the 1930s the promotion of teachers often depended on the profits from the school vegetable gardens, and in the town primary schools the emphasis was on the training of artisans.

There were a few, particularly from the four communes of Senegal, who acquired a higher education in France. They were more likely than the Nigerians and Gold Coasters to remain in Europe after they had qualified. Arthur Girault, one of the most influential French writers of the colonial period, saw this aspect of assimilation as a 'Safety-valve' and maintained that 'To the man whom we prevent from being the first in his country because his country is a colony, there must be the possibility of being first among us'.[4] A more recent French historian, Henri Brunschwig, has asserted that 'Alone among the Western nations, the French found it normal to entrust their interests to black lawyers, their health to black doctors, their children to black professors and their recruits to black officers. . . . They were lost to Africa to the profit of France'.[5]

Three general points of difference between French and British educational practice in Africa were to influence the way in which the government services developed. First, in French Africa, unlike British Africa, the vernacular languages were never used in any schools at any level. All teaching was in French. Secondly, while in British Africa almost all primary and most secondary eduction was until a very late stage in the hands of the missionaries, in French Africa the majority of the schools were run by the State. Thirdly, in French Africa education was free. In short the French regarded the school system as an important instrument of French policy and French culture, in which equality of opportunity was provided to enable a restricted number to proceed to higher education. By contrast the British on the West Coast made little effort to correlate education and employment, and until 1925 virtually pursued a policy of educational laissez faire.

A great change in French policy took place immediately after the Second World War. During the War Eboué in Equatorial Africa had shown a greater understanding of the aspirations of the African middle class than his predecessors and his views had prevailed at the Brazzaville Conference of 1944. Under the Constitution of 1946, although self-government for the colonies was excluded, all subjects became citizens and all African territories now returned deputies to the French Parliament in Paris as well as at the Federal and territorial level.

In French Africa, unlike British Africa, civil servants were eligible to be elected to the legislature. Most of the African deputies who were now returned, both in Paris and in the local assemblies, were former officials, the majority being teachers in government schools. In 1960 eight of the Presidents of the eleven new states of French Africa were former teachers. The new deputies immediately made their influence felt both on the education system and on the position of Africans in the government services.

One demand, as in Nigeria and Ghana in this post-war period, was for a wide extension of primary education. The number of children enrolled in French West Africa rose from 121,000 to 428,000 between 1948 and 1959. The proportionate rise in secondary education was even greater. The Ponty School became a University Institute in 1948 and in 1959 became the University of Dakar. By 1957 6,600 Africans were undertaking Higher Education in France.

At every level, in primary, secondary and higher education, the curriculum was closely linked with that of France. It was the Africans themselves who insisted that there must be 'no education on the cheap', no reduction of standards. President Senghor of Senegal, who had been a professor in Paris, was as insistent on this as President Houphouet-Boigny of the Ivory Coast, who had been a medecin-africain from the William Ponty School. Africanization was delayed by the bottleneck in the secondary schools; not only did the French examinations have to be passed, but the same age limits were enforced as in France. In 1955 two-thirds of the places in secondary schools in French Equatorial Africa were thus empty and the rate of failure in the baccalauréat in both West and Equatorial Africa was very high.[6] The insistence on diplomas valid in France was a natural reaction against the humiliating status of the auxiliary, but it also fitted with French policy, which attached greater importance to cultural ties than did that of Britain. The University of Dakar and those at Abidjan and Brazzaville which were set up after independence granted degrees whose validity were recognized in France. Because university teachers are civil servants under the French system, this in effect gave the Africans who took the more advanced degrees the possibility of teaching in France. Reciprocally the African universities, even after independence, were obliged to accept any changes made in the French curriculum and examination systems: they might only appoint teachers whose qualifications were approved by France, and they were not allowed to appoint foreigners other than Frenchmen to their staff.

The new deputies also insisted on the equal status of the African and the Frenchman in the government services. Although in 1934 the Popular Front government in France had announced that all overseas posts should be open to Frenchmen and colonials on equal terms, this declaration had little effect. In 1950, however, the Senegal deputy, Lamine Gueye, sponsored a law in the French Assembly which guaranteed identical conditions of recruitment, pay and promotion for all metropolitan and overseas officer, even enabling the latter to take holidays in France. Intensive Africanization measures, such as were taken in Ghana and Nigeria in the 1950s, only really started in 1956, after the loi-cadre of that year. The loi-cadre greatly strengthened the territorial governments at the expense of those of the West African and Equatorial Federations: the bulk of the civil service was transferred to the territorial governments. The African civil servants were not entirely happy at the change, for they no longer automatically obtained the salary increases which were applied when the cost of living rose in Paris. In the following year a further law reserved 66% of all posts for indigenous officers. Between then and 1960, when the territories became independent states, much was done, but progress was quite uneven. In general Africanization was most rapid in teaching, and in the departments of health, labour and public works.

Patterns which had appeared balanced within the old federations were sometimes senseless when these broke up into a dozen successor states, some with a population of less than a million. The countries on the coast were considerably more advanced educationally than those of the interior. Senegal had Africanized all posts of commandant de cercle by independence. The Ivory Coast had Africanized twelve of these posts and had three African Commissioners of Police. Dahomey, 'the Latin Quarter' of Africa, had previously provided much of the staff for the West African Federation and now found itself with a surplus of teachers, customs officers and midwives. In the interior the position was much weaker. Upper Volta was only producing twenty 'bacheliers' a year from the secondary schools. Niger had only three African doctors. Jealousies accentuated some of the inherited difficulties. The Ivory Coast expelled officials from Senegal and Dahomey and withdrew its students from the University of Dakar.

There had always been proportionately more French than British officials in West Africa. Africanization had started later in French Africa than in British Africa, and the creation of twelve fully sovereign states meant that a larger staff was required than if the federations had remained in being. The situation could have been disastrous but for the realistic measures taken by the French government to meet it.

On the one hand everything possible was done to persuade French administrators and professional officers to remain. Since 1948 those in the general cadre had been paid by the French Government and seconded from their respective ministries in Paris. There was thus no problem of compensation or of reintegration. As soon as an officer became redundant in Africa he knew that his ministry would have a post for him in France. Meanwhile he was paid a handsome overseas allowance, and his savings were considerably enhanced by a favourable rate of exchange. Another advantage which he had over his British counterpart was that the local educational system was fully integrated with that of France. In 1964 one-third of the students at Dakar University were French, most of them being the children of officials and experts. After independence the salaries and expenses of the French officials were carried on the French technical assistance budget, and the successor states were charged a small monthly fee for each expert, graduated according to their ability to pay. The new governments were neither required to pay pensions nor compensation. Indeed the poorer governments in the interior received budgetary subventions from France in order to pay their indigenous civil service. An imaginative measure taken by France was to allow her nationals to choose to serve as teachers or technical assistance experts overseas instead of doing military service.

In addition, in the last few years before independence, the scholarship scheme in France was greatly expanded and continued to receive even larger numbers after independence. Apart from formal higher education, considerable attention was given to organizing practical training for Africans who were already in government service. The cult of the diploma, however, went even further than in British Africa. A student who completed his studies of economics in Paris would somehow manage to remain to write a thesis on the history of the light opera: the student who qualified in medicine would continue to become a specialist, while French Army doctors were sent out to work as general practitioners in the bush. These students did not, they said, intend to be a 'sacrificed generation' just because their governments were in a hurry to have their services.[7]

As in Nigeria and Ghana, the earliest students to go abroad from French West Africa had studied medicine, law, commerce and journalism because there were openings in these professions outside government service. By 1957 law and economics became favourite courses, leading to the senior administrative posts which were now open to Africans. By 1964, as these posts were filled, science had become more popular as a qualification for the professional posts in which there were still senior vacancies.

The territories on the coast, wealthier and more advanced than those in the interior, continued to receive more fellowships and experts from France because they had more highly developed services to maintain. The proportion of French professional officers as compared with administrators gradually increased after independence. In Senegal there were more French doctors, teachers and agricultural officers in 1964 than in 1960.[8] In general the ministers of the former French territories seemed in less of a hurry to dispense with the French administrators than were the ministers in the neighbouring

English speaking territories in respect of their British Permanent Secretaries. This was particularly true of those who had sat for years in the French Parliament and had become more at ease with Frenchmen than with their unsophisticated compatriots. But even those who had stayed at home seemed less troubled on this point than their contemporaries in the former British territories. A lasting advantage of the French colonial system was that it had allowed African children to sit beside French children in school and take the same examinations: as a consequence there was less often than in the former British states an inferiority complex to trouble race relations.

Perhaps because so many of the ministers were schoolmasters, perhaps because a few of the most influential had lived for so long in Paris, the new states mostly maintained administrative standards as closely linked to France as were those of the universities. The old general, upper and local cadres were exactly succeeded by cadres A, B, and C, for which the former educational qualifications were still required. Most of the new states set up an École Nationale d'Administration, with the same 'equivalence' of its qualifications with the French Institut des Hautes Études d'Outre-Mer as the Universities had with the University of France. It was agreed between the states that only officials who passed through these schools should enter the 'A' cadre.

The rigidity with which the standards were maintained can be seen from the experience of the Senegal Government. In 1960, the year of independence, when it opened its National School of Administration, it offered two alternative methods of entry. University students might enter through a written examination, whilst serving government officers from the 'B' cadre could enter by a shortened written examination and interview. No university candidates presented themselves, and of 29 government officers who applied, only 5 were admitted. In subsequent years university graduates were accepted without having to sit an examination but standards remained rigorous. The course lasted two years for serving officers and one year for graduates, including three months in a district, a month in the secretariat and a month at the Supreme Court office. Most of the lectures were given by university professors, in contrast to the practice in the institutes of administration in the former British territories, where the bulk of the instruction was given by former administrators.[9]

As the French administrators became advisers they were often succeeded by Africans with professional qualifications such as teachers, veterinarians and medical aides. The Senegal School of Administration held a six months' course in 1964 for such officers who had become Governors of Provinces, Chiefs of Districts and permanent heads of ministries, in order to enable them to be regularly classified in the administrative, or 'A' cadre. Amidst considerable consternation, 30 out of 60 candidates were failed.

It was easier for the former French than for the former British territories to continue to use civil servants as district officers, for this seemed to reflect not a colonial system but the centralized administrative system of France itself. After independence in most of the States civil servants remained as the government's representatives in the districts, but as 'Prefects' rather than 'Commandants de Cercle'. The demarcation between political and civil service appointments was less clear than in the former British territories. There was no tradition of a Public Service Commission: in most states the President himself made appointments and transfers of Prefects, and though these usually could not sit in Parliament, the Chefs du Cabinet of the ministries could.

While statistics are not available as to the number of African officers in the armies of the new states in former French tropical Africa, it appears that in West Africa at least there were some African officers in each of them at independence. In Europe during the First War, the French made extensive use of 'Senegalais' troops who were in fact mostly recruited not from Senegal but from the interior. Even at that time there were African officers who had been through the French military schools. From 1907 Africans could in principle become officers in the French Colonial Army, and the commander of the Senegal Army after independence was a Colonel who had led a battalion in the Second War. A number of officers from West Africa who were serving in the French Army were recalled at independence to their countries and N.C.O.s were also promoted: by 1964 in Senegal there were no French officers in executive posts, though some still remained as advisers. Candidates for direct commissions had to have the 'baccalauréat' of full secondary education, and there appeared to be no difficulty in finding them. The French, unlike the British, had conscripted their troops in Africa. Independent Senegal continued this policy. During their eighteen months' service the conscripts were used on development schemes and the training was as much directed to civil as to military purposes.

Shortly after independence there were army revolts in Togo, Dahomey, and Gabon. These were led by the officers against the civil regimes, on the Latin American pattern. They were not mutinies against the officers, such as occurred in East Africa.

The French heritage was criticized after independence from various sides. Some of the most interesting comments came from President Sekou Touré of Guinea, from which France withdrew all administrative and technical aid in 1959 when it voted to leave the French community. Sekou Touré himself had failed to obtain a place at the Ponty School but went into government service as a postal clerk, became a trade union organizer, and studied in Prague. He suggested that under the French system far too much emphasis was placed on formal education and diplomas. As a consequence, he maintained, Africans were 'depersonalized' by having to attend professional courses in France which were unnecessarily long compared with those in other countries. He also questioned traditional salary scales by which a clerk was paid twice as much as an artisan, and by which the top salaries in the civil service were fifty times as high as those at the bottom.[10]

This line of criticism was broadened by Professor René Dumont, a French socialist and agronomist whose book, *L'Afrique Noire est mal partie*, caused something of a sensation in former French Africa in 1962. Dumont suggested that the Balkanization of the former federations had led to an intolerable burden being carried by the successor states for costs of ministerial salaries, embassies and the civil service, so that 66% of Dahomey's budget, for example, was being spent on administration. The new 'bourgeoisie of the administration', he maintained, was considerably less useful than the bourgeoisie of Western Europe, which had both worked hard and had invested in production. The school system still had its roots in a system originally devised to produce Latin-speaking clerics in the Middle Ages, and was a positive impediment to agricultural production. Dumont advocated a drastic reduction in the salaries and numbers of the civil service and a closer association of the rural schools with agricultural life.[11]

Criticism did not only come from the Left. A number of French academics attacked the educational system for being too closely tied to that of France. After independence in several of the new states modifications of the primary and secondary curricula were made, but the African universities were still accused of being preoccupied with the possibility of access to the French universities instead of with the problems of training men for the government service. The French university system, it was suggested at a conference in Dakar, in 1962, was 'a victim of its own monopoly' and did not allow sufficient autonomy or flexibility to its African members; an obsession with the 'equivalance' of degrees and diplomas had led to a neglect of local needs.[12] Mali after independence showed a strong desire to follow Guinea in breaking away from the system.

The French started on Africanization later than the British. Until 1957 they were still insisting that Africans must have exactly the same qualifications as Frenchmen before they could replace them, and the French and French speaking Africans were throughout the period of decolonization generally less flexible about 'standards' than were the British and their successors. The French political and administrative arrangements were, however, outstandingly successful in enabling Frenchmen to maintain the government services after independence while Africans were trained. The main unanswered question four years after independence was perhaps that which Dumont had raised – how much longer would the man in the street be prepared to tolerate the enormous gap between his own standard of living and that of the officials? Or for that matter, how much longer would French taxpayers be prepared to carry the burden of financing the heavy administrative superstructure in these tiny states? Already the articles of Raymond Cartier in Paris had coined a new word – 'Cartierisme' – for their protest.

If the Africanization of the civil services was less advanced at independence than in British West Africa, in the army it had probably gone further. In one other area the French record also seemed to have been more successful. The mandate and trusteeship systems of the League of Nations and the United Nations had curiously different consequences in the territories for which the British and French were responsible. In Tanganyika, as we have seen, the government services were poorly prepared for independence because secondary education had lagged behind that of the neighbouring British territories. By contrast, the French Cameroun had a literacy rate much higher than that of the neighbouring states of French Equatorial Africa, since under the mandate and trusteeship arrangements missionaries of many denominations and nationalities were allowed to set up schools there, whilst their activities had not been encouraged in the French colonies.

THE BELGIANS IN TROPICAL AFRICA

The collapse of the administration in the former Belgian Congo at independence in July 1960 is the classic example of the catastrophic result of the failure of the colonial power to localize the higher ranks of the services.

The Belgians had done much in the Congo which was greatly admired by visitors in the 1950s. Industry was more developed than in any other part of tropical Africa. Thirty-five per cent of the active population were wage earners, and there was a comprehensive system of social and health services for them. As early as 1946, half the children of primary age were in school and by independence this had risen to 70%. Although there were many Belgians in the Congo in mining and large business enterprises, immigration of foreign artisans and middlemen was more strictly limited than in neighbouring territories and thus an African class of self-employed craftsmen, shopkeepers and small manufacturers emerged. Technical and vocational training was well developed, and visitors familiar with other African territories were impressed to find Africans operating I.B.M. machines or as captains of Congo steamers.

Yet, as an American observer remarked in 1955, everywhere Africanization stopped just short of that critical point which separates policy responsibility from routine responsibility. The power to make decisions, whether in the administration or in business, was never left in African hands.[13]

In the administration posts requiring not only higher education but even secondary education were reserved for Belgians until 1959. There were no institutions of higher education in the Congo until Louvanium University was opened in 1954 and the University of Elizabethville in 1956; and even then the courses at Louvanium were professional rather than general. Congolese students, except those studying for the priesthood, were rarely admitted to Belgian universities. As Van Bilsen pointed out at the time, there were only 15 Congolese students in the Belgian universities in 1956 while 1,300 Africans were studying in the French universities.[14] The Belgian policy was defended in a speech by the Minister for the Colonies in 1954–'Civilization cannot be limited to a few individuals or even to a few thousand, for its purpose is to raise the whole people to a higher level. I do not think that the method which some countries have applied has had very favourable results. We have seen that those natives who have been shown Europe and given a very advanced education did not always return to their homelands in a spirit favourable to civilization and to the mother country in particular. In our view civilization founded on a solid basis in their own environment offers greater guarantees'.[15]

Within this framework a school of public administration was opened in each province by the Government in 1955 in order to train future chiefs and young men for local government and the courts, and in co-operative and community development activities. But these schools were closed in 1957 as a result of pressure from the Church, which resented a potential elite being trained outside its own educational system.[16]

The Belgian change of policy on decolonization was late and sudden. When Professor Van Bilsen had proposed a thirty-year plan for the independence of the Congo in 1954, he incurred great unpopularity and his warning was unheeded, that 'unless we form an elite there will be chaos'.[17] Only from January 1959, eighteen months before independence, were steps taken to Africanize the administration, when 700 Africans were appointed to posts previously reserved for Europeans. But these were at a relatively low level. At independence there were only 3 Congolese graduates in the government and about 30 graduates in the whole country, apart from some 400 trained as priests.

The Belgian educational policy in the Congo had been based on recommendations of the Phelps-Stokes mission in 1924.[18] Although almost all post-primary education had been vocational, that training had not continued to the higher level. Except for Nigeria, the Congo with its ten million inhabitants was the largest state in tropical Africa, but at independence there were no fully trained Congolese doctors or engineers. Nor was the immediate future encouraging. There were no Congolese secondary school teachers except for the priests, and in the year of independence only 136 children completed secondary education and became available for higher education.

André Ryckmans, a Belgian district officer who was the son of a former Governor General, wrote desperately to the government in June 1959 that it was much more important to appoint ten Congolese as district officers, army lieutenants and commissioners of police than as cabinet ministers. He was convinced that candidates could be found and trained in a few months, and eventually in defiance of his superiors he handed over charge of his own district to a Congolese assistant before Independence.[19] But in general the steps taken to Africanize the district administration were too late to be effective. Each Belgian subdivisional officer was asked to select an African for training, but these were only to have taken up their posts six months after the date of independence. In April 1960, African assistant district officers were appointed, but by this time relations between the Belgian administration and the political parties were so strained that these officers were branded as 'collaborators' and usually received little co-operation from the local population. A fatal mistake made by the Belgians in the Congo, as compared with the British and French in their African territories, was to fail to provide for a period of internal self-government before independence during which the political parties could obtain experience in office and come to terms with the civil service.

The disintegration of the Federal Government in the first week after independence was immediately caused by the mutiny of the Force Publique, or army, of 24,000 men, which had no Congolese officers. For months before independence, letters from Congolese soldiers had been published in the local newspapers demanding that Africans should be appointed as officers. 'Adolf Hitler was only a simple corporal,' wrote one anonymous soldier. 'Dear leaders, do not forget this lesson'.[20] It should not be supposed that General Janssens, the Commander in Chief, had no programme of Africanization. In 1958, the Government announced that the first African second lieutenants would be appointed in ten years' time. Contemptuous of the country's educational system, the army opened its own primary and secondary schools. Only when a boy had passed through these would he be eligible to enter an officer's school. Questioned on this policy, Belgian army spokesmen maintained that the training of officers must depend on international criteria, just as much as that of doctors and engineers; and five years' study of Greek and Latin were included in the curriculum.[21] General Janssens in February 1960 stated that no preference would be given in promotion to Congolese, and explained that it would be highly dangerous to weaken the efficiency of the Force Publique by reorganization before independence in view of the heavy responsibility which it was likely to carry at that time.[22]

Jealousy of the rapid promotion of politicians and civil servants was an important factor in precipitating the mutiny. When it broke out General Janssens summoned the Congolese N.C.O.s to his headquarters and, after stating that there would be no Africanization, wrote on a blackboard the memorable words 'Before Independence = After Independence'. Next day he was dismissed by Lumumba and on his way back to Belgium to write his memoirs, which throw considerable light on the Congo disaster.[23]

Even if there had been no revolt of the army, there would perhaps have been a revolt of the clerks. Throughout the first half of 1960, the trade union of Congolese government employees had been demanding the complete Africanization of administrative (though not of technical) posts before independence. Paradoxically enough, their demands were not very different in object from those of the union of Belgian officials which was petitioning the King at the same time. After pointing out that a number of Congolese publications contained virulent invitations to racial hatred, and even encouragement to murder Belgians and take possession of their wives and daughters, the Belgian officials demanded that instead of being transferred integrally to the Congo Government's employment they should be treated as advisers lent by Belgium. They did not succeed on this point, but did obtain a law, passed by the Belgian Parliament in March 1960, by which if the King ascertained that for reasons outside their control they were unable to carry out their work in the Congo they would be transferred to equivalent posts in the civil service of their home country. When the mutiny broke out, this act was invoked, and there was a wholesale departure of Belgian officers. The desire to get into the home service before the best jobs were taken appears to have contributed to this exodus as much as the breakdown of law and order, for the civil servants departed far more rapidly than the businessmen. The numbers were very considerable. At independence, there were 10,000 Belgian officials in the Congo. About 3,500 of these had higher educational qualifications, including about 500 doctors and the same number of engineers. It had never been envisaged by the Belgian Government that almost all of these officials would return from the Congo simultaneously to demand integration. Under pressure from the trade unions of metropolitan government officials, who were afraid that their future promotion would be blocked for years by the returning colonials, the law of March 1 was revoked. Thus the colonial officials were left with the conviction that they had been betrayed by the home government, while the services of the Congo virtually collapsed.[24]

Belgium was also the administering authority for the United

Nations trust territory of Ruanda-Urundi, which became independent as two separate states in July 1962. Here the same law of January 1959 which applied to the Congo opened the higher ranks of the services to Africans, so that they had two years longer in which to acquire experience. In Rwanda and Burundi, unlike the Congo, the Belgians granted internal self-government some months before independence. In the period between the independence of the Congo and that of Rwanda and Burundi, a few more graduates returned and a certain amount of in-service training took place. There was an almost total lack of Africans trained however as doctors or in the professions.

The public services of Rwanda and Burundi would have been in a considerably better position at independence if the governments had made full use of their few trained men after independence. The Belgians had governed in each country by indirect rule through the King and Chiefs of the Tutsi tribe which, though in a minority, had received most of whatever secondary or higher education was obtained. In Rwanda the Hutu majority overthrew the Tutsi feudal system shortly before independence and most of the educated Tutsi fled or were eliminated from government service. In Burundi, though the political parties were not organized along straight tribal lines, the Belgian-supported party which was in office before independence subsequently lost the elections: a number of the men who had obtained administrative experience before independence were thus subsequently removed from office.

In each of these two countries some two or three hundred Belgian officials and professionals remained after independence and prevented the collapse of the services. They were able to do so because their security appeared assured by a strong ruler in Burundi and by a homogeneous ruling political party in Rwanda; and by now the Belgian Government had arranged favourable financial conditions for them. Without the prestige or good-will which the British and French experts still enjoyed in most of Africa as a result of a more skilful policy of decolonization, Belgian agricultural officers continued to strive to maintain the remarkable system of anti erosion works and coffee cultivation which they had built up over forty years. But to the Hutu peasant the tedious labour involved often appeared a relic of colonial and feudal rule, and the coffee exports, which had financed the administrative budget, fell disastrously.

THE FRENCH AND OTHER EMPIRES

THE AMERICANS IN THE PHILIPPINES

American colonial policy in relation to the development of the government services can best be studied in the Philippines, which were acquired by the U.S.A. in 1898 after the War with Spain and became fully independent in 1946. The Americans had to defeat the Filipino nationalist forces who were first on their side against Spain but later fought for independence. In the United States, the Democratic Party was bitterly critical of the 'imperialism' of the Republican Presidents McKinley and Theodore Roosevelt, and throughout the period of occupation American policy varied considerably according to whether the Republican or Democratic Party was in power.

The Spaniards had built up an educational system which was largely in the hands of the church; though restricted in scope, it enabled the Filipino elite to enter the University in Manila, which dated from the 17th century, as well as the universities of Europe. On the other hand this educated class occupied practically no senior positions in the government. The Americans instituted mass education and gave Filipinos access to all posts in the administration.

Immediately after the American occupation, President McKinley issued a directive that preference should be given in the civil service firstly to qualified Filipino nationals and secondly to discharged American soldiers. There was general agreement that it would be disastrous to allow the 'spoils system' to develop in a colony; and the method of recruitment which was introduced was more based on merit, and the tenure of office more permanent, than that in the Federal Service of the United States at the time. Examinations were held locally, not in the United States, and Filipinos competed on an equal basis with Americans, though they were handicapped by their lack of English. In practice in early years some senior posts were reserved for Americans by exemptions from competition, which were granted by the Governor General with the consent of the Senate, as well as through temporary appointments which did not have to be approved by the Civil Service Board.[25]

The early American civil servants had no special training. Many of them were either young and inexperienced or promoted from quite subordinate offices in the United States. Between 1900 and 1905 there was a series of scandals in which ten American provincial treasurers or deputy treasurers were convicted of embezzlement.[26] Successive Republican Governors-General considered that the

American occupation would be, and should be, long enough to justify building up a career service whose senior positions would be held by Americans. In 1913, however, the Democrats came into office in Washington on a platform which included the early grant of independence to the Philippines, and a rapid Filipinization of the services took place. While in 1913 there were 2,600 American officials occupying 23% of civil posts, by 1919 they were reduced to 600 or 6%. By 1921, 30 of the 40 Bureaux of Government were headed by Filipino Directors, including that of the Civil Service.[27]

This period provided probably the earliest example of a compensation scheme. From 1903 Americans who served three years in the Philippines had been eligible for appointments to Federal government posts in the U.S.A.: in 1913 Americans who had served six years in the Philippine Government became entitled to a compensation benefit which rose after ten years' service to a sum equivalent to a year's salary.[28]

The Democrats went out of office in 1921 without granting independence to the Philippines, and the pace of advance was slowed down by the Republicans, who had described the Filipinization programme as premature and cataclysmic.[29] They did not however reverse the process. In a sense they even strengthened the position of the Filipino civil servants. The Democratic administration in 1917 had appointed Filipino civil servants as Under Secretaries, or permanent heads of departments, who were responsible to a political Secretary, on the British model. The Republican Governor General Wood quarrelled with the political Secretaries, five of whom resigned in 1923. For the next five years the Filipino permanent undersecretaries remained directly responsible to the Governor General for the business of their departments.

When the Democrats returned to power, the Philippines became a 'Commonwealth', with a ten year period of internal self government which was intended to lead to full independence in 1946, and did so in spite of Japanese occupation during the Second World War. By 1932 Americans held only 2% of the civil service posts and these were mostly teachers. From 1928 they were mainly recruited on contract as advisers and from 1938 the President of the United States was authorized to lend the services of U.S. federal officers to the Philippines in an early technical assistance programme.[30]

An interesting survey of the senior civil service was published in 1933 just before internal self government.[31] Of the 8 permanent under-secretaries, the average age was 48 and the average length of government service 26 years. Of the 55 under-secretaries and Chiefs of Bureaux 38 had visited the U.S.A. and 17 Europe, a remarkable proportion in a period before air travel had developed. Most seem to have had higher education, many having started with only secondary education but having studied for university degree while in government service. Thirty-one out of these 55 top officials had substantial private incomes: about half were the sons of landowners and half of former government officials. The Americans left a senior civil service in the Philippines with a high degree of education, experience and continuity. The criticism that has been made is that it was too narrowly drawn from the class of 'caiques' or landlords.[32]

Other legacies were less fortunate. The American practice of exemptions from the normal civil service recruitment procedure was widely extended by the Commonwealth and independent governments to cover posts which were 'technical' or 'confidential'. By 1954, the number of posts which were 'unclassified' or exempt considerably exceeded those to which recruitment was made by competition.[33]

The achievement of which the Americans were proudest was in education; the American soldier with a rifle in one hand and an English grammar in the other became a national legend. Twenty per cent of the annual budget of the Philippines under American rule was devoted to education, compared with about 5% in British India or the Dutch Indies.[34] Primary education was taken out of the hands of the church and so expanded that when the Americans left, the Philippines had the highest literacy rate of any Asian colonial territory. Education was conducted entirely in English, with great emphasis on civics and the inculcation of patriotism.

The pattern which then developed was not unlike that in India. Progressively between 1905 and 1929 the requirement for entry into government service was raised from a primary education to a university degree. By this time the Americans were trying with little success to encourage vocational and technical education. After independence the inflation of qualifications continued. The law, medicine and accountancy remained the gentlemanly professions even though at times doctors and dentists could only find employment as clerks. By 1960 there were twenty-four universities in the Philippines, some being run on a profit-making basis with shares quoted on the stock exchange. It was almost impossible to get the young graduate to go to the rural areas. Doctor or lawyer, engineer or biologist, teacher or administrator, if he could not find work in Manila he sought it abroad. Applications for the civil service arrived in such thousands that no one had time to read them before the examinations, and the entry examinations had to be suspended for years at a time because already more candidates had been selected than posts were available.[35]

The Dutch were in Indonesia for 300 years. Its natural resources were more intensively developed and its administration was more elaborate than those of other Asian colonies. In 1930 it was estimated that in proportion to the population there were nine times as many imported civil servants in the Dutch East Indies as in British India and four times as many as in the Philippines.[36]

The Dutch administrators undertook a five year special course of training at the University of Leyden before going out to the Indies. The Indonesian administrators were given a course of three to five years within their country which was intended to give them an insight into western attitudes. They were selected with regard to the social and political background of their families. Senior administrative posts were reserved for the Dutch, who supervised the activities of the hereditary Indonesian Regents under a system of indirect rule whilst the Indonesian administrators worked within the services of the Regencies. Indonesians were eligible, however, on equal terms with the Dutch for appointment to senior professional posts, and at one time an Indonesian was head of the Education Department. In 1940, of the senior posts in the government only 221 out of 3,039 were held by Indonesians and less than half of the 27,000 intermediate level posts.[37]

A striking feature of Dutch rule was the extent to which Eurasians were used in the administration. These, unlike their counterparts in India, were treated as nationals of the metropolitan power. For a short time in 1913 their representatives co-operated with the Indonesian nationalists in demanding 'equal pay for equal work' because heads of government departments were inclined to appoint Indonesians instead of Eurasians on grounds of economy. Once this demand was granted, the Eurasians identified themselves completely with the Dutch and sometimes rose to the very highest positions in the service. But they suffered severely for the identification. Of some

300,000 'Dutch' who left or were expelled from Indonesia between 1945 and 1960, probably three-quarters were Eurasians.[38] At the same time, the Netherlands Government did more than other colonial powers after independence to welcome the Eurasians and find them employment in the metropolitan country.

Just as the Eurasians occupied the middle positions in government, so the Chinese blocked the way in commerce, and an Indonesian middle class was thus slow to emerge. The Dutch considered that the British in India and the Americans in the Philippines had developed western education too widely.[39] They concentrated therefore on professional rather than literary education. A technical college was established in 1919, a medical college in 1926, and a law college in 1934; a university was not created until 1940. But the law college was initially reserved for the sons of the nobility, and in 1940 only thirty-seven Indonesians graduated from any institutions of higher education, though a few more were studying in the Netherlands. Only a quarter of the boys who graduated from high schools in this year were Indonesian.[40] Even this modest flow led to some unemployment and consequent discontent. As the nationalist leader Sjahrir wrote in 1937 'the large increase in the number of educated Indonesians requires that more of them be absorbed into the colonial government unless the government itself wants to make these people into an ever-growing source of opposition to it'.[41]

The Dutch did not hold competitive examinations for entry to the government service. In some fields Indonesians were chosen from amongst the qualified candidates neither by examination nor by interview but by lot.[42] The standards and curriculum of the Dutch language secondary schools also remained exactly the same as those of the metropolitan country, in order that the Dutch residents might send their children on from them to the universities at home. In the last stage of colonial rule, the classical colonial educational dilemma was described in Indonesia by Amry Vandenbosch. 'The nationalists on the one hand complain that the educational system is too western and has for its object the denationalization of the Indonesians: on the other hand, whenever a limitation of Western education is proposed the nationalists accuse the government of wishing to deprive them of just that type of schooling which will most rapidly prepare them for self government. In Dutch circles a reversal on this question has taken place. Two decades ago the imperialist elements advocated western education, whereas the liberals were the protagonists of practical national education. Today the conservatives have turned against western education, probably largely because of its effect in stimulating nationalism, and are now advocating vocational and indigenous education.'[43]

Dutch rule was cut short, and it is fruitless to speculate how far and with what results their policies might have altered after 1941. In that year the Japanese not only invaded the country and put the Dutch officials in concentration camps but liquidated many of their closest Indonesian collaborators. The junior Indonesian officials who succeeded them were preoccupied first with the problems of the occupation and then of war with the Dutch. Once the independent government was established there was a great expansion in education and of the services. The number of pupils in senior secondary schools rose from 4,400 to 69,000 between 1940 and 1956. In the same period the number of government servants rose from 140,000 to 700,000.[44]

REFERENCES

[1] V. Thompson and R. Adloff, *Emerging States of French Equatorial Africa*, London, 1960, p. 68.

[2] C. Gray Cowan, *Memorandum on Africanization* (typescript), 1955.

[3] G. Hardy, *Nos Grands Problèmes Coloniaux*, Paris, 1949 edition, p. 78.

[4] A. Girault, *Principes de Colonisation et de Legislation Coloniale*, Paris, 1927 edition. This passage first appeared in 1903.

[5] H. Brunschwig, *L'Avènement de l'Afrique noire*, Paris, 1963, p. 190.

[6] V. Thompson and R. Adloff, *Emerging States of French Equatorial Africa*, London, 1960, p. 298.

[7] P. Chaleur in *Études*, Paris, March, 1963, p. 356, and examples encountered in Africa by the author.

[8] *Plan quadriennal de Developpement* (1961–64), Dakar N.D., p. 104.

[9] In some of the other former French territories the National Schools of Administration were not part of the university and more of the instruction was given by technical assistance experts.

[10] Sekou Touré, *La Guinée et l'Emancipation Africaine*, Paris, 1959, p. 125 and p. 168.

[11] Rene Dumont, *L'Afrique noire est mal partie*, Paris, 1962.

[12] Prof. J. C. Groshens and Prof. P. Ardant, *Annales Africaines*, University of Dakar, 1962, Vol. II, p. 533.

[13] L. Gray Cowan, op. cit., 1955.

[14] A. A. J. Van Bilsen, *Vers l'Indépendance du Congo*, Brussels, 1958, p. 140.

[15] Andre Duquae, quoted in Ruth Sloan, *The Educated African*, London, 1962, p. 192.

[16] G. Brausch, *Belgian Administration in the Congo*, London, 1961, p. 53.

[17] Van Bilsen, op. cit., p. 150.

[18] R. Lamarchand, *Political Awakening in the Congo*, Univ. of California, 1964, p. 134.

[19] 'J.K.', *André Ryckmans*, Brussels, 1961.

[20] CRISP, *Congo 1960*, Vol. I, p. 346.

[21] ibid., p. 345.

[22] ibid, p. 346.

[23] E. Janssens, *J'étais le general Janssens*, Brussels, 1961.

[24] CRISP, *Congo 1960*, Vol. II, pp. 518–536.

[25] H. P. Willis, *Our Philippine Problem*, New York, 1906, p. 60.

[26] H. P. Willis, op. cit., p. 68.

[27] J. R. Hayden, *The Philippines*, New York, 1942, Chapter IV.

[28] J. R. Hayden, op. cit., Chapter V.

[29] J. R. Hayden, op. cit., p. 94.

[30] G. Fischer, *Un Cas de Decolonisation*, Paris, 1960, pp. 41–48.

[31] R. Hayden, *American Political Science Review*, Vol. XXVII, 1933, p. 218.

[32] G. Fischer, op. cit., p. 46.

[33] E. O. Stene and Associates, *Public Administration in the Philippines*, Manila, 1956, p. 102.

[34] A. Vandenbosch, *The Dutch East Indies*, Univ. of California, 1944, p. 216.

[35] Stene, op. cit., Chapter VI.

[36] A. Vandenbosch, op. cit., p. 173.

[37] G. T. Kahin, *Nationalism and Revolution in Indonesia*, New York, 1952, p. 34.

[38] L. Palmier, *Indonesia and the Dutch*, London, 1962, p. 103.

[39] L. A. Mills, *British Rule in Eastern Asia*, London, 1942, p. 369.

[40] Kahin, op. cit., p. 32.

[41] S. Sjahrir, *Out of Exile*, New York, 1949, p. 181.

[42] G. H. Bousquet, *A French View of the Netherlands Indies*, London, 1940, p. 97.

[43] A. Vandenbosch, op. cit., p. 221.

[44] Palmier, op. cit., p. 159.

CHAPTER XII

Standards and Prejudices

'Everybody was making a fetish of Standards.'
REPORT OF THE AFRICANIZATION COMMISSION,
EAST AFRICAN COMMON SERVICES
ORGANIZATION, 1963

Throughout this study a recurring theme in the reports and correspondence which have been quoted has been the necessity of 'maintaining standards'. Sometimes this phrase served to impede or slow down the replacement of the British by local officers in the services and with a variety of motives between which it is useful to attempt to distinguish. Among the most important were the security of the colonial power, racial prejudice and professional interests.

The argument of security was an obvious one on which little need be said. In India, Curzon and some other Viceroys were frank in stating that as long as British rule lasted the top administrative and army posts must remain in British hands. There was an embarrassing conflict of principle here with Queen Victoria's declaration of equality between the races, but even the nationalists usually realized that an imperial power was almost bound to reserve certain key posts for its own nationals and hardly expected, for example, that Indians would be appointed as governors or generals.[1] The disagreement was partly one of degree: Indians could probably safely have been appointed earlier and more often as Secretaries of Departments and Commissioners of Divisions; for the Indian officers proved, as it turned out, remarkably loyal to the imperial government in times of civil disobedience campaigns. In very small colonies such as the West Indian islands, it was not found necessary to keep more than two or three posts in British hands, and the services in Malta were

234

almost entirely staffed by Maltese for the whole 150 years of British rule. But in India the generals in particular took fifty years to recover from the shock of the Indian Mutiny and in Africa it was believed that the admission of the educated native to senior posts would disturb the systems of Indirect Rule.

Racial prejudice, because it was often submerged and sometimes unconscious, deserves more attention. It has been seen how at the end of the 19th century the process of localization was reversed in West Africa and halted in India. There were important local factors in both regions. Control of diseases made them safer for Europeans, and improved communications with Europe brought out English women in greater numbers and accentuated racial segregation. The consolidation of British administration throughout the Empire at this time was, of course, a natural consequence of the triumph of imperialist policies over those of the liberal Little Englanders who only wanted to maintain trading posts. To some extent the conscious establishment of a more permanent administration naturally brought about for reasons of efficiency the replacement of local people by Europeans with higher professional or educational qualifications.

But these were not the only reasons for the change of policy. Joseph Chamberlain was not unrepresentative in proclaiming that the British were the greatest ruling race in history. Rosebery, who had been a Liberal Prime Minister, asked the students of Glasgow University in 1899 'what is Empire but the predominance of race?'.[2] Curzon declared 'I sometimes think that in the catalogue of our national virtues we hardly lay sufficient stress upon the enormous administrative ability of the English race'.[3] Kipling popularized this feeling with his poem on the White Man's Burden.

Such attitudes might have astonished some of the Colonial Secretaries and Governors of fifty years earlier. Darwinism contributed to the change, for the Social Darwinists believed that races, like animals, could be arranged in an order of development. Even before Darwin published the *Origin of Species*, Herbert Spencer had put forward, with similar effect, an organic concept of society in which national traits were hereditary. Both these theories at least allowed for the evolution, however slow, of primitive races. The most prominent members of the Anthropological Society of London in the 1860s, among them James Hunt, Richard Burton and Winwoode Reade, went much further. They maintained, quite fallaciously, that the Negro cranium had, and always would have, a smaller capacity than that of the European. Hunt, during the American Civil War, used this argument to support slavery and the Confederate Cause.[4] It was primarily against these pseudo-scientific theories that James Africanus Horton of Sierra Leone, himself a living refutation of them, wrote his *West African Countries and Peoples*.

Other influences developed outside the stream of Darwinism. Curzon was responsive to Carlyle's cult of the Hero, born to rule over lesser men and lesser races. Though Winwoode Reade's *Martyrdom of Man* was one of Rhodes' favourite books, it was Ruskin's inaugural lecture at Oxford on the Empire which he described as the turning point in his life.[5] Another Oxford professor who played an important part in developing racial pride was Freeman whose lectures and writings in the sixties and seventies eulogized the virtues of the Anglo-Saxons in contrast to the Latin races. Many of those who reached high positions in government service by the eighties and nineties had thus been influenced by racial theories which had developed over the previous twenty years. The remarkable Western scientific discoveries and technological achievements of the 19th century accentuated the feeling of racial superiority. In 1783, Burke had described India's great cities with their merchants and bankers, and 'their ingenious manufacturers and mechanics' and her 'most diligent and not least intelligent tillers of the soil' with a respect which was seldom repeated a hundred years later.[6]

Missionaries as well as government officials were affected, and some of the consequences in West Africa in the 1890s have been seen. In Ceylon, A. G. Fraser when he went out in 1904 was advised by European missionaries not to allow the Ceylonese further into his house than the verandah in case they got swollen-headed.[7] There were, however, many missionaries such as Fraser and C. F. Andrews who spent much of their lives fighting racial prejudice both in relation to government and non-official employment policies.

A similar change of fashion in racial theories influenced contemporary French colonial policy. The French revolutionary leaders of 1789 believed that all men were born equal and that education could correct environmental differences. At each subsequent revolution in 1830, 1848 and 1870, the principle was reaffirmed. Until this time the French policy was one of 'assimilation'. The free inhabitants of territories colonized before 1870 were citizens of France and there were no limits on the positions to which they might attain at home and abroad. But by the 1890s 'assimilation' changed to 'association'. The citizens of the newly acquired territories were not given votes.

Gobineau had written his essay 'Sur l'inégalité des races' before Darwin published his great work. Gustave Le Bon was perhaps even more influential in teaching that mankind was permanently divided into four groups, primitive, inferior, intermediate and superior, and that belief in the efficiency of education was 'one of the most harmful illusions that the theorists of pure reason had ever engendered'. By the end of the century there was wide support for the view that the education of the individual on French lines should be replaced by the education of the group in terms of their environment, though the new theories never prevented the French, however, from accepting the exceptional educated individual into their society and government.[8]

The intense phase of racial prejudice in the British Empire did not last very long. By the 1930s, as Dr. Perham has pointed out, the interest of the British in continuing to occupy the former German colonies caused them to emphasize the difference between their own racial attitudes and those of Hitler's Germany.[9] There were too always some officials who were ahead of their time in insisting that the local people had a right to be considered for senior posts in the government on an equal footing with the British.

Two who immediately come to mind are Ripon in India and Guggisberg in Ghana, whose memories are still venerated even by ardent veterans of the independence movement. Among the military leaders who were concerned with localization, Kitchener, though a staunch imperialist, appears to have been unusually devoid of the prejudices of his contemporaries; he could view almost with detachment their 'deep-seated racial repugnance to any step which brings near the day when Englishmen in the Army may have to take orders from Indians', and went further than most of them in proposing Indianization in the Army.[10] He also showed remarkable imagination, immediately after the Battle of Omdurman, in founding the Gordon College in Khartoum to educate the sons of his leading opponents; and he spent his leave in England raising money for the purpose.

Perhaps the only characteristic which Ripon, Kitchener and Guggisberg had in common was that none of them had a conventional English upper class upbringing. Ripon was educated at home by private tutors to the age of 21; Kitchener went to school in

France and Germany; and Guggisberg, though he went on to an English school and to Woolwich, had been brought up in Canada. This common factor may have been accidental, but there can be no doubt that the traditions of the English preparatory and public schools of the period, though admirably suited to produce conscientious rulers, also tended to inculcate a deep, if seldom expressed, consciousness of race and class superiority.

The concern of the British in reports on localization that standards of integrity would be as difficult to maintain as standards of efficiency had of course a very real basis. The local officer, surrounded by dependent relatives seeking jobs or contracts, was under much greater pressure than his expatriate predecessor. The attitudes towards government of the society in which he grew up were quite different from those of the Englishman. In most developing countries loyalties to family or tribe were generally regarded as more important than loyalty to the state. Often the legal system was so alien that to break its regulations brought no social disapproval. Sometimes the bureaucracy moved so ponderously that small bribes were almost essential in order to grease the wheels and keep the files moving.

All this is now better understood than it was in the 19th century. To many British officials of the evangelical tradition Asians and Africans lied and stole simply because they were sinful. Their remedy in Africa and Ceylon was to train a new generation in English modelled public schools where sin could be exorcized by Christianity, caning and compulsory games. The results were not unimpressive. Those who entered government service from the new schools proved in general as incorruptible as their British colleagues, and equally class conscious. The massive corruption continued at the middle and lower level of the services, on which the well paid successors had little influence.[11]

An aspect of 'standards' which has been less studied is the effect which strict application of the educational and professional qualifications of the metropolitan power had on the development of the government services in the colonial territories.

It has been seen how after the Asquith and Elliott Reports of 1945 the United Kingdom Government adopted a much more active policy in higher education in the colonies, under which new University Colleges were established and brought temporarily into a special relationship with London University, while an Inter-University Council for Higher Education in the Colonies, representative of all the British universities, was created in London in order to help to set up and staff the new colleges. The I.U.C. Report on progress over the first eight years of the scheme in 1954 stated their attitude to standards. 'This is the heart of the matter. There can be no compromise on this issue of standards. . . . The price for this fundamental decision of aiming at first class universities has been deliberately paid. It has meant that initially student numbers are small: that the staff student ratio is high: that the institutions require very large funds, both capital and recurrent: that only a few of these university institutions can be established at this stage. We do not doubt that this policy has justified itself.'[12]

Had the Committee foreseen that not only the West African but the East African territories would become independent within the next decade they might have been less complacent about 'ivory tower' policies which restricted the output of graduates at a time when the governments were in desperate need of administrators and specialists to replace the British; which took virtually no account of manpower needs, and which drove the local youth to study abroad because the entry requirements of the African universities were more severe than those of the two most technically advanced countries in the world.

The 'Asquith doctrine' had been to a considerable extent developed in reaction to the policies which had resulted in low standards and large numbers in the Indian universities. The approach of the Asquith and Elliott reports themselves was flexible: it was the interpretation of the doctrine which was rigid. Neither the adoption of a curriculum in which the balance of subjects was different from those of the English universities nor the organization of diploma or pass degree courses, honestly labelled as such, need have implied a debasement of standards.

By 1964, as the territories in Southern Africa moved towards independence, another reaction set in. The new Universities of Zambia and of Malawi as well as that of Basutoland, Bechuanaland and Swaziland decided to admit entrants at the Ordinary School Certificate level and to concentrate on four year pass degrees. In their plans there was much more emphasis than there had been in West and East Africa on meeting the most urgent needs of the countries for administrators and agricultural officers.

Neither the governments nor the universities had full control of the standards maintained by the professional services in the British

239

territories: in most cases a professional association in London had the final decision. In the first half of the 19th century in Britain professional associations were set up to which Parliament gave the right to examine, and in effect to license, for practice in the principal professions. In due course these professional associations also became the controlling bodies who were responsible for deciding what qualifications were necessary to enable members of their professions to practise in or enter government service in the colonies. Here was a complication which was to cause standards to be applied in the colonies which sometimes were irrelevant and hampered the rapid development of the profession. A striking example was in the veterinary field. No one could either work as a government veterinarian in the colonies or practise privately without a British university degree which was registrable with the Royal College of Veterinary Surgeons in London. An African who obtained the London external degree at Makerere or Ibadan would automatically be entitled to claim registration as a member of the Royal College of Veterinary Surgeons, and would thus be entitled to practise in Britain. The R.C.V.S. insisted on facilities for teaching which neither Makerere nor Ibadan were able to provide. It was therefore impossible either in West or East Africa before independence to organize degree courses in a field which was of great importance for the economies of the territories.[13] In East Africa a veterinary diploma course was started but had to be closed for lack of candidates. It suffered from the same weakness as the old Yaba course in medicine: the diploma course was almost as long as the full degree course which could be taken in Britain, but the diploma holder would only earn half the salary of the man with the full degree.

Medicine was in almost all the colonial territories the first profession in which fully trained local people were admitted to government service. Here it was the General Medical Council of Great Britain which had to recognize the medical degrees of the new universities in order for their holders to be registered to practise. In India the G.M.C. recognized the degrees of the Indian universities for this purpose at the end of the 19th century. Considerable difficulties were to arise, however, in Africa. Both in Ibadan and Makerere very expensive teaching hospitals had to be built in order to satisfy the standards of the G.M.C., that at Ibadan costing £5 million. The African student, since his London degree enabled him to practise in England, had to concentrate on the study of diseases prevalent in

240

England. The curriculum at Ibadan did not allow sufficient emphasis on preventive medicine, social medicine and child health, the real problems of Africa, and the students instead 'were obliged to follow an inflexible course designed for an affluent society with an infant mortality among the lowest in Europe'.[14]

Of the government departments, however, Health was often the most realistic and flexible in its treatment of standards. Tanganyika provides a good example. In this poor territory, the officers who set up the medical department after the British occupation in the First World War realized that it would be many years before the economy could afford to make fully skilled medical treatment universally available. They started therefore by giving a three months course to tribal dressers, selected by the chiefs, who on their return to their villages were provided with simple buildings, medicine and equipment at the expense of the community which they served. Gradually Africans were trained at higher levels. By the time that the British departed, the tribal dresser, now called 'tribal medical aid', remained at the base of the pyramid, running a small dispensary. At the next level a larger dispensary was run by a 'rural medical aid' with two years training. At the district level a health centre was run by a medical assistant with three years training; he was gradually being replaced by the assistant medical officer, who had four years training and a year's in-service experience in hospital and virtually functioned as a rural general practitioner. At the top level there were a few fully qualified African doctors. The one who took over as Chief Medical Officer at independence had qualified sixteen years before at Makerere and had taken postgraduate courses in Britain. A striking feature of the Tanganyika service was that a considerable proportion of the doctors and assistant medical officers had started as dispensers. One assistant medical officer who qualified in 1962 had joined as a dispenser in 1932.[15]

While it is hard to generalize in so wide a field, it appears that there were times when standards even in the health services were probably unnecessarily high. Ghana's Africanization Commissioner found that there was no need for a nurse to have to serve ten years as sister before becoming eligible for promotion to ward sister: three years now seemed sufficient.[16] The Singapore localization commission was surprised to learn that a higher qualification was required for Senior Registrars' posts in Singapore than in the United Kingdom.[17] But the medical service by and large was the most advanced in localization. The advantages of this policy could be seen particularly in preventive medicine where the local doctor could often get closer to the people than could the foreigner. An example was the achievement of Dr. Milton Margai, subsequently Prime Minister of Sierra Leone, who while serving as a government medical officer, was able to make use of the tribal initiation ceremonies for girls in order to introduce courses of instruction in hygiene.[18]

Many of the great engineers who made the industrial revolution in Britain were men with little formal education: George Stephenson, who invented the steam locomotive, is said to have been unqualified to join the Institution of Civil Engineers and to have founded the Institution of Mechanical Engineers for this reason.[19] From the mid-19th century, however, practice of engineering at the higher level in Britain and the colonies was confined to those who had obtained membership of the Institutions of Civil, Mechanical or Electrical Engineers, either by passing their examinations or by obtaining a university degree or diploma recognized by the Institutions.

In India the Roorkee Engineering College was founded at a very early stage. In Africa, apart from the Sudan, the development of training in engineering was not very fortunate. Although at Yaba, Achimota and Makerere, engineering courses had been run before 1945 for intermediate London examinations, the new University Colleges assumed no responsibility in this field. The Institutions in London, conscious of the importance of the status of the engineer, urged in vain on the Secretary of State for the Colonies that engineering should be taught at the University Colleges. Instead separate Colleges of Arts, Science and Technology were set up to offer courses of general scientific and technical education which would lead to professional, or near professional, qualifications, but not to degrees. Boys with sufficient education to get into these technical colleges were not content to do so, but preferred to go to a university. Eventually the Colleges of Arts, Science and Technology became the engineering faculties of the universities: indeed as a further stage in Ghana, Nigeria and Kenya, they became themselves the nucleus of new universities. Valuable time, however, had been lost on the way.[20]

To enter government service as an engineer the local officer, as well as the expatriate, needed to acquire Associate Membership of the appropriate Institution of Engineers in London. This required him not only to pass the Institution's examinations but to spend a period as a pupil to a member or to an approved body. The pupillage requirements, however reasonable in the United Kingdom, were to frustrate the development of the profession in some of the colonies. For Malayan irrigation officers to have to be trained in the United Kingdom, which had no large irrigation schemes and grew no rice, made little sense. Australian training facilities were more relevant, but the Institution of Civil Engineers in London only recognized one year's pupillage as valid under an engineer with Australian qualifications, while two years had to be served altogether.[21] In Nigeria, Ghana and Malaya, it was a grievance that nationals who held American engineering degrees could not enter government service because their qualifications were not recognized by the British Institutions.

While West Africa was very short of African engineers at independence, in East Africa there were practically none, nor was the future encouraging. At the Royal College, Nairobi, in the Faculty of Engineering only two Africans survived in 1961 in the fifth year of the course out of twenty-four who had embarked on it: of fifteen Kenya Africans who studied engineering in British universities between 1951–61, none obtained a degree.[22] While this heavy failure rate was attributed to inadequate science teaching and lack of prior contact with engineering devices, perhaps 'standards' were also relevant. One of the British staff members at the Royal College told Sir Willis Jackson in 1961 that 'the present inability of African students to match up to our standards in engineering subjects had been interpreted and quoted as another aspect of British colonialism, and that he and his colleagues feared a reduction, in due course, in the standard of the degree award towards that of the American first degree. He said that the increasing availability of scholarships for study in America was a considerable embarrassment in this connection'.[23] It seems remarkable that the standards of engineering education of the United States were considered too low for East Africa in 1961.

The profession which perhaps maintained the most parochial attitude was that of accountancy. The annual report of the Association of Accountants in the Gold Coast for 1954 stated that recognition of any accountancy qualification other than those of the associations which were based in the United Kingdom would be 'detrimental to the profession and to the Gold Coast'. By 1956 they broadened their horizon to accept the qualifications also of the

Society of Chartered Accountants of South Africa and now defined the 'universally recognized professional accountancy bodies' as those of Scotland, England, Wales, Ireland and South Africa. Only in 1960, three years after independence, was recognition extended to include any body which was recognized by the International Congress of Accountants. By now it began to be suggested that the syllabus of the United Kingdom bodies covered subjects such as executorship law and accounts which had little practical application in Ghana.[24] An article by a Ghanaian on the subject in 1961 asserted that the American and Scandinavian systems, by which accountants were given part of their training at universities, was more appropriate to Ghana's conditions than apprenticeship in the British tradition.[25] Training in universities might have provided a more practical method for some other colonies also. For, as a Malayan localization committee complained, the professional etiquette which required that a prospective pupil should be introduced in person to the accountant to whom he is to be articled 'occasions difficulty when 8,000 miles separate the prospective pupil from the accountant'.[26]

Was British training, in general, as has sometimes been alleged, unnecessarily long? The traditions of some of the professional associations can be traced back to those of the medieval guilds, which had deliberately restricted the numbers of their practitioners by imposing very long periods of apprenticeship. The Nigerian National Manpower Board in its report in 1963 suggested that a review of professional and technical entry qualifications was required. 'Hitherto,' they said, 'the qualifications and periods required have corresponded with those demanded in the U.K. and it is by no means clear that requirements for the U.K. are necessarily appropriate to Nigeria. In the United States, for example, similar standards of competence are reached in substantially shorter periods'. In Kenya it was asked why African students should have to take three years to obtain a degree because they could only spend 24 weeks a year in residence at the university according to traditional Oxford practice, although in America it was possible to obtain a degree in 14 months of continuous study. At the other end of the scale the government in Kaduna failed to appreciate why a Nigerian house painter required three years training because this was a regulation in Great Britain.[27]

The question was perhaps particularly relevant in agriculture. The Colonial Service agricultural officer, like the veterinarian and forestry officer, was required to have an honours degree in his subject and subsequently to have taken a special course in tropical studies, usually at the Imperial Agricultural College in Trinidad. For research work such high qualifications were probably needed. It is less certain that they were essential for extension work. Experience since independence, when these services were left short-handed after the departure of expatriates and before the graduation of Africans, on the whole defied predictions of disaster. The African with a diploma or with long practical experience usually proved capable of carrying wider responsibilities in extension work and considerable dilution was possible.

Africans sometimes assert that the British deliberately kept local people out of the senior professional posts. This attitude, they maintain, started during the thirties when there was unemployment among British professional officers. The policy of forming unified colonial services, formulated at a time when the colonial empire was expected to last a hundred years, seems to have proved a particular obstacle to Africanization in the agricultural services. As we have seen in earlier chapters, despite the importance of agriculture for the economies of most of the colonial territories only a small proportion of students were studying in this field by independence.[28] Agricultural faculties naturally took longer to organize than those in Arts. But it was also true that the profession was less attractive than many others in government service. Much of the criticism directed by the British at young Indians, Ceylonese and Africans for preferring other professions was somewhat beside the point. The agricultural officer was usually less well paid than the administrator or doctor. His prestige was not so great, which meant that his bride would bring a lower dowry, in countries where this applied, than the girls who married into other professions. He was likely to be stationed in rural areas, with inadequate schools for his children, and which were often infected by malaria and other diseases. Only if there were a salary differential in the favour of the agricultural officer, or if promotion were easier to obtain in this than in other branches of government, was it likely that an adequate number of candidates would be found.

In the administrative service and the police it was much more difficult for professional yardsticks to be used. There was normally an initial insistence that locally appointed administrative officers must have honours degrees. This requirement seemed particularly unfair to the Africans after the Second War, when many of the British administrative officers had no degrees but had been appointed on grounds that their experience in the army was an equally good qualification. Ahmado Bello pointed out that at one time none of the three Lieutenant Governors in Nigeria had degrees.[29] The requirement also discouraged students in the universities from taking pass degrees. Until a few years before independence standards were usually maintained to be inviolable. When the Acting Commissioner of Police was asked by the Malayanization Committee of 1954 'whether it would not be possible to accelerate the promotion of local officers in order to make a fairer proportion between the local and expatriate gazetted officers,' he replied that he 'could not agree to promotion being governed by political considerations, and that merit must be the only consideration'.[30]

It is striking that in the 20th century both in West and East Africa, unlike India, local doctors, who required a much longer period of training, were recruited by the government before local administrative officers. But in the closing stages of British rule, when Commissions or Commissioners for Africanization were appointed, it was possible to accelerate localization of the administrative and police services much more rapidly than in the professional services. It appeared more feasible to promote executive officers with long service to the administrative grade than to promote professional officers with diplomas to posts previously held by men with degrees.

In considering the influence of the professional associations on localization it must not be forgotten that many of them did much to foster education in their fields in the colonies. Their membership was often a considerable source of encouragement and strength to men in the colonies, of whatever race, who were working in isolation from their colleagues. Standards which may have been too high were far better than no standards at all. The associations, which were primarily concerned with conditions in the United Kingdom, cannot perhaps be blamed if their qualifications proved inappropriate in the colonies. Nevertheless, as the Inter-University Council observed in 1954, 'the link between academic awards and professional, particularly registrable, qualifications introduces a factor into colonial university development that is to some extent distracting, frustrating and conservative. . . . Clearly if a doctor trained in a colony automatically has the right to practise in the U.K. his training must fit him for that, even if this means reducing the emphasis on tropical and other local conditions which would otherwise be desirable'.[31] The Ashby Commission still found, six years later, that there was a belief that

STANDARDS AND PREJUDICES

standards of attainment for Nigerians practising in Nigeria must be acceptable to the bodies which legislate for Englishmen practising in England.[32]

This belief arose, on the African side, from the bitter experience of the men with local diplomas, the doctors from Yaba, the veterinarians from Makerere, the *medecins africains* from Dakar, whose qualifications had doomed them to a perpetual place in the second grade of their professions. Only after independence could the issue be faced by setting up national professional associations, as India had done much earlier, whose standards and curricula could be related to local needs and accepted by national governments. The Royal Institute of British Architects, which had previously controlled the development of the profession in the dependent territories, found a formula after they became independent which might become a model for other professions. The function of assessing educational standards in schools of architecture, and of facilitating recognition of degrees, was transferred to a Commonwealth Association of Architects, which the R.I.B.A. joined as a member on an equal footing with national bodies of other countries.

REFERENCES

[1] Lord Sinha was appointed as a Governor in the 1920s but the appointment remained unique until within a few years of independence.
[2] Lord Rosebery, *Questions of Empire*, London, 1900, p. 13.
[3] T. Raleigh, *Lord Curzon in India*, London, 1906, p. 50.
[4] James Hunt, *On the Negro's place in Nature*, London, 1863.
[5] J. G. Lockhart and C. M. Wodehouse, *Rhodes*, London, 1963, pp. 62–67.
[6] Edmund Burke, op. cit., p. 182.
[7] W. E. F. Ward, *Fraser of Trinity and Achimota*, London, 1965, p. 56.
[8] R. F. Betts, *Assimilation and Association in French Colonial Policy*, New York, 1961.
[9] M. Perham, *The Colonial Reckoning*, London, 1962, p. 49.
[10] Sir G. Arthur, *Life of Lord Kitchener*, London, 1920, Vol. II, p. 181.
[11] See R. Braibanti, 'Reflections on Bureaucratic Corruption' in *Public Administration*, London, 1962, Vol. 40 and R. Wraith and E. Simpkins, *Corruption in Developing Countries*, London, 1963.
[12] Report of Inter-University Council for Higher Education Overseas, 1946–54, London, HMSO, Cmd 9515, p. 4.
[13] A. M. Carr-Saunders, *New Universities Overseas*, London, 1961, p. 145–6.
[14] E. Ashby, *African Universities and Western Tradition*, London, 1964, p. 34. See also report of Professor Graham Bull quoted in same.

[15] D. F. Clyde, *History of the Tanganyika Medical Service*, Dar-es-Salaam, 1962.

[16] A. L. Adu, *Civil Service in New African States*, London, 1965.

[17] Colony of Singapore, *Interim Report on Malayanization Commission*, Singapore, 1956, p. 227.

[18] D. L. Sumner, *Education in Sierra Leone*, London, 1963.

[19] S. Smiles, *Lives of the Engineers*, London, 1862, Vol. III, p. 479. The legend was disputed and disappeared from further editions.

[20] A. M. Carr-Saunders, op. cit., pp. 147–150.

[21] Federation of Malaya, *Report of the Committee on Malayanization of the Public Service*, Kuala Lumpur, 1956, p. 109. Also *Report of the Committee on Malayanization*, 1954, p. 40.

[22] Sir Willis Jackson, 'Some Impressions of Electrical and Educational Developments in East and Central Africa', *Electrical Supervisor*, October, 1961, p. 4.

[23] ibid., p. 4.

[24] From papers made available privately.

[25] E. H. Boohene in *Journal of Management Studies*, Accra, Vol. I, June, 1961.

[26] Federation of Malaya, *Report of the Committee on Malayanization*, Kuala Lumpur, 1956, p. 43.

[27] *Report of Nigerian National Manpower Board*, Lagos, 1963, and observations of the author in Africa in 1964.

[28] The proportions are shown in Carr-Saunders, op. cit., table 6, p. 122.

[29] Ahmadu Bello, *My Life*, London, 1962, 0p. 110.

[30] *Report of Committee on Malayanization of the Government Service*, Kuala Lumpur, 1954, p. 91.

[31] I.U.C. Report, 1946–54, op. cit., p. 14.

[32] *Ashby Report*, op. cit., p. 23.

CHAPTER XIII

Reflections on Localization

'Civil Servants have got the double role of being custo-
dians of what is best in the old traditions of the civil
service and being innovators in building new traditions.
. . . It would be a pity if they proved to be old bottles
that cannot carry the new wine.'

—DR. MILTON OBOTE, PRIME MINISTER OF
UGANDA, 1964[1]

T he process of decolonization was still unfinished while this
book was being written. After East Africa became independent the focus of interest moved south as the Central African
Federation broke up and as constitutional agreements were made
with Basutoland, Bechuanaland and Swaziland.

Nyasaland became independent as 'Malawi' and Northern
Rhodesia as 'Zambia' in 1964. One of the most incisive of all
Africanization reports had been that of the Localization Committee
set up by Dr. Banda to advise the Nyasaland Government in 1960.
Adu was Chairman and the report reflected many of his ideas which
have been seen in West and East Africa. While the Nyasaland
Government service required 430 officers with university degrees or
professional qualifications, only 33 local people possessed these
qualifications in 1960, with 40 more in training. At the current rate
only 120 altogether would be available by 1971.[2] The Committee
suggested that in many cases the British educational qualifications
which were demanded were irrelevant and urged that Nyasalanders
who had school certificates should be sent to the U.S.A. and Canada
to obtain degrees in agriculture, forestry and engineering.[3] They
recommended that an immediate policy decision should be made to
place the civil service in the hands of Nyasalanders. To those who
had spoken to them of the dangers of going too fast, they suggested

that the dangers of going too slow were even greater; they pointed to the lesson of the Congo to show that chaos could follow the withdrawal of foreign personnel if indigenous people had not been given the opportunity to take responsibility and acquire experience before independence.[4]

Despite this report, all Malawi's Permanent Secretaries remained British at independence, and though two-thirds of the district officers were Africans these reported to headquarters through the nearest British official. The pace of Africanization was reported to be one of the points at issue in the breach between Dr. Banda and his ministers shortly after independence.[5] Dr. Banda's own approach to the question may have been influenced by the fact that he had been living in the 1950s in Ghana, which retained British officers in a number of senior positions after independence. The contrast between Malawi and Zambia was striking. In Zambia Africans were appointed as understudies to the Permanent Secretaries several months before independence and were given an intensive training course, together with the politicians who were already designated to succeed the Provincial Commissioners.

Further south still, the former British Protectorates of Bechuanaland, Basutoland, and Swaziland faced the special administrative problems which confront countries with very small populations at independence. How, it was asked, could an independent Swaziland, for example, with a population of only 250,000 continue to support 500 'European' officials or their African replacements, if paid on a similar scale? In the Protectorates compensation arrangements for the expatriates reached extremes of complexity, when distinctions were made between eligibility of 'Europeans' recruited locally or from South Africa or from London. In these territories the political aspects of localization were as difficult as those which were economic. Could independent governments continue to employ the white South Africans who had been the mainstay of their professional services – or could they avoid a collapse of the services without them? Or, for that matter, what would their attitude be to the black South Africans who by reason of their better education sometimes held posts senior to the local people in the services?

While the consecutive study of localization of the services in India, West Africa and East Africa has a natural sequence, it should be remembered that developments in other territories also affected the pattern.

One of the most important influences was that of the Sudan, though its administration was untypical in several ways, for it was the responsibility not of the Colonial Office but of the Foreign Office; and in a Condominium its services were staffed by Egyptian as well as by British officers. A twenty year programme of Sudanization which was drawn up in 1946 was rapidly overtaken by political events, and in the last year before independence almost 90% of the expatriate officers were terminated or resigned.[6] Despite this sudden exodus, the Sudanese, whose University College had been one of the earliest to be established in Africa, carried on the administration with more success than had been anticipated. The Sudan experience was to cause the British Government to become preoccupied in West Africa with the equitable compensation of expatriate officers who might be terminated, rather than with devising arrangements which could encourage them to remain over the difficult period of transition in countries which, unlike the Sudan, had no desire to dispense with their services immediately.

In Southeast Asia the reports of localization commissions in Malaya and Singapore, which consisted of politicians rather than of civil servants, were important not so much for their effect on Colonial Office thinking as for their influence on political commissions elsewhere. A Ceylon Commission used them as a precedent to justify the establishment of quotas for racial groups in the services.[7] In Nigeria the Malayan reports were quoted by a Parliamentary Committee to support their view that all key posts, such as those of Permanent Secretaries, must be placed in the hands of nationals at independence.[8]

The history of localization in the West Indies lies somewhat outside the main stream and has unusual features. Longer than anywhere else a system of patronage continued into the 19th century by which West Indian posts were held by politicians in London and the duties discharged by deputies. Localization, however, developed relatively early. In 1945, of 1,318 posts with salaries of over £600 a year, only 287 were held by expatriates. Unlike the other British territories there were no separate administrative, executive and clerical grades. A West Indian, even if a graduate, had to start as a second class clerk.[9] Though it was alleged that the transfer of British officers from other colonies sometimes blocked the promotion of better qualified local men,[10] the existence of the unified colonial services and subsequently of the Federal West Indian services had evident advantages for the smaller islands. With the dissolution of the Federation, the separate administrations faced serious problems in offering worthwhile careers to graduates and professional officers, and the way in which they handled these might prove to be of considerable interest to the other scattered islands of the Commonwealth which were still not independent.

No account has been given in this study of the development of the government services in the white colonies; in these, after the lessons of the American War of Independence, the colonies encountered little difficulty in obtaining approval to staff their services from their own resources even before the stage of self-government. The colonists who filled the posts sometimes had careers in the service of the United Kingdom as well as in their own countries. Amery recruited Australians and Canadians into the Colonial Service. Crocker, who had vehemently criticized indirect rule after serving as an administrative officer in Nigeria, went on to serve as an Australian High Commissioner, and R. G. Casey served as Governor of Bengal before becoming Australia's Foreign Minister.

Lord Milner and his friends would have liked to go further and create an imperial legislature with an imperial secretariat, though the Canadians and Australians eventually killed the idea. But Milner specifically excluded the non-white races from his scheme. India at the Imperial Conference, he said, was 'an embarrassment and a weakness. . . . It is no use pretending that bonds of family feeling exist or can exist between peoples of a dependent empire and those of the British Nations'.[11] This racial view, so much more restrictive than that of Macaulay and Trevelyan, prevailed. Lord Sinha became a British Parliamentary Secretary in 1919, but there were no Indian proconsuls on the frontiers of the British Empire such as Gaul, Spain and even Africa had provided for Rome. British colonial history has no Governor to match Eboué, the West Indian who rallied Equatorial Africa to De Gaulle while West Africa under its French Governor General collaborated with Vichy; nor in the Colonial Office would a visitor be received, as in the Ministries in Paris, by an Asian assistant secretary or an African doctor.

Throughout this study a thread of continuity has been the relation of the British experience in India to their policies in Africa. In education we have seen how continuously the experience of the British in India affected African policies; how the recommendations of Phelps-Stokes and of the Advisory Committee in the 1920s, which emphasized mass education in terms of the rural environment, were a reaction against the problems of educated unemployment which the Indian policies had created; and in turn how the Asquith doctrine with its insistence on British academic standards was again influenced by the spectre of the Calcutta University.

Of Indian administrative experience, however, the Colonial Office, though separated only by a courtyard in Downing Street from the India Office, seems to have made little use. Of 100 colonial governors appointed between the Wars, only one came from the I.C.S., though seven came from the home civil service and twenty-eight from the army.[12] Lugard, who as a youth had failed to pass the I.C.S. examination, wrote in the *Dual Mandate* in 1922 that 'perhaps it was as well that Great Britain, following the tradition of the Empire, did not (as she might have been expected to do) select from her most experienced servants, trained in the school of Indian administration, those who should grapple with this sudden emergency, but trusted to the men on the spot. The pioneers of African administration came to their tasks with minds unbiassed by traditions unsuited to the races and conditions of Africa and more ready to make bricks without straw'.[13] Yet when at last Lord Hailey, who had been Governor of the Punjab and of the United Provinces and a member of the Viceroy's Council, published his massive *African Survey* in 1938 it could be seen how much might have been learnt from India. As he looked into the administrative and professional services all over tropical Africa, Hailey pointed out how little had been done and was being done to train Africans for the middle level positions which in India had been staffed by nationals for 50 or 100 years.[14]

Sometimes precedents from India were unreal. Lugard's idealistic picture of life in the Indian Native States would have surprised many officers of the Indian Political Service: it would have been more convincing to let Indirect Rule stand on its own legs without this kind of historical support.[15] Sometimes Indian precedents may have been unconscious or subconscious. Those who in the 1930s described the administrative service in Nigeria as a 'scaffolding' around native administrations, which would disappear at independence, were using the same phraseology as Sir Charles Trevelyan had employed in giving evidence to a Parliamentary Committee about the future of the I.C.S. in 1873.[16]

That more reflection in the Colonial Office on the lessons of India could have been profitable has been seen on two major questions. Chamberlain in 1895 found himself faced with the same kind of problem in West Africa as Cornwallis had encountered in India a hundred years earlier. Action was required to deal with corruption and inefficiency both among European and locally recruited officers. Cornwallis's solution was to create a well paid and virtually exclusive British service. It has been seen how Parliament insisted on breaking down the principle of exclusiveness and how much bitterness was subsequently created in the rising Indian middle class by the practical obstacles which were placed in the way of their admission. Yet the Colonial Office followed much the same road and alienated the small but influential educated middle class in West Africa by excluding it from senior government posts.

A precedent which Amery might have considered thirty years later could perhaps have been even more illuminating. A study of the consequences of the separation of Europeans into 'Imperial' services and Indians into 'Provincial' services in the 1890s might have caused more attention to be given to the obstacles to African promotion and ambitions which would ensue from the creation of the unified colonial services, restricted to officers of 'pure European descent' in the 1930s. In this case indeed, as Professor Kenneth Robinson has pointed out, the Colonial Office officials need hardly have crossed the courtyard to the India Office. Their own files could have shown the instructive history of the services in Ceylon,[17] where the introduction of the Donoughmore Constitution prevented the progress of Ceylonization from being affected by the creation of the unified services.

It was only in 1960 that there is evidence to show that localization was seen by the Colonial Office as a general rather than a territorial problem. In that year a Public Services Conference, sometimes referred to as 'the Localization Conference', was called in London and attended by representatives of the governments of West, East and Central Africa as well as of Somaliland and the Protectorates. The Conference discussed a pooling of experience on the approach to localization, higher education and training, and compensation schemes, and agreed on the need both to clarify principles and to keep policy under consideration. 'The Colonial Office,' the Report stated, 'had not hitherto been organized to consider the problems of localization as a general issue. Arrangements were, however, to be made, under which one Department of the Office would in future be the focal point for handling this subject'.[18] These arrangements do not seem to have been made. Probably it was too late to matter. To the historian there is an air of unreality about this conference: Kenya, Uganda, Tanganyika, Zanzibar, the various East African Common Services, Northern Rhodesia and Nyasaland were all represented at it exclusively by Europeans, who were about to be swept away by the wind of change over the next four years.

No more perhaps can reasonably be expected of a colonial power which considers itself to be a trustee than that it should seek to establish institutions in the colonies which are the best possible at the time by enlightened contemporary metropolitan standards. The confident assertions, for example, by educational officers of the 1920s that 'the traditions and values of the English Public School are of universal validity' may seem quaint now in an age in which the Public Schools appear to be generally regarded as an embarrassing obstacle to modernization in the metropolitan country itself; at the time few would have questioned the principle.

Yet in practice colonial institutions tended to reproduce the British characteristics not only in an outdated but an exaggerated form. Dr. Arnold, who appointed his prefects on intellectual ability, would hardly have recognized a system such as that in the government schools of Tanganyika where they were chosen for distinction in drill: nor would he have appreciated the situation in which the new headmaster, on arrival at Trinity College, Kandy, found 100 boys waiting to be caned by him in person. A system which was not anti-intellectual in England often became so in the colonies.

Exaggeration of British administrative practice was particularly unfortunate. The financial and office procedures, in the form in which they evolved in India, became capable in times of strain or emergency of almost paralysing the machinery of government. Curzon, dealing with files which had drifted between London, Calcutta and the North West Province for over six years, described the Government of India as 'a gigantic quagmire or bog into which every question that comes along either sinks or is sucked down; and unless you stick a peg with a label over the spot at which it disappears and from time to time go round and dig out the relics you will never see anything of them again'.[19] Forty years later the combination of rigid financial procedures and labyrinthine filing routes contributed to the loss of hundreds of thousands of lives in the Bengal Famine, and in Ceylon government factories which had been established in the Second World War stood idle while the papers had to pass between four or five government offices and the Crown Agents in London before a few rupees could be sanctioned to buy spare parts. In Britain the tradition of Treasury control served a wholesome purpose in preventing extravagance but did not inhibit urgent decisions in time of emergency. In a democracy the elector whose letters to a government department remained unanswered could jolt the machine into action by having a question asked in Parliament. But in the colonies only a rare white settler was capable of a spirited gesture such as that of Lord Delamere in Kenya who, according to local legend, set fire to a government office in order to obtain attention to his communications. The monstrous unchecked bureaucratic growth which the Successors inherited in some of the territories was one of the worst of the British legacies.

It is possible that if the British officers had remained longer in the same departments or posts they might have discovered how to control the enormous volume of paper produced by the hundreds of local clerks who worked permanently in the Secretariat. Here again there was an exaggeration of the national practice of administrative amateurism. Although in the home Civil Service the administrative officer who was recruited by written examination received no formal training, he would normally spend most of his career in one ministry in whose procedures, problems and precedents he would eventually become an expert after twenty years of experience. In India and Africa, however, it was unusual for an officer to remain in the same post for more than a couple of years. John Bright told the Commons in 1859 of an I.C.S. officer who had held 21 posts in 17 years.[20] Chettur in Madras in the 20th century was transferred 13 times in 12 years.[21] Partly this was because frequent interchange between secretariat and the field was considered healthy in order to prevent the development of a 'secretariat mentality'. Leave in West Africa was also frequent enough to hamper continuity. But the principle of 'Buggins's turn' was equally important. G. O. Trevelyan told the House of Commons in 1868 of the I.C.S. – 'Good or bad, they must be promoted in their turn or something like their turn'.[22] Ninety years later an American described the policy of automatic promotion in Eastern Nigeria as 'little short of disastrous'.[23] Fairness to officers in rotation and in promotion generally took precedence over efficiency. Nowhere was this more apparent than in the Education Departments: government schools and training colleges could often have made a far greater impact if they had enjoyed the same continuity of staff as the mission schools.

The consequences of the amateur attitude to secretariat administration were sometimes serious for the successor governments. Early Africanization was concentrated almost entirely on training district officers at a time when secretariat work was becoming increasingly complicated, as money became available for development schemes. It was mainly American advice which at a late stage established the principles that methodical training was necessary for secretariat officers and that continuity in the administration of departments was desirable.

Another exaggeration can be seen in the development of the Public Service (or Civil Service) Commissions. In Britain, when patronage was abolished in government offices, the Civil Service Commission was established in order to carry out recruitment and hold examinations for the public service. It had no responsibility for promotions. In Africa, however, the Public Service Commissions which were established not only undertook recruitment but advised the governments on promotion. As soon as the stage of internal self-government was reached, the Commissions became executive instead of advisory. The object was to protect the position of British civil servants against the African ministers. By placing what sometimes was construed as an insulting limitation on the authority of the Prime Minister, considerable irritation was, however, caused. The Commissions were usually made advisory again after independence. Meanwhile the ministers were not entirely inhibited. In Kenya, though under the Constitution the Public Service Commission was required to be consulted by the Prime Minister on the appointment of Permanent Secretaries, its members only learnt on the radio on Independence Day that the expatriates had been replaced in these posts. In Malawi the first candidates selected for training as administrative officers were chosen not by the P.S.C. but by a committee of ministers.

In the introduction of competitive written examinations as the means of entry to government service, the British were giving India and Ceylon what was at the time a very modern device. Examinations for entry to the public services in the United Kingdom followed logically from the triumph of the middle classes over the aristocracy with the passing of the Reform Bill of 1832; for the sons of the former, educated at the new or revitalized Public Schools, had a better chance of selection by competition than by patronage. The procedure had the same appeal for the new middle classes in Asia and West Africa, which had good reason to believe that under a system of patronage the relatives of chiefs and princes would obtain the best appointments. The embarrassment of the British was considerable when they found that the sons of the Indian and Ceylon middle classes absorbed European culture so rapidly that they soon became capable of defeating British candidates in open competition. Thus they began to experiment with quotas, sometimes with considerable justification in defence of the less educated minority groups, while the principle of written competitive examination became firmly embedded in the nationalist platform.

Macaulay and his school were responsible for much unhappiness and waste. In order to produce a relatively small elite, the whole educational system was harnessed to a course of studies which was unrelated to agriculture or to increased productivity or to the national culture. Because the British generally failed to develop industry or agriculture, the prizes at the top of government service had an almost universal attraction. The question of salaries in the colonial governments was particularly intractable. In Ceylon Colebrooke caused the British salaries to be reduced to local levels, with the result that the British officers spent half their time growing coffee in order to supplement their income. In East Africa the Holmes Commission recommended that Africans receive only three-fifths of the European salary in order that a local 'Mandarin class' should not be created: but the British Government was unable to withstand the consequent criticisms of racial discrimination. It was successfully argued that the African officer ought to be able to live in the same style as his British colleague. Eventually, both in the British and French colonies, the salary rates for expatriates and local officers became the same. After independence the enormous discrepancy between the standard of living of those at the top and the bottom of the services thus became a major source of political discontent, particularly in West Africa. On the other hand in Malawi, Dr. Banda encountered serious difficulties with his African civil servants when they demanded, but did not receive, the same salaries and allowances as the British after independence.[24]

It was certainly better for the colonial power to be able to hand over the services to an educated and experienced elite, however remote from the masses than, as in the Congo, to leave no successors. In East Africa, where political advance far outstripped higher and professional education, the British brooded too long over the evils of creating a class of unemployable 'baboos', when the real danger was of administrative collapse for lack of trained Africans. And when they embarked on higher education, the approach was leisurely and perfectionist. Their defence was that the process could not be hurried, that primary and secondary education had to be improved and expanded before the output of graduates for the government service could be increased. Consideration of the practice in the two countries which were technologically leading the world might have suggested that there were other ways of producing qualified men in this emergency. In both the U.S.A. and the U.S.S.R., in marked contrast to the United Kingdom, there was a proud tradition that the door to higher education was never closed, and almost any qualification could be acquired through part-time classes and correspondence courses. As a consequence there was in these countries in general more upward mobility in the government services than there was in the British system, even though in Nigeria, by great effort, clerks did sometimes manage to take external degrees from London University. Articles by a British education officer from Kenya who visited the Soviet Republics of Asia in the fifties suggest that much might have been learnt there not only in respect of the use of correspondence courses, but in ensuring that secondary school and university students did not lose touch with their environment.[25] The impact of American educational methods, of course, has been considerable since independence in Africa and Asia.

Before 1945 it would perhaps have been unreasonable to expect the British, who were themselves governed by an elite, not to consider that the creation of an elite was the best solution to the problems of the succession. The most serious criticism arises from the failure in timing. Even in West Africa, let alone in East Africa, the graduates of the new universities were not ready to take major responsibilities by independence.

Sir Alexander Carr-Saunders, who was more than anyone responsible for the implementation of the Asquith doctrine after 1945, found the British Colonial Service unsympathetic to the establishment of the new universities.[26] In earlier days a senior official admitted to Ward of Achimota his dislike for a policy of training Africans for government service because 'I do not wish to shut in my son's face the door I myself have passed through'.[27] It would be imprudent, however, to generalize about the attitude of the British officers to their potential successors. In India, even at the worst days of racial tension at the end of the 19th century, I.C.S. officers like Cotton, Wedderburn and A. O. Hume could identify themselves with middle class aspirations. At the end in India there was probably not much jealousy or resentment on the British side. It had, after all, been known that it was the government's policy to replace the British officers since 1917, before some of the last of them were born. Many of them, without leave through the Second War, were tired and frustrated. One of them has left a convincing account of the I.C.S. welcoming the advent to power of Nehru, who although anti-British, could carry on the struggle more effectively than they had been able to do against the old problems of caste and rural indebtedness and the seclusion of women.[28]

By contrast, there were quite young men in the British service in East Africa at independence who had been confidently told by Colonial Office officials that British rule would certainly outlast their time. They received their compensation, but the suddenness of the change and the manifest lack of preparations for it made some of them embittered with politicians, with the United Nations, with everyone deemed to be responsible. In the months before independence, these showed an unwillingness to compromise, an insistence on a rigid distinction between a right and a wrong way of doing things: the new government could make up its mind, but they were not themselves prepared to be associated with lower standards. Yet as some of the African leaders recollected, in a different sort of emergency in Britain in the War, there had been no complaints when crash training courses were organized, when men were promoted in months instead of years to staff expanded departments, and when professors and businessmen were made into Permanent Secretaries. In those territories where there was a longer period in which to adjust to the prospect of independence, British officers seemed readier to change their attitudes on 'standards'. The adjustment thus appeared easier in Kenya and Uganda than in Tanganyika. In technical services like Posts and Telegraphs, where senior expatriate staff had been temporarily seconded from Britain, the transition to African management was often notably smoother and the training of Africans undertaken with more enthusiasm.

It may not be fanciful to suppose that the attitudes of British colonial officers both to the rising local middle class and to reforms emanating from London were sometimes coloured between the

Wars by their contempt for politicians as a class both at home
and abroad. This had not been a prevalent feeling in the 19th
century: it was possible to hate Palmerston, Gladstone or Salisbury
but hardly to despise them. The scorn started from the time when
Lloyd George sold Honours, whose values have always been treated
more seriously by civil servants than by most other elements in
British life: it continued for various reasons to embrace Baldwin and
MacDonald and many of their ministers. There was a widespread
belief that the men who ought to have been leading Britain had either
perished on the Somme or had found politics a disreputable profession. By contrast, the dignified local relations with traditional chiefs
appear to have had a romantic and even escapist attraction.

The position of the minorities in the services was part of the wider
political problem. Almost always claims for quotas of places in the
services received parallel treatment to the demand for seats in the
legislatures. Minorities such as the Muslims and Scheduled Castes
in India required special consideration because they were educationally backward. But often the problem was precisely the opposite,
as in Ceylon and in East Africa and in Nigeria, where the minorities
were over-represented. In India the drastic solution of partition
was adopted; in Nigeria the public services were placed on a regional
basis. In Ceylon and East Africa the proportional rights of the
majority were much more firmly asserted by the successor governments than by the British. Though there was an element of 'divide
and rule' under most colonial regimes, the problem did not disappear with independence. Pakistan continued to allocate quotas to its
two wings in the civil service, and in 1965 India appeared to be considering adopting a similar policy between its states in light of its
language problems. A conference of senior African civil servants
in 1964 concluded that it was necessary to relax standards of admission for candidates from less developed areas as part of the price
which had to be paid for national unity.[29]

Localization can only be studied in the margins of political history.
Where it failed the failure was usually due to lack of political fore-
sight. Sometimes the local people were educated by the government,
but denied entry to senior ranks of the services. More often they were
educated by the missionaries, at first to the delight of the government, which wanted clerks, and later to its consternation, fearing
unrest. In the opposite situation, the pace of political advance raced
ahead of education and the risk of administrative breakdown was

accepted as the price of retaining the political initiative. West Africa was the last area where self-government proceeded at a controlled pace, to which localization could fairly adequately be geared. Shortly after the general election of 1959 it would appear that the MacMillan Government in Britain decided to withdraw from Africa as rapidly as possible. The subsequent series of constitutional conferences which the British Government held with representatives of the political parties of the colonial territories seem to have given little, if any, consideration to the relation of the constitutional timetable to the tempo of Africanization, except in safeguarding the financial position of the expatriate civil servants.

Up till this time there had been little sense of urgency about localization in East Africa; and Central Africa was still part of the Federation. The degree to which the governments adapted them-selves to the new situation as the timetable of independence was accelerated depended on local initiative, rather than on the Colonial Office. Some administrators seemed almost to despair. Others profited by the experience of West Africa, rapidly organized inten-sive training courses, and appointed African understudies to ex-patriates in key positions. As the territories became independent expatriates from their services joined other administrations: these 'retreads', as they were vulgarly called, were often of great assistance in enabling old errors to be avoided.

Not much has been said in this study of the actual techniques of localization, a somewhat specialized aspect of public administration which has been fully treated elsewhere.[30] By 1964 Institutes of Public Administration had been set up in most of the former British terri-tories, often with American or United Nations aid. That at Zaria might almost be said not only to have saved the administration of Northern Nigeria but to have saved those of East Africa by its example. Concentrated training courses were organized, and methods which had evolved experimentally and pragmatically became recog-nized and systematically applied in job dilution, the appointment of supernumeraries, the establishment of trainee grades and the acceptance of experience in place of formal qualifications. Eventually Africanization programmes merged into permanent training institu-tions, as the old British traditions of 'learning by apprenticeship' were modified.

No judgement of the relative success of localization could usefully be made except within the much wider context of the history of decolonization. And in any case judgement would be premature. It remains to be seen, in Africa at least, to what extent the immediate successors will be able to retain their positions and to carry out their duties, and whether the services established by the British can be successfully adapted to the orders of new masters and the demands of new electorates.

While the colonial civil service had been primarily concerned with the maintenance of law and order, the Successors were to spend a greater proportion of their time in administering development programmes. American critics have described the British colonial administrators as the best in the world, but with the pervasive defect of an ignorance of sound technology which often hid from them simple solutions to administrative problems.[31] Most of their successors shared this technological illiteracy. The new emphasis on development raised the question after independence as to whether a new type of senior administrator was required with a scientific rather than an arts degree. And this in turn caused reflection on the relative status of the administrative and professional officer. A change of social attitudes was necessary, it was agreed by a seminar of senior African civil servants in 1964, by which society gave the same respect to its agricultural specialists and engineers as to its administrators.[32]

To serve a one party state was not necessarily unfamiliar, for the powers of the new President were sometimes hardly more comprehensive than those of the old colonial governor. Dr. Obote, the Prime Minister of Uganda, in 1964 put forward a concept of the relationship between Minister and Permanent Secretary which was not very different from the British tradition. The Permanent Secretary, he said, must give frank advice to the Minister, withholding nothing from him, and must then accept and implement his decisions. But he added that on the other side civil servants must show a greater awareness of the role of the Party man, who had a duty to bring the grievances of the people before the administrator.[33] It was here that the greatest difficulties in adaptation seemed likely to arise.

In India and Pakistan the civil service faced a less serious adjustment at independence than elsewhere. They continued to be the essential instrument of the central government in huge and complex administrations: to some extent also the system was indigenous and constructed on the foundations of pre-British rule. In Ceylon, a much smaller country, the position of the senior civil service suffered in the keener reaction against cultural decolonization.

In Africa the adaptation from the spirit of British colonial rule to that of African socialism was most difficult, but on the other hand the traditions were shortest. The earliest Africans to enter the administrative service had done so at most fifteen years, and in some countries only five years, before independence. The problem of adjustment was stated frankly by the Committee on the review of the Kenya Institute of Administration in 1964.

'The inherited traditions of the public service,' they wrote, 'at their best encouraged attitudes of objective impartiality and detachment from the processes of party politics but . . . the civil servant can no longer afford to remain detached, and the concept of emotional involvement in national objectives becomes more and more fundamental to the evolution of the public service. . . . There is a widespread belief that it [the civil service] has inherited from the past a formal attitude of mind which, if a rift is not to develop between it and the political leadership of the nation, must quickly give place to something more than a sense of patriotism, that is to say a heart and soul commitment to new policies, new approaches, and a new impetus towards national reconstruction and national development'.[34]

More needs to be known of the verdicts of the Successors themselves on the British inheritance. Some impressions of these in India were given in Chapter IV. In Africa the services were localized so late that only A. L. Adu of Ghana, one of the first of the Successors, has yet given his views on the question at all fully. In his book on the Civil Service in New African States[35] he repeated the criticisms which have been seen in his reports of the slowness with which the administrative services were Africanized. He insisted on the need to adapt the structure and orientation of the services to the new political and constitutional framework. But, he said in his Introduction, 'Such traditions of the Colonial service as integrity, impartiality, efficiency of service, loyalty to the government of the day and devotion to duty are worth preserving. How to preserve them at a time of rapid turnover of personnel in responsible positions in the service is the problem and challenge presented to all those with responsibility for building the new nations and for shaping the New Civil Service in particular. Without these traditions, it would be impossible to preserve standards and pride of service and the New States would be poorly served by those who are responsible for executing the policies of their governments'.[36]

REFLECTIONS ON LOCALIZATION

REFERENCES

[1] *Third Public Administration Seminar*, Makerere College, 1964, p. 7.

[2] *Report of the Localization Committee* (Adu Report), Zomba, 1960, p. 22.

[3] ibid., p. 24.

[4] ibid., p. 15.

[5] *Africa Digest*, February, 1965, p. 96.

[6] K. Younger, op. cit., p. 68.

[7] *Final Report of National Education Commission*, Colombo, 1961, S.P. 7, p. 150.

[8] *Interim Report of Parliamentary Committee on Nigerianization*, Nigeria, S.P. 7 of 1958, p. 11.

[9] Sir M. Holmes, *Report of the Commission on Unification of the Public Services in the British Caribbean*, 1948–49, London, Col. 294, 1949.

[10] Ulric Lee, *Report on Reorganization of the Public Service in Trinidad and Tobago*, Trinidad, 1959, Introduction.

[11] Lord Milner, *Questions of the Hour*, London, 1945, p. 205.

[12] K. Robinson, *The Dilemmas of Trusteeship*, London, 1965, p. 121.

[13] Lugard, *Dual Mandate*, op. cit., p. 607.

[14] Lord Hailey, *African Survey*, London, 1945 ed., pp. 257–259.

[15] Lugard, *Dual Mandate*, op. cit., p. 226.

[16] P.P. 1873, Vol. XII, p. 96.

[17] K. Robinson, op. cit., p. 43.

[18] *Report of the Public Services Conference*, London, Col. 347, 1960, p. 3.

[19] Lord Ronaldshay, *Life of Lord Curzon*, London, 1928, Vol. II, p. 64.

[20] J. Bright, *Speeches*, London, 1868, Vol. I, p. 100.

[21] S. K. Chettur, op. cit., p. 13.

[22] Hansard, House of Commons Debates, 5 May, 1868, Col. 1844.

[23] J. D. Kingsley, *Staff Development in the Eastern Nigerian Public Service*, op. cit., p. 17.

[24] See article by C. Sanger reproduced in *Africa Digest*, December, 1964, p. 67.

[25] N. Larby in *Times Educational Supplement*, 20 January, 1961 and unpublished material.

[26] Carr Saunders, op. cit., p. 30.

[27] W. E. F. Ward, *Fraser of Trinity and Achimota*, London, 1965, p. 243.

[28] M. and T. Zinkin, *Requiem for Empire*, London, 1964, pp. 68–81.

[29] *Third Public Administration Seminar*, Makerere College, Kampala, 1964, p. 11.

[30] Notably by A. L. Adu in *The Civil Service in New African States*, London, 1965.

[31] e.g. Prof. de Kiewiet, quoted by E. Lucas, *Inaugural Lecture as Professor of Education*, Makerere College, 1959.

[32] *Third Public Administration Seminar*, Makerere College, 1964, p. 21.

[33] ibid., p. 6.

[34] Kenya Institute of Administration, *Report of Committee of Review*, November, 1964, Chairman A. L. Adu, mimeographed copy, p. 21.

[35] A. L. Adu, op. cit.

[36] A. L. Adu, op. cit., p. 13.

SELECT BIBLIOGRAPHY

As full references have been included at the end of each chapter, only the more important reports and other publications need be mentioned. In addition to these there are many official reports on localization which have only contemporary interest. The memoirs of many Indians in public life before independence and those of many colonial administrators also contain frequent references to the development of the public services.

Abbreviations
C.O.   Colonial Office confidential prints.
P.P.   Parliamentary Papers, England.
S.P.   Sessional Paper.

INDIA AND PAKISTAN

OFFICIAL REPORTS

Parliamentary Papers, England
    1812–13, Vol. X., Charles Grant's pamphlet on the *State of Asia.*
    1831–32, Vols VIII and IX, *Report and evidence of Select Committee on Affairs of East India Company.*
    1852–53, Vol. XXVIII, Sir Charles Trevelyan's pamphlet on *Education of the People of India.* Vol. XXVII and Vol. XXVIII, *Report and evidence of Select Committee on Affairs of East India Company.*
    1854–55, Vol. XL, *Report of Committee on Examination of Candidates for the Indian Civil Service.*
    1878–79, Vol. LV, *Papers Relating to Admission of Natives to the Civil Service in India.*
    1884–85, Vol. LVIII, *Correspondence on Age of Civil Service Candidates.*
    1893–94, Vol. LXIV, *Correspondence on Simultaneous Examinations.*
Report of Indian Education Commission (Hunter Report), Calcutta, 1883.
Report of the Public Service Commission (Aitchison Report), Calcutta, 1888.

SELECT BIBLIOGRAPHY

Report of Royal Commission on the Public Services in India (Islington Report), London, 1917, Cmd 8382.

Report on Indian Constitutional Reforms (Montagu-Chelmsford Report), London, 1918, Cmd 9109.

Report of Calcutta University Commission (Sadler Report), Calcutta, 1919.

Report of the Royal Commission on the Superior Civil Services in India (Lee Report), London, 1924, Cmd 2128.

Indian Statutory Commission Report (Simon Report), London, 1930, Cmd 3568, 3569.

Report of Indian Military College Committee, London, 1931.

Indian Round Table Conference, London, 1931, Cmd 3778.

Report of the University Education Commission (Radhakrishnan Report), New Delhi, 1949.

Report of the (Pakistan) Commission on National Education, Karachi, 1959.

Hansard, House of Commons Debates

10 July, 1833, Macaulay's speech on the East India Company Charter Bill.

24 June, 1853, Macaulay's speech on civil service entry.

5 May, 1868 and 2 June, 1893, Debates on examinations for the I.C.S. and other services.

2 August, 1922, Lloyd George's speech on the I.C.S.

OTHER PUBLICATIONS

Paul Appleby, *Public Administration in India*, Delhi, 1957.

Sir G. Arthur, *Life of Lord Kitchener*, London, 1920.

A. H. Aslam, *The Deputy Commissioner*, Lahore, 1957.

Sir Surendranath Banerjea, *A Nation in Making*, London, 1925.

A. C. Banerjee, *Indian Constitutional Documents*, Calcutta, 1948.

R. Braibanti (ed.), *Administration and Economic Development in India*, Duke University, 1963.

R. Braibanti (ed.), *The Civil Service of Pakistan*, Duke University, 1959.

Cambridge History of India, Vol. VI, 'The Indian Empire', London, 1932.

D. Chakrabarty, *Congress in Evolution*, Calcutta, 1958.

Asok Chanda, *Indian Administration*, London, 1958.

Sir George Chesney, *Indian Polity* (3rd ed.), London, 1894.

S. K. Chettur, *The Steel Frame and I*, London, 1962.

267

SELECT BIBLIOGRAPHY

Sir Valentine Chirol, *Indian Unrest*, London, 1910.

Sir H. Cotton, *New India*, London, 1886.

J. C. Curry, *The Indian Police*, London, 1932.

A. Embree, *Charles Grant and British Rule in India*, London, 1962.

A. C. Ewald, *Guide to the I.C.S.*, London, 1870.

H. Fawcett, 'Indian Finance', in *Nineteenth Century*, October, 1879.

G. R. Gleig, *Life of Sir Thos. Munro*, London, 1831.

H. F. Goodnow, *The Civil Service of Pakistan*, London, 1964.

A. D. Gorwala, *Role of the Administrator, Past, Present and Future*, Bombay, 1952.

J. N. Gupta, *R. C. Dutt*, London, 1911.

W. F. Gutteridge, *Military Institutions and Power in the New States*, London, 1965.

Indian Armed Forces in the Second World War, volume on 'Expansion of the Armed Forces', Calcutta, 1956.

G. N. Joshi, *Indian Administration*, London, 1953.

J. W. Kaye, *History of the Sepoy War in India*, 9th ed., London, 1880.

Sir Henry Lawrence, *Essays Military and Political Written in India*, London, 1859.

D. MacDonald, *Surgeons Two and a Barber*, London, 1950.

J. Ramsay MacDonald, *The Government of India*, London, n.d.

Arthur Mayhew, *The Education of India*, London, 1926.

R. Maher, *These are the Anglo-Indians*, Calcutta, 1962.

Sir R. P. Masani, *Dadabhai Naoroji*, London, 1939.

F. Maurice, *Life of Lord Rawlinson*, London, 1928.

James Mill, *History of British India*, London, 1820.

Lady Minto, *India, Morley and Minto*, London, 1934.

B. B. Misra, *The Indian Middle Classes*, London, 1961.

R. J. Moore, 'Abolition of Patronage in the I.C.S.', in *Historical Journal*, Vol. VII, 1964.

F. Max Müller, *India, what can it teach us?*, London, 1883.

J. Nehru, *Autobiography*, London, 1936.

S. Nurullah and J. P. Naik, *A History of Education in India*, Bombay, 1951.

L. S. S. O'Malley, *The Indian Civil Service*, London, 1931.

C. H. Philips (ed.), *Select Documents on History of India and Pakistan*, Vol. IV, London, 1962.

Sir Thomas Raleigh, *Lord Curzon in India*, London, 1906.

P. C. Ray, *Life and Experiences of a Bengali Chemist*, Vol. I, 1932, and Vol. II, 1935.

SELECT BIBLIOGRAPHY

Lord Ronaldshay, *Life of Lord Curzon*, London, 1928.

N. C. Roy, *The Civil Service in India*, Calcutta, 1958.

Hira Lal Singh, *Problems and Policies of the British in India*, London, 1963.

H. Sharp and J. A. Richey (eds.), *Selections from Educational Records*, Pts. I, II, Calcutta, 1920 and 1922.

T. N. Siquiera, *Modern Indian Education*, London, 1960.

H. A. Stark, *Hostages to India or the life story of the Anglo-Indian race*, London, 1936.

E. P. Stebbing, *The Forests of India*, London, 1923.

V. Subramaniam, 'Graduates in the Public Services', in *Public Administration*, Vol. XXXVI, 1958.

E. T. Stokes, *The English Utilitarians and India*, London, 1959.

Sir John Strachey, *India*, 1888.

R. Symonds, *The Making of Pakistan*, London, 1950.

D. Tagore, *My Boyhood and My Life in Bombay*, Calcutta, 1915 (in Bengali).

Prakash Tandon, *Punjabi Centenary*, London, 1961.

H. Tinker, *India and Pakistan*, London, 1962.

G. O. Trevelyan, *The Competition Wallah*, London, 1864.

G. O. Trevelyan, *Life and Letters of Lord Macaulay*, London, 1889.

P. Woodruff, *The Founders*, London, 1963.

P. Woodruff, *The Guardians*, London, 1963.

M. and T. Zinkin, *Requiem for Empire*, London, 1964.

CEYLON

OFFICIAL REPORTS

Colonial Office Confidential Prints 54/353, 54/434, 54/528 and 55/115.

Ceylon Government
S.P. 27, 1897, *Reclassification of the Ceylon Civil Service.*
S.P. I, 1919, *Further Employment of Ceylonese in the Public Service.*
S.P. 5, 1948, *Report of Commission on Organization, Staffing and operative methods of government departments.*
S.P. 3, 1961, *Report of the Salaries and Cadres Commission.*
S.P. 7, 1961, *Final Report of the National Education Committee.*
S.P. 16, 1963, *Ceylon Universities Commission Report*, 1962.

United Kingdom Government
Report of the Special Commission on the Constitution (Donoughmore Report), Cmd 3131, 1928.

SELECT BIBLIOGRAPHY

Report of Rt. Hon. W. G. M. Ormsby-Gore on visit to Ceylon, Cmd 3235, 1928.

Correspondence relating to the Constitution of Ceylon, Cmd 5910, 1938.

Report of the Commission on Constitutional Reform (Soulbury Report), Cmd 6677, 1945.

OTHER PUBLICATIONS

Sir Chas. Collins, *Public Administration in Ceylon,* London, 1951.

Community, Vol. 4, No. 3, Colombo, 1963. (Volume devoted to discussion of the public services.)

Handbook of Ceylon National Congress (1919–1928), Colombo, 1928.

Sir Chas. Jeffries, *Ceylon, The Path to Independence,* London, 1962.

Sir I. Jennings, 'The Foundation of the University of Ceylon', in *University of Ceylon Review,* Vol. IX, 1951.

R. N. Kearney and R. L. Harris, 'Bureaucracy and Environment in Ceylon', *Journal of Commonwealth Political Studies,* November, 1964.

E. F. C. Ludowyk, *The Story of Ceylon,* London, 1962.

G. C. Mendis, *The Colebrooke-Cameron Papers,* London, 1956.

L. A. Mills, *Ceylon under British Rule,* London, 1933.

S. J. Tambiah, 'Ethnic Representation in Ceylon's high administrative services', *University of Ceylon Review,* Vol. XIII, April, 1955.

J. R. Toussaint, *Annual of Ceylon Civil Service,* Colombo, 1935.

T. Vittachi, *The Brown Sahib,* London, 1962.

W. E. F. Ward, *Fraser of Achimota,* etc. See under West Africa.

Leonard Woolf, *Growing,* 1961.

WEST AFRICA

OFFICIAL REPORTS

Report of the Commission on Higher Education in West Africa (Elliott Report), Cmd 6655, London, 1945.

Gold Coast (Ghana):

Report of the Select Committee of the Legislative Council on Africanization, S.P. 1, 1950, Accra.

Report of the Commission on the Civil Service of the Gold Coast (Lidbury Report), S.P. IV, 1951, Accra.

Report of Select Committee on the Lidbury Report (Gbedemah Report), S.P. III, 1952, Accra.

SELECT BIBLIOGRAPHY

Final Report of Working Party to Review the Africanization Programme (Adu Report), unpublished, 1953.

Statement on Programme of the Africanization of the Public Service, Accra, 1954.

Nigeria:

Report of a Committee appointed by the Governor (Walwyn Report), Colonial Office, London, 1942, mimeographed.

Report of the Commission on Recruitment and Training of Africans for Senior Posts in the Government (Foot Report), Lagos, 1948.

Sir S. Phillipson and S. O. Adebo, *Nigerianization of the Civil Service*, Lagos, 1954.

Annual Report of Nigerianization Officer for 1957, Lagos, 1958.

Interim Report of Parliamentary Committee on Nigerianization and *Views of the Government of the Federation on the Interim Report of the Committee on Nigerianization*, S.P. 7 of 1958, Lagos.

Final Report of Parliamentary Committee on Nigerianization, S.P. 6 of 1959, Lagos.

Government Statement on Final Report of Parliamentary Committee on Nigerianization, S.P. 2 of 1960, Lagos.

Investment in Education (Ashby Report), Lagos, 1960.

Report of Nigerian National Manpower Board, Lagos, 1963.

Seminar on Manpower Problems, Lagos, 1964. Unpublished mimeographed papers.

Manpower Situation in Nigeria, Lagos, 1963.

Seventh Report on the Federal Public Service Commission, Lagos, 1965.

Western Region of Nigeria:

Seventh Report of the Public Service Commission, Ibadan, 1963.

Eighth Report of the Public Service Commission, Ibadan, 1965.

Nigerianization of the Public Service of Western Nigeria, Ibadan, 1960.

The Role of the Administrator, F. D. McGrath, Ibadan, 1963.

The Public Service Commission, L. G. Coke Wallis, Ibadan, 1960.

Northern Region of Nigeria:

A Short History of Education in Northern Nigeria, D. H. Williams, Kaduna, 1959.

Eastern Region of Nigeria:

Public Service Policy Paper, Official Document No. 5, Enugu, 1963.

Annual Report of the Public Service Commission for 1962, Enugu.

271

SELECT BIBLIOGRAPHY

Sierra Leone:

Report of the Commission on the Civil Service of Sierra Leone (Sinker Report), Freetown, 1953.

Report of the Commission on the Civil Service of Sierra Leone (Gorsuch Report), Freetown, 1957.

Government Statement on Africanization, S.P. 4 of 1959, Freetown.

OTHER PUBLICATIONS

A. Adedeji, *The Public Service in a Developing Country*, University of Ife, Seminar on Public Administration, 1964.

J. F. A. Ajayi, *Milestones in Nigerian History*, Ibadan, 1962.

O. Awolowo, *Path to African Freedom*, London, 1947.

O. Awolowo, *Awo*, Cambridge, 1960.

Ahmadu Bello, *My Life*, London, 1962.

M. J. Bennion, 'Institute of Administration, Zaria,' in *Journal of Local Administration, Overseas*, January, 1963.

R. W. Cole, *Kossoh Town Boy*, London, 1960.

Taylor Cole, 'Bureaucracy in Transition, independent Nigeria', in *Public Administration*, Winter 1960.

J. S. Coleman, *Nigeria, Background to Nationalism*, London, 1958.

W. R. Crocker, *Nigeria*, London, 1936.

H. R. Fox-Bourne, 'Blacks and Whites in West Africa', *Transactions of Aborigines Protection Society*, 1901–1903.

S. F. Graham, 'History of Education in Northern Nigeria', unpublished London Ph.D. thesis, 1955.

D. K. Greenstreet, 'Development of the Ghanaian Public Service', in *Journal of Management Studeis*, Universtiy of Ghana, September, 1963.

F. H. Hilliard, *Short History of Education in British West Africa*, London, 1957.

J. A. B. Horton, *West African Countries and Peoples*, London, 1868.

J. D. Kingsley, *Staff Development, East Nigeria Public Service*, Enugu, 1961.

J. D. Kingsley, *Staffing, Organization and Training Problems in the Public Service of the Western Region of Nigeria*, mimeographed, Ibadan, 1958.

J. D. Kingsley and Sir A. Rucker, *Staffing and Development of the Public Service of Northern Nigeria*, mimeographed, Kaduna, 1961.

SELECT BIBLIOGRAPHY

A. H. M. Kirk-Greene, 'A Training Course for Northern Nigerian Administrative Officers', in *Journal of African Administration*, Vol. XI, No. 2, 1959.

Lord Lugard, *Instructions to Political Officers*, London, 1919.

K. Mellanby, *The Birth of Nigeria's University*, London, 1958.

C. Newbury, *West African Commonwealth*, Cambridge, 1965.

M. Perham, *Native Administration in Nigeria*, London, 1937 and 1962 editions.

S. S. Richardson, 'The Institute of Administration, Zaria', in *Journal of Local Administration Overseas*, Vol. III, No. 1, January, 1964.

M. J. Sampson, *Gold Coast Men of Affairs*, London, 1937.

E. W. Smith, *Aggrey of Africa*, New York, 1930.

M. G. Smith, *Government in Zazzau*, London, 1960.

D. L. Sumner, *Education in Sierra Leone*, London, 1963.

W. E. F. Ward, *Fraser of Trinity and Achimota*, London, 1965.

C. G. Wise, *A History of Education in West Africa*, London, 1956.

R. Wraith, *Local Government in West Africa*, London, 1964.

EAST AFRICA
OFFICIAL REPORTS

Report of the Commission on the Civil Services of Kenya, Tanganyika and Zanzibar (Holmes Report), London, Col. 223, 1948.

Report of the Commission on the East African Territories and East African High Commission (Lidbury Report), London (Crown Agents), 1954.

East Africa Royal Commission Report (Dow Report), Cmd 9475, 1955.

Report of the Commission on the Public Services of the East African Territories and the East African High Commission (Flemming Report), Entebbe, 1960.

Report on the Localization of the Civil Service of the East African High Commission (Ramage Report), Nairobi, 1961.

Report of the Africanization Commission (Udoji Report), East African Common Services Organization, Nairobi, 1963.

East African Common Services Organization, *Memorandum on Report of Africanization Commission*, S.P. 1 of 1963, Nairobi.

Proceedings of the Central Legislative Assembly, Vol. II, No. 2 East African Common Services Organization, Nairobi, 1963.

SELECT BIBLIOGRAPHY

Report of Commission on Financial Position of Kenya (Pim Report), Col. 116, 1936.

Report of the Economy Commission, Kenya Government, Nairobi, 1962.

Annual Reports of the Education Department, 1924–1962, Kenya Government.

Annual Reports of the Department of Education, 1923–1960, Tanganyika Government.

Reports of Visiting Missions of the United Nations, 1948, 1951, 1954, 1957, and 1960, and observations of the Administering Authority, Government of Tanganyika.

Annual Reports on the Administration Submitted to the United Nations, 1950–1960 (Tanganyika), London, HMSO.

Report of the Africanization Commission (Maswanya Report) 1962, Tanganyika Government, Dar-es-Salaam, 1963.

Africanization of the Civil Service, Annual Report for 1963, Tanganyika Government, Dar-es-Salaam, 1964.

Tanganyika Five Year Plan, Dar-es-Salaam, 1964.

Annual Reports of the Education Department, 1925–1962, Uganda Government.

Final Report of Standing Committee on Recruitment, Training and Promotion of Africans (Wild Report), Uganda Government, Entebbe, 1955.

Future Developments in the Public Services in Uganda, S.P. 2 of 1961, Entebbe.

Report of the Commissioners for Africanization, Uganda Government, Entebbe, 1962.

Statement on Report of the Commissioners for Africanization, S.P. 7 of 1962, Uganda Government, Entebbe.

OTHER PUBLICATIONS

History of East Africa, ed. Harlow, et. al., Vol. II, London, 1965.

Sir Hesketh Bell, *Glimpses of a Governor's Life*, London, 1946.

Sir Michael Blundell, *So Rough a Wind*, London, 1964.

Mrs. C. J. Bryant, 'Some Problems of Public Administration in Uganda', Unpublished London University thesis, July, 1963.

Sir Donald Cameron, *My Tanganyika Service and Some Nigeria*, London, 1939.

B. Chidzero, *Tanganyika and International Trusteeship*, London, 1961.

SELECT BIBLIOGRAPHY

D. F. Clyde, *History of the Tanganyika Medical Service*, Dar-es-Salaam, 1962.

Sir Chas. Dundas, *African Crossroads*, London, 1955.

R. M. Gatheru, *Child of Two Worlds*, London, 1964.

Guy Hunter, *Education for a Developing Region*, London, 1963.

Guy Hunter, *High Level Manpower in East Africa*, mimeographed, 1962.

Sir Willis Jackson, 'Some Impressions of Electrical and Educational Developments in East and Central Africa', in *Electrical Supervisor*, October, 1961.

Norman Leys, *Kenya*, London, 1926.

Norman Leys, *Last Chance in Kenya*, London, 1931.

Tom Mboya, *Freedom and After*, London, 1963.

R. Oliver, *The Missionary Factor in East Africa*, London, 1952.

J. R. P. Postlethwaite, *I Look Back*, London, 1947.

Public Administration Seminar, University College, Dar-es-Salaam, 1962.

Third Public Administration Seminar, Makerere College, 1964.

J. Clagett Taylor, *Political Developments of Tanganyika*, London, 1963.

G. Tobias, *Survey of High Level Manpower Requirements in Tanganyika*, Ford Foundation, 1962.

J. L. Thurston, *Human Resources and Manpower Planning in Tanganyika*, Mimeographed, Dar-es-Salaam, 1960.

AFRICA, GENERAL

OFFICIAL REPORTS

Advisory Committee on Native Education in the British Tropical African Colonies, *Educational Policy in British Tropical Africa*, Cmd 2374, 1925.

Higher Education in Africa (De la Warr Report), Col. 142, 1937.

Organization of the Colonial Service, London, Col. 197, 1946.

Post-War Training for the Colonial Service, London, Col. 198, 1946.

Report of Inter-University Council for Higher Education Overseas 1946–1954, Cmd 9515, London, 1954.

OTHER PUBLICATIONS

A. L. Adu, *The Civil Service in New African States*, London, 1965.

SELECT BIBLIOGRAPHY

Sir Eric Ashby, *African Universities and Western Tradition*, London, 1964.

T. Balogh, 'The Problem of Education in Africa', in *Centennial Review*, Vol. VI, No. 4, 1962.

E. Bethune and A. Wembi, 'Le Problème de la sous-administration dans les pays d'Afrique noire indépendante', *Civilizations*, Vol. XII, No. 4, 1962.

Godfrey N. Brown, 'British Educational Policy in West and Central Africa', *Journal of Modern African Studies*, 2, 3, 1964.

R. L. Buell, *The Native Problem in Africa*, New York, 1928.

P. C. C. Evans, 'Western Education and Rural Productivity in Tropical Africa', *Africa*, October, 1962.

L. Gray Cowan, *Memorandum on Africanization*, typescript, 1955.

Lord Hailey, *An African Survey*, London, 1945 and 1956 eds.

G. Hunter, *New Societies in Tropical Africa*, London, 1962.

L. J. Lewis, *Education and Political Independence in Africa*, London, 1962.

J. G. Lockhart and C. M. Wodehouse, *Rhodes*, London, 1963.

Lord Lugard, *The Dual Mandate in British Tropical Africa*, London, 1922.

Nuffield Foundation, *African Education*, London, 1953.

M. Perham, *Life of Lord Lugard*, Vol. *II*, *The Years of Authority*, London, 1960.

Phelps-Stokes Fund, *Education in Africa*, New York, 1922, and *Education in East Africa*, New York, 1925.

S. S. Richardson, *The Evolving Public Service in Africa*, University of Wisconsin, 1964.

R. Robinson (ed.), *African Development Planning*, Cambridge, 1963.

Ruth Sloan Associates, *The Educated African*, London, 1962.

FORMER FRENCH AFRICA

H. Brunschwig, *L'Avènement de l'Afrique noire*, Paris, 1953.

P. Chauleur, 'Le Formation des Cadres Supérieurs Africains', in *Etudes*, Paris, March, 1963.

H. Deschamps, *Méthodes et Doctrines Coloniales de la France*, Paris, 1953.

René Dumont, *L'Afrique noire est mal partie*, Paris, 1962.

J. C. Froelich, *La Vie d'un Commandant de Cercle*, Paris, 1959.

SELECT BIBLIOGRAPHY

A. Girault, *Principes de Colonisation et de Legislation Coloniale*, Paris, 1927 ed.

J. C. Groshens and P. Ardant, 'L'enseignement supérieur et la formation des cadres', *Annales Africaines*, Vol. II, University of Dakar, 1962.

G. Hardy, *Nos Grands Problèmes Coloniaux*, Paris, 1949 ed.

Teresa Hayter, 'French Aid to Africa – Its Scope and Achievements', *International Affairs*, Vol. 41, No. 2, April 1965.

R. Hoffherr, 'Le problème de l'encadrement dans les jeunes états', *Tiers Monde*, October, 1962.

M. Ligot, 'La co-opération militaire dans les accords passés entre la France et les états Africains', *Revue Juridique et Politique* d'Outre Mer, No. 4, 1963.

H. B. Mbarga, *Problèmes Africains de l'Éducation*, Paris, 1962.

A. Moumouni, *L'éducation en Afrique*, Paris, 1964.

Sekou Touré, *La Guinée et l'Emancipation Africaine*, Paris, 1959.

Senegal Government, *Plan Quadriennal de Developpement 1961–1964*, Dakar, 1962.

A. Tevoedjre, *L'Afrique Révoltée*, Paris, 1958.

V. Thompson and R. Adloff, *Emerging States of French Equatorial Africa*, London, 1960.

V. Thompson and R. Adloff, *French West Africa*, London, 1958.

CONGO

A. A. J. Van Bilsen, *Vers l'Indépendance du Congo*, Brussels, 1958.

G. Brausch, *Belgian Administration in the Congo*, London, 1961.

CRISP (Centre de Recherche et d'Information Socio-Politique), Brussels
Congo, 1960.
Congo, 1961
Rwanda Politique 1958–1960

W. J. Ganshof Van de Meersch, *Fin de la souveraineté Belge au Congo*, Brussels, 1963.

C. Hoskyns, *The Congo since Independence*, London, 1965.

E. Janssens, *J'étais le général Janssens*, Brussels, 1961.

R. Lamarchand, *Political Awakening in the Congo*, University of California, 1964.

P. Lumumba, *Congo, My Country*, London, 1962.

'J.K.', *André Ryckmans*, Brussels, 1961.

SELECT BIBLIOGRAPHY

INDONESIA

G. Bousquet, *A French View of the Netherlands Indies*, London, 1940.

G. T. Kahin, *Nationalism and Revolution in Indonesia*, New York, 1952.

L. Palmier, *Indonesia and the Dutch*, London, 1962.

S. Sjahrir, *Out of Exile*, New York, 1949.

Amry Vandenbosch, *The Dutch East Indies*, University of California, 1944.

THE PHILIPPINES

G. Fischer, *Un cas de decolonisation – Les États-Unis et les Philippines*, Paris, 1960.

J. R. Hayden, *The Philippines*, New York, 1942.

R. Hayden, 'Higher Officials in the Philippine Civil Service', *American Political Science Review*, Vol. 27, 1933.

E. O. Stene and Associates, *Public Administration in the Philippines*, Manila, 1956.

H. P. Willis, *Our Philippine Problem*, New York, 1906.

GENERAL AND MISCELLANEOUS

OFFICIAL REPORTS

Report of the Committee on Malayanization of the Government Service, Federation of Malaya, Kuala Lumpur, 1954.

Report of the Committee on Malayanization of the Public Service, Federation of Malaya, Kuala Lumpur, 1956.

Report of the Localization Committee (Adu Report), Nyasaland (Malawi) Government, Zomba, 1960.

Interim Report of Malayanization Committee, Colony of Singapore, Singapore, 1956.

Report of the Commission on Unification of the Public Services in British Caribbean, 1948–49 (Holmes Report), London, Col. 294, 1949.

Report on Reorganization of the Public Service in Trinidad and Tobago (Lee Report), Trinidad, 1954.

Report of the Commission on Higher Education in the Colonies (Asquith Report), Cmd 6647, London, 1945.

Report of the Public Services Conference, London, Col. 347, 1960.

Report on the Development of a University in Northern Rhodesia, Zambia (Northern Rhodesia) Government, Lusaka, 1964.

SELECT BIBLIOGRAPHY

OTHER PUBLICATIONS

T. Balogh, 'Economics of Education and Planning', *Comparative Education*, October, 1964.

R. F. Betts, *Assimilation and Association in French Colonial Policy*, New York, 1961.

R. Braibanti, 'Reflections on Bureaucratic Corruption', *Public Administration*, Vol. 40, London, 1962.

Sir Alan Burns, *History of the West Indies*, London, 1954.

A. M. Carr-Saunders, *New Universities Overseas*, London, 1961.

A. M. Carr-Saunders and P. A. Wilson, *The Professions*, London, 1933.

Sir Christopher Cox, 'The Impact of British Education on the Indigenous Peoples of Overseas Territories', *Colonial Review*, December, 1956.

Adam Curle, *Educational Strategy for Developing Countries*, London, 1963.

J. S. Furnivall, *Colonial Policy and Practice*, London, 1948.

Sir R. Furse, *Aucuparius*, London, 1962.

R. Heussler, *Yesterday's Rulers*, London, 1963.

James Hunt, *On the Negro's Place in Nature*, London, 1863.

R. Hofstadter, *Social Darwinism in American Thought*, Boston, 1955.

Sir Chas. Jeffreys, *The Colonial Empire and its Civil Service*, London, 1938.

Institut International des Civilisations Differents, *Staff Problems in Tropical and Subtropical Countries*, Brussels, 1961.

Institutes of Public Administration in the Commonwealth, *Report of Conference of Directors* 1963, R.I.P.A., London, 1963.

J. P. Lapalombara (ed.), *Bureaucracy and Political Development*, Princeton, 1963.

W. M. MacMillan, *The Road to Self Government*, London, 1959.

A. Mayhew, 'A Comparative Study of educational aims and methods in British India and British Tropical Africa', *Africa*, Vol. VI, 1933.

A. Mayhew, *Education in the Colonial Empire*, London, 1938.

L. A. Mills, *British Rule in Eastern Asia*, London, 1942.

Viscount Milner, *Questions of the Hour*, London, 1925.

Hla Myint, 'The Universities of South East Asia and Economic Development', *Pacific Affairs*, Summer, 1962.

Margery Perham, *The Colonial Reckoning*, London, 1961.

SELECT BIBLIOGRAPHY

J. Pope-Hennessy, *Verandah*, London, 1964.

Margaret Read, *Education and Social Change in Tropical Areas*, London, 1955.

Samuel Smiles, *Lives of the Engineers*, London, 1862.

V. Subramaniam, 'Graduates in the Public Services', *Public Administration*, Vol. 36, 1958.

R. Wraith and E. Simpkins, *Corruption in Developing Countries*, London, 1963.

K. Younger, *The Public Service in New States*, London, 1960.

Index

INDEX

East African Common Services Organization (formerly East African High Commission), 177, 179–183

East India Company, British, 26, 28, 30, 45, 46, 48, 51, 59, 66, 92, 93, 98; Charter of 1813, 46; Charter of 1833, 29, 46, 47, 93; Charter of 1853, 48

Eboué, Félix, 212, 214, 252

Ècole Nationale de la France d'Outre-Mer, 212, 213

Economics, teaching of, 142–3

Education: terminology, 12; British policies, 238–40, 258–9; in Belgian Africa, 222–6; in Ceylon, see Chapter V, 98–114; in East Africa, 180–1, 183–4 and see Chapter X, 187–207, passim; in French Africa, 213–221; in India, see Chapter II, 44–54; 138, 139; in Indonesia, 230–2; in the Philippines, 229–30; in West Africa, see Chapter VII, 133–47

Elliott Report, 141, 142, 143, 145, 238, 239

Elphinstone, Mountstuart, 19, 26, 28

Engineering: in Ceylon, 105, 111; in the Congo, 223; in Ghana, 155; in India, 67–80; in Malawi, 244; in West Africa, 142, 144, 145, 167; 'standards' in, 242–3

Eurasians, 230–1, see also Anglo-Indians

Evangelicals, 27, 28, 45, 238

Fafunya, Professor B., 133, 146

Fawcett, Henry, 35

Ferguson, G. E., 121

Flemming Report, 178

Foot, Sir Hugh, 157, 162

Ford Foundation, 161, 163, 191

Forestry: in East Africa, 193; in India, 70–2, 73; in Malawi, 249; in West Africa, 145

Fourah Bay College, 134, 136, 140, 141, 165

Fowler, Sir Henry, 37, 38

Fraser, A. G., 140, 141, 196, 236

Fraser Commission, 74

Freeman, E. A., 16, 236

French Colonial Administration, 128, 211–21, 236–7

Furse, Sir Ralph, 127, 151

Gandhi, Mahatma, 52

General Medical Council, 67, 105, 240

Germans, in Tanganyika, 187–8

Ghana (see also Gold Coast): administrative service, 152–6; 'Africanization' in, 152–6; armed forces, 166; education in, 140–7

Ghulam Mohammad, 90

Girault, Arthur, 213

Gladstone, W. E., 81

Gobineau, J. A., Comte de, 237

Goderich, Lord, 100–1

Gokhale, G. K., 76

Gold Coast (see also Ghana), 121, 123, 124, 129, 130–1

Gold Coast, University College of (see also Ghana), 141, 142, 144, 155

Goonitilleke, Sir Oliver, 113

Gorsuch Commission (Sierra Leone), 165

Gorwala, A. D., 86–7

Gosse, Edmund, 80

Grant, Charles, 27, 45, 46

Guggisberg, Sir Gordon, 130–1, 140, 237–8

Gupta, Bihari Lal, 79–85

Gupta, J. N., 83, 86

Hailey, Lord, 14, 136, 151, 253

Haileybury College, 26, 28, 30

Hamilton, Lord George, 37, 57

Hardinge, Lord, Governor General, 47, 94

Hardy, Georges, 213

Hare, David, 47, 79

Hastings, Warren, 45, 46, 73

Hayford, Casely, 127, 136, 151

Hindu College, Calcutta, 47, 79

283

INDEX

INDEX